Methods Of Operations Research

METHODS OF
OPERATIONS
RESEARCH

METHODS OF
OPERATIONS
RESEARCH

PHILIP M. MORSE

PROFESSOR OF PHYSICS
MASSACHUSETTS INSTITUTE OF TECHNOLOGY
FORMERLY DIRECTOR OF RESEARCH
WEAPONS SYSTEM EVALUATION GROUP
OFFICE OF THE SECRETARY OF DEFENSE

GEORGE E. KIMBALL

PROFESSOR OF CHEMISTRY
COLUMBIA UNIVERSITY
FORMERLY DEPUTY DIRECTOR
OPERATIONS EVALUATION GROUP
UNITED STATES NAVY

FIRST EDITION REVISED

Published jointly by

**THE TECHNOLOGY PRESS OF
MASSACHUSETTS INSTITUTE OF TECHNOLOGY**

and **JOHN WILEY & SONS, INC. · NEW YORK**

CHAPMAN & HALL, LTD. · LONDON

SECOND PRINTING   JULY, 1951

PREFACE

IN A SENSE, this book should have no authors' names or else several pages of names. Parts of the book were written by various persons during and at the end of World War II. What the undersigned have done is to collect the material, rewrite some in the light of later knowledge, expand some to make it more generally intelligible, add chapters on organization and general procedures, and cement the mosaic into what is hoped to be a fairly logical structure.

Since the undersigned were members of the Operations Research Group, U S Navy, it is perhaps not surprising that the examples given are drawn chiefly from the work of this group, though an effort has been made to include examples from the work of other groups. Many persons have helped by discussions and editorial criticism, including members of other operations research groups in this country and in England. To mention a few would slight many others, so none will be named.

During the war the scope, methods, and triumphs of operations research were not appreciated by most scientists or by most military men because no information was freely available. If we are not to lose this valuable experience and background, some of it must be made available *to the scientists and engineers as well as to the armed services*. This is particularly important if the methods of operations research have important peacetime applications—as it is believed they do.

The first publication of this work was in classified form, just after World War II. To further the purposes mentioned in the preceding paragraph, however, the volume has now been declassified, after suitable modification of a few examples. The first and last chapters have been entirely rewritten, to bring the discussion up to date, in particular with respect to nonmilitary applications.

There has been growing interest in the application of the techniques of operations research in industry and other nonmilitary operations. This is evidenced by the formation of a committee on operations research of the U. S. National Research Council and of an Operations Research Club in London, and by the institution of classes in operations research in several American Universities. It is hoped that the present, unclassified edition of METHODS OF OPERATIONS RESEARCH will be equally of interest and of use to industrial, merchandising, and nonmilitary governmental executives as the earlier, classified edition seems to have been in military circles.

PHILIP M. MORSE.
GEORGE E. KIMBALL

Washington, D C, April 1950

CONTENTS

Chapter 1

INTRODUCTION

Operations research is a scientific method of providing executive departments with a quantitative basis for decisions regarding the operations under their control It first developed as a recognized activity in response to the military needs of World War II where it was sometimes known as operations analysis or evaluation (or in one case weapons systems evaluation) Although its techniques and methods of approach have earlier been used sporadically in industrial, governmental, and military activities, sometimes under different names, its systematic applications have to date been predominantly military However, as the definition suggests, as the examples in this book will indicate, and as experience since the war has shown, the techniques and approach of operations research can be of help in arriving at executive decisions concerning operations in any field, industrial and governmental as well as military After four years of war experience and four subsequent years of peacetime experience most experts in the field have agreed on the definition given in the first sentence, with all its implications and generality *

1 1 DEFINITION OF OPERATIONS RESEARCH

Let us first point out some of the more obvious implications of the definition given in the first sentence above, we will then mention a few examples of the methods used and devote the rest of the first chapter to a discussion of techniques, organization, and personnel First of all operations research is a *scientific method* It is an organized activity with a more or less definite methodology of attacking new problems and finding definite solutions Executives have often in the past used some of the techniques to be explained herein to help themselves arrive at decisions, military staffs have used some of its techniques, and "efficiency experts" have exploited some of its methods But the term "scientific method" implies more than sporadic application and occasional use of a certain methodology, it implies recognized and organized activity amenable to application to a variety of problems and capable of being taught

1.1.1 An Applied Science

Next we see that operations research is of service to *executive* departments the commanding general of a military force, the vice-president in charge of operations in an industry, or the director of some governmental activity Operations research, therefore, is *an applied science* utilizing all known scientific techniques as tools in solving a specific problem, in this case providing a basis for decisions by an executive department As we shall see, operations research uses mathematics, but it is not a branch of mathematics It utilizes the results of time and motion studies, but it is not efficiency engineering It often helps in the introduction of new equipment but it is not an adjunct of a development laboratory. Just as civil engineering uses the results of science in order to build a bridge, so operations research utilizes these various techniques as tools to help the executive It is likely, however, that operations research should not be classed as a branch of engineering For the branches of engineering recognized at present are involved in the construction or production of equipment whereas operations research is involved in their use The engineer is the consultant to the builder, the producer of equipment, whereas the operations research worker is the consultant to the *user* of equipment

The next important word in the definition is "quantitative" It is to some extent implied in the earlier phrase "scientific method," but it is worth the iteration Certain aspects of practically every operation can be measured and compared quantitatively with similar aspects of other operations It is these aspects which can be studied scientifically

The phrase "basis for decisions" implies that these quantitative aspects are not the whole story in most executive decisions Many other aspects can enter politics, morale, tradition, items often important but impossible to express in numbers It is the prerogative and responsibility of the executive officer to add these factors to the quantitative basis provided by the operations research group, to reach the final decision The task of the operations research worker

---

See Bibliography of unclassified articles at the end of this book

is to present the quantitative aspects in intelligible form and to point out, if possible, some of the nonquantitative aspects that may need consideration by the executive before he reaches his decisions But the operations research worker does not and should not make the decision

1.1 2   Separation of Operations Research from Executive Decision

This separation of the duties and activities of the operations research worker and the executive officer is important, the experience of the past ten years has only emphasized this importance Experience has shown, for instance, that a person with operations research training, when placed in an executive position, loses a great deal of his usefulness as an operations research worker (though he may become an excellent executive) The requirement that the executive reach a decision concerning an operation is to some extent antagonistic to the requirement that he look at it scientifically and impersonally, as would be required in operations research The proper use of an operations research group by an executive department implies a sort of symbiosis, requiring, on the part of each, trust in the other's activities and respect of the other's prerogatives

Since operations research is to provide the executive with a quantitative basis for decision, it is easy to see that the techniques of presentation of a result are very important parts of the activity All scientific method implies the imparting of scientific results to other workers In this work however the results are usually to be imparted to nonscientists, and no project in this field can be considered completed until the findings obtained by the scientist are imparted to the executive in a manner that will aid the latter to make his decisions

The word "operations," in the definition, itself requires definition Its use in military terminology is quite specific, but this usage differs somewhat from that current in industrial or other governmental activities A specific definition will not be attempted this early in the text, though several implications of the usually understood meanings of the word should be pointed out The term "operation" implies to some extent a repetition of some action or some parts of an action This has come to be more and more true as operations of modern times have come to involve machinery as well as men The repetitive factor in the usual operation is of course the factor that makes it amenable to scientific attack Often the repetition, the similarity between parts of different operations,

is not at all obvious A standard task of any scientific research is to find similarity between apparently different things and to isolate these similarities so that they can be studied quantitatively Such techniques are all-important in operations research

The last phrase "under their control" emphasizes again that this is an applied science, concerned chiefly with the problems of immediate importance to the executive department An operations research group should not report to the research department of a military service or of an industrial organization, for example It must have direct and personal contact with the officer who makes the executive decisions, so that the group can know from him what are the important questions requiring decision and so that he can hear directly from them the results of their studies, which are to form a basis for his decisions

The concept of staff function is perhaps more clearly understood in military organizations than in industrial or other governmental ones Clearly operations research is a staff function For this reason the group should be as small as possible, and all contact should be as personal as possible Research activity need not be all short-range, however There is need for long-range research in any operational problem Yet, as with any applied science, the work must be directed towards the main goal As with much scientific research, it is often the operations research group that can best decide whether a certain research is pertinent to the problem at hand or not

1 1 3   Early Development

It should be apparent by now that there is no fundamental reason why operations research, as a distinct activity, should be less useful in nonmilitary operations than it has been in military operations, nor even that its major application should continue in the military field The reasons for its start in World War II are not hard to find, however During that struggle lives and national freedom were at stake, whereas with most industrial problems only money is at stake The urges for scientists to enter the field were thus much greater, and the benefits, to begin with, were perhaps more obvious In addition, more men of higher ability were available to turn to this field than there are usually in peacetime The creation of a new field of applied science involves nearly as much ability and scientific initiative as does the creation of a field of pure science In the present case it appeared necessary for research scientists of high caliber to take part in the initial effort

Naturally these same scientists would be of similar great utility later in the development of the field, but during peacetime they are usually engaged in more important research (more important to them) in pure science and so are unavailable to start a new field of applied science Perhaps it required a great war to provide the proper combination of needs and willing intellects The requirements for scientific experience and research ability are still quite high, in operations research, however

1 1 4   Value of Operations Research

During the war operations research proved its worth in military applications, and today the Services, both in the United States and England, are provided with groups attached to the planning and operational parts of the higher staffs An interesting appraisal of this work was given by Admiral E J King in his Final Report, issued December 8, 1945

The complexity of modern warfare in both methods and means demands exacting analysis of the measures and countermeasures introduced at every stage by ourselves and the enemy Scientific research can not only speed the invention and production of weapons, but also assist in insuring their correct use The application, by qualified scientists, of the scientific method to the improvement of naval operating techniques and material, has come to be called operations research Scientists engaged in operations research are experts who advise that part of the Navy which is using the weapons and craft—the fleets themselves To function effectively they must work under the direction of, and have close personal contact with, the officers who plan and carry on the operations of war

∗   ∗   ∗

The late war, more than any other, involved the interplay of new technical measures and opposing countermeasures For example, the German U-boats had to revise their tactics and equipment when we began to use radar on our anti-submarine aircraft, and we, in turn, had to modify our tactics and radar equipment to counter their changes In this see-saw of techniques the side which countered quickly, before the opponent had time to perfect the new tactics and weapons, had a decided advantage Operations research, bringing scientists in to analyze the technical import of the fluctuations between measure and countermeasure, made it possible to speed up our reaction rate in several critical cases

Since the war operations research has been applied in a variety of industrial and governmental activities, with fairly universal success If the subject is to develop in a healthy manner, its basis of support requires widening, and courses of training for work in the field are needed It is the purpose of this book to indicate the techniques utilized by operations research, to indicate to students in science the existence of a career in this subject, and to illustrate by

examples the possible range of usefulness of the techniques Most of the examples chosen are from military applications, because these applications were first to be worked upon and the implications have had a longer time to be digested The implications of these examples with regard to other, nonmilitary applications, should be obvious to the reader, however It is expected that another five years of experience in this field will provide an equal number of industrial and nonmilitary governmental examples

1 2   SOME SIMPLE EXAMPLES

Before we attempt even a preliminary discussion of the techniques, personnel, and organization of operations research it will be well to quote a few examples of its working These examples will be chosen, not for their importance or for the value of the results, but primarily to illustrate one or more of the points already made or to be made in this chapter Many other examples illustrating these and other points will be given later in this volume

1 2 1   Rearrangement of Use of Equipment

The first example, simple to the point of triviality, involves the line-up of soldiers washing their mess kits after eating at a field mess station An operations research worker during his first day of assignment to a new field command noticed that there was considerable delay caused by the soldiers having to wait in line to wash and rinse their mess kits after eating There were four tubs, two for washing and two for rinsing The operations research worker noticed that on the average it took three times as long for the soldier to wash his kit as it did for him to rinse it He suggested that, instead of there being two tubs for washing and two for rinsing, there should be three tubs for washing and one for rinsing This change was made, and the line of waiting soldiers did not merely diminish in size, on most days no waiting line ever formed

This example, trivial as it is, illustrates a number of the points already discussed in the first section and to be amplified later In the first place the solution, when seen, was absurdly simple, anyone could have seen it, and it seems surprising that it required a trained scientist to point it out Perhaps the scientist's preoccupation with problems involving flow had given him a predisposition to see the possibility of a solution and to ask the right questions Here the right question concerned the relative time spent at each tub

The next point to note is that the improvement was obtained *with no added requirement in equipment* The tubs were merely rearranged as far as use goes No "gadgetry" was needed

The third point of interest is that the observation concerning the waiting line and the suggestion for improvement were made to someone who could do something about it and did No doubt many of the soldiers waiting in line could, and perhaps did, make the observations made by the operations research worker If so, the results of their observations and their possible suggestions for improvement never got to the person who could make the necessary operational decision, and so no improvement occurred

One more point of interest here, to be expanded later in this volume, concerns the result of the suggested change In theory, a change from two wash tubs plus two rinse tubes to three wash tubs plus one rinse tub should increase the flow through the line by 50 per cent The result, however, was that the waiting line reduced practically to zero, in other words the dividends obtained were even greater than those predicted It is an operational property of waiting lines that, the longer they get, the longer they tend to get Many operations have this same self-aggravating property A high-speed arterial highway, for instance, may carry Sunday traffic easily as long as no accident or other perturbation occurs to cause a momentary slowing down, as soon as a slowdown does occur, a traffic jam results Some of the most rewarding applications of operations research turn up in the study of such self-aggravating operations Although they are primarily nonlinear effects, they can usually be handled by known mathematical techniques and by the probability theory outlined in Chapter 2

1 2 2   Changes in Setting, Rearrangement of Unit Size

In this first example the solution could have been given in a short time by any qualified efficiency expert, indeed a solution should have been arrived at by any intelligent person who took the trouble to look at the problem In many cases, however, considerably greater amount of technical background is needed before the nature of the problem is seen and its solution is obtained In the example quoted in section 3 4 8, where a simple change in the depth-setting of the aircraft antisubmarine depth charges was recommended to improve U-boat sinkings, a detailed probability study and some knowledge of the physical properties of depth charge fuzes

was needed in order to arrive at the solution Here again, however, an improvement in results by a factor of 2 was obtained with no substantial change in the equipment involved, simply a change in the depth-setting of the fuze To have attempted to obtain an equivalent improvement by increasing the explosive charge, or by improvement of fire control, would have required years of development time and millions of dollars in production and installation cost

The decision to increase the size of convoys and the result, that of reducing average ship loss, outlined in section 3 2 2, is another example of large effects being obtained with no change in equipment used, only change in the way it was used Here again it was necessary to have a certain amount of knowledge concerning the behavior of ships in port and in convoy in order to see that an increase in size of a convoy would not bring concomitant deleterious effects The operations research worker need not be an expert in the operation involved (indeed, too great familiarity with its details may handicap him), but he must have enough technical background to understand the fundamentals of the operation, enough mathematical ability to carry out the analysis involved, and, above all, the sort of impersonal curiosity that is the prime requisite of any scientific research worker

Here again the study was made at the request of the authority controlling convoys This authority was in a position to try out the effect of the predictions of the study and to prove their worth A similar report, handed to any other authority, would have had no effect because it could not have been acted upon

It is also of interest to note that, in many cases, much of the problem is solved once it is decided what criteria are to be used in analyzing the operation From looking at the raw data on sinkings, it was apparent that approximately *the same number of ships* were lost, per attack, from large convoys as from small, and so one might thoughtlessly conclude that large convoys would not help It was only when it was realized that the correct criterion was the *percentage* lost of the total number of ships crossing the ocean that the correct solution was apparent In many cases the choice of the proper *measure of effectiveness* of the operation is the all-important decision to make in the analysis Sometimes this choice is not easy to make (for example, is the correct measure of a traffic system the reduction of accidents or the increase of traffic flow or the ratio of the two?) and the executive in charge of the operation must help decide

1.2 3 Determination of Dependence on Operational Parameters

One other point comes up in connection with the convoy study that operations research is often an experimental science as well as an observational one Its object is, by the analysis of past operations, to find means of improving the execution of future operations In the convoy study enough data were available on convoys of different size to enable preliminary conclusions concerning losses to be reached Prediction that large convoys would result in smaller percentage losses could then be made, and it was then possible to institute *trials* to check this prediction When the results justified the prediction it was then possible to reduce the findings to standard practice

The use of chance fluctuations in the operation, to give an insight into the dependence of the results on the various operational parameters involved, is a standard technique of operations research, one that will be exemplified throughout this volume Sometimes an astonishing number of answers can be obtained from apparently unpromising data by proper statistical manipulation An example from the commercial world is of interest here For reasons that should be apparent to any operations research worker, it would be important to know what percentage of the total retail sales in a given city, for a given week or month, are made by the particular store under study It would then be possible to obtain a really objective criterion of the utility of advertising and other means of sales promotion But reasons of commercial security, which are at times as strict as military security, prevent any given store from learning the total sales of its competitors for a given week or month All that is published in the press is a statement concerning the total retail sales in a given city per week in comparison with the corresponding sales the year previously Totals are not given otherwise the problem would be simple, ratios only are published Similarly the ratio of total retail sales for a given month to the total of the preceding month is also given From these data, by the use of simultaneous equations, comparing the weekly and monthly ratios, it is possible to compute the magnitude of total sales in the city for each week or month, with the exception of one overall, constant, multiplicative factor Once this factor is obtained, it is possible, from then on, to obtain approximate figures for the total sales each week or month, and thence, the sales for the store under study being known, the required fraction

could be computed The overall constant, however, could not be computed from the published data

It was then noted that during the preceding five years mistakes had occasionally occurred in reporting sales These mistakes had later been corrected, and the corresponding total sales ratios had then been rectified and rereported in the press The relation between the known size of the mistakes and the resulting size of the published corrections was sufficient to enable the analyst to obtain a reasonably accurate figure of this overall factor and consequently to solve the problem From then on that particular store knew, each week, what share of the total retail sales it had made

In other problems chance fluctuations are not enough to give complete data concerning the dependence of the operation on the various parameters In such cases, whenever possible, some of the parameters should be changed temporarily so as to determine the effect A decision to make such a change in operations is usually a serious decision, and it often must be made by the senior executive Changes made should be as small as possible to give positive results until one knows in which direction the effect is going to go

In the complex series of operations involving radar countermeasures, reported in section 5 3, recourse to changes in tactics was frequently made Radar sets were shut off for periods, intermittent operation was tried, and so on, in order to see the change in results In many traffic studies certain roads are artificially reduced in width in order to learn the effect of road width on traffic flow, since it is much easier to reduce the width of the road than it is to increase its width One here assumes that for small changes in parameters a linear dependence is a good approximation, consequently the degree of reduction of traffic flow owing to a reduction in width should be simply related to the corresponding increase in traffic flow for a corresponding increase in width This technique of small variations is discussed later In this present case, as in many others, corrections must be made for the self-aggravating property of traffic flow, as mentioned earlier

1 2 4 The Problem of Finding the Problem

It often occurs that the major contribution of the operations research worker is to decide what is the real problem In section 3 4 4 is reported a case where it was nearly decided that it was not worth while to put antiaircraft guns on merchant vessels, because they did not shoot down enemy planes It took an operations research worker to point out that, even though the enemy planes were not shot down, the antiaircraft guns were valuable because they decreased the accuracy of the enemy planes enough to lessen the chance that the merchant vessel be sunk Here again, a choice of the proper measure of effectiveness was crucial

A recent analysis of a merchandising concern brought out the fact that its advertising material went chiefly to its satisfied customers Statistical studies had shown that the "results" from such advertising were quite gratifying It was pointed out, however, that it was possible that satisfied customers did not need the amount of advertising that was being sent out and that perhaps it was more important to find out why some customers were changing from satisfied to dissatisfied ones and why some potential customers never became regular ones It was suggested that perhaps other criteria than those that had been used were required to evaluate properly the usefulness of advertising Studies along this line have been initiated but are not yet completed

1 2.5   Finding the Sensitive Parameters

The analysis of the dependence of an operation on the various operational parameters involved is, of course, made so that one can determine to which parameters the operation is most sensitive All operations depend on a large number of parameters, the less sensitive ones must be eliminated from the first analysis in order that any progress can be made at all Sometimes a statistical examination of past operations, combined with an analytic study of the elements of the operation, will indicate that certain parameters are important that had never been suspected previously In one analysis of a mail order concern, selling extensively to low-income rural families it was discovered that there was a sharp dependence of COD refusals on time between the writing of the original order by the family and the delivery of the item by the mailman Evidently, in this case, there was a "mean free time" of ready cash in such families, whether because of other financial pressures or impatience or simple shortness of memory If the item ordered did not arrive within a certain time, the money was spent somewhere else and the COD item had to be refused From this simple observation came a reorganization of selling methods of the firm, resulting, incidentally, in considerable reduction in such lost sales

The final aim of operations research, of course, is to predict future operations and to understand them well enough so as to be able to modify them to produce new or better results The aim is not simply to record past operations or just to explain them, in this respect the work differs from the usual statistical analysis In the example just cited the simple correlation between refusals and length of time between order and delivery could provide the clue to enable one to reduce the number of returned COD packages, by limiting the market area covered or by speeding delivery But in order to take more positive action than this, to lengthen the mean free time, so to speak, it was necessary to understand the reason for this correlation in terms of the economic and psychological factors involved

A good example of the need for a detailed understanding of the operation occurs in the problem of the search of submarines by aircraft Before the operational data on the visual sightings of submarines by aircraft were completely understood it was necessary to develop a new theory of sighting, which required considerable mathematical analysis and also a certain amount of physiological and psychological experimental work Now that all this has been done it is possible to predict the results of search operations for many other things besides submarines Examples of the need of a complete understanding of the operation, in its physical, mathematical, biological, and psychological aspects, are found in later pages

1 2 6   Mathematical Analysis

In a number of cases a certain amount of mathematical analysis is required before the necessary predictions can be made This was already mentioned in connection with the problem of retail sales A detailed analytical study of the flow of buses through a city is at present being carried on, using fairly comprehensive mathematical techniques in its pursuit Circular routes rather than back and forth linear routes are being investigated, and the effect of the self-aggravating behavior mentioned earlier is coming under study A number of problems, mentioned in Chapters 4 and 5, have involved a great deal of mathematical analysis This analysis, of course, was only a means to an end and would have been omitted if simpler means had been found to arrive at the result

In many cases the reasoning used in reaching a solution needs only simple arithmetic In others the complexity of the operation is sufficient to require the machinery and precision of advanced mathematical techniques, even, in a few instances, to the extent of using modern computing machines However, in most cases where operations research studies produced striking effects the analysis was cogent but not complicated, recondite but not highly symbolic Usually the answers had not been found before the scrutiny of the operations research worker, not because the answer was a complex one but because the problem had not been looked at from the right point of view

_{1 2 7}   **Requirements of Secrecy**

It is interesting to note here that the majority of the examples, both military and industrial, quoted here had to be worked out in secrecy and had to be kept secret for some time after executive action was taken As every historian knows, the "true" reasons for an action, whether emotional or logical, must often be disguised and often are lost forever, though the action and its results may eventually be known in some detail The reasons for this sometimes stem from the competitive nature of the operation and sometimes from ever-present questions of personalities and morale They are just as compelling in non-military operations, industrial or governmental, as they are in military operations Problems of secrecy, encompassed in the military term "security" will nearly always obtrude in operations research in any field, and the worker must be prepared to cope with them intelligently and not emotionally Because of this, many extremely instructive examples of operations research will never be reported in the open literature Some of the details of the final decisions and the outcome of these decisions, for some of the problems mentioned in this book, cannot yet be told

1 3   METHODS OF OPERATIONS RESEARCH

Having discussed what operations research is, and having given a few simple examples of its techniques and results, we are now in a position to make a more formal statement regarding its methods and organization Many of the comments in the next few sections are phrased in connection with military applications and with respect to military organizations, but the translation to other applications and organizations is obvious

The methodology of this new application of science is, of course, related to the type of data that can be obtained for study, in the present case, it usually turns out that few numerical data are ascertainable about phenomena of great complexity The problems are therefore somewhat nearer, in general, to many problems of biology or of economics rather than to most problems of physics, where usually many numerical data are ascertainable about relatively simple phenomena However, operations research, like every other science, must not copy in detail the technical methods of other sciences but must work out methods of its own, suited to its own special material and problems The object here is to assist in finding means of improving the efficiency of operations in progress or planned for the future. To do this, past operations are studied to determine the facts, theories are elaborated to explain the facts, and finally the facts and theories are used to make predictions about future operations This procedure insures that the maximum possible use is made of all past experience

_{1 3 1}   **Statistical Methods**

The most important single mathematical tool of operations research is probability and statistical theory The data upon which the research is based will come, for the most part, from statistical studies of operations These operations are often uncontrolled in the scientific sense and therefore cannot be considered as the equivalent of experiments In such cases the data are observational, therefore, rather than experimental, and naive statistical techniques may lead to serious errors in the results obtained

Statistical analysis is not fruitful unless there are available for study a large number of reports on operations that are roughly similar in nature For this reason, operations research is at first most successful in those fields where the individual operations are numerous, simple, and roughly similar Bombing operations on a target of a given type satisfy these requirements, for a great number of such operations are carried out under similar weather conditions and under somewhat similar conditions of enemy opposition Other examples such as sales and traffic have been mentioned earlier in this chapter

When we come to the larger actions of warfare or industry, however, the occasions are few, the complexities of the action are great, and the outcome will depend on a large number of independent factors In studying such actions in a statistical manner, the progress of operations research will naturally be slow Certain aspects of these larger operations can be studied in detail, and the whole picture perhaps can eventually be put together From what has been said, however, it can be appreciated that the classical naval engagement between surface vessels, for example, or the classical land battle is, in general, difficult for operational research to attack early in its development Only after the simpler cases mentioned previously have been thoroughly understood, can an attempt be made to analyze these more complex operations Strategy and tactics in the large will always be an art, though operations research may help its practice by providing tools of increasing power, just as the study of physiology has improved the art of medicine

1 3 2   Field Assignments, Collection of Data

The rapid collection of operational data is immeasurably improved by the assignment of a scientifically trained observer as close to the operations as is feasible In peacetime applications this is usually not difficult, but in military operations it often involves special hazards In World War I, for instance, it became exceedingly difficult, primarily because the scope of the operations was so large that, if the scientist got close enough to see the details of operations, he inevitably became a participant rather than an observer The problem became somewhat more simplified in World War II, owing primarily to the introduction of the airplane In all combat involving aircraft, the technical observer can be placed at a forward air base and get his reports at first hand from the participants immediately after they have returned from the operations It has been found by experience that important facts concerning the operations can often only be determined by having a technically trained observer question the operational personnel at first hand

Another important function of the men in the field is to see that the usual action reports contain as many useful data as possible Because these men know the kind of data that are most amenable to analysis, they can try to see that the reports are as complete as possible and are as "painless" as possible for the person making them out, and that the reports get sent as quickly as possible to the headquarters group for analysis They can also detect at first hand what kinds of intelligence material are likely to be unreliable, because of local factors which are not always appreciated at headquarters

The observers' reports, together with the usual operational reports, must then be sent in to a central group which analyzes the results from all theaters and compares them for differences and similarities The importance of the close interrelation between the field observers and the central group is obvious. In practice it has been arranged that members of the central group spend a certain part of their time in the field, to return later to the central group with increased insight into the operations they are studying

1 3 3   Limitations of Operational Data

Statistical analysis is part of the observational aspect of operational research The operations cannot always be controlled in the scientific sense, and insight into the reasons for their success or failure can sometimes be obtained only by studying large numbers of similar operations, so as to find out by statistical methods the effects of the variation of one or more components of the operation This imposes certain limitations on the usefulness of the results of the statistical analysis, for the range of variation of the various components in the operation will, by the nature of things, be rather limited Once successful tactics have been devised, it becomes less and less likely that the protagonists in the individual operation will deviate widely from the accustomed mean Consequently the operational data can only be utilized (by the variational method) to find whether small changes in components will improve or diminish the results

The results of such variational studies are quite useful, and the applications sometimes quite striking, since often the enemy's reaction (for "enemy" we can substitute "customer" or "competitor" as the case requires) to a *quantitative* change in our operation is a *qualitative* change in his counteraction However, a study of small variations is not usually sufficient In many cases what is interesting is not a small change in the tactics used but a completely different combination of actions, a "mutation" of the operation, as it were These new tactics may not be predictable from the old operations by variational calculation, for the extrapolations are, in this case, by definition too large for first-order terms Here a mathematical analysis of the whole operation, or of parts of it, may supply the necessary knowledge, or it may be possible that a series of discussions with the operating personnel may bring the necessary insight

1 3 4   Limitations of "Expert Opinion"

It should be mentioned, however, that the opinions of a few dozen persons who have had operational experience provide an extremely shaky foundation for any operations research It is unfortunately true, though not often realized, that people seldom estimate random events correctly, they always tend to remember the "exciting one" and forget others, and as a result their *opinions* are nearly always unconsciously biased Their *actions* in an operation or an operational experiment are important and worth recording, however The need for unbiased, impersonal *facts*, not opinions, must always be borne in mind, military personnel (and indeed most people without rigorous scientific training) tend to take the opposite opinion of the relative validity of opinion versus facts One often hears the question, "Why do you need detailed action reports (or why should you witness this operation) when so-and-so can tell you all about it?" If science has learned one thing in the past three centuries, it is that such a point of view must be avoided if valid scientific results are to be achieved For these reasons, "public opinion polls" are of limited usefulness in this field, since they represent only opinions, not actions

The statistical analysis of past operations is a vitally important part of operations research, but it has its limitations, and it must be supplemented by other methods of scientific attack

1.3.5 Operational Experiments

In some cases experimental methods can be used Some of the parameters under control can be varied An operational exercise can be laid out so that quantitative measurements of the behavior of the forces engaged may be obtained Such controlled experiments are sometimes difficult to arrange, so that they are really measured experiments rather than training exercises Many more could and should be carried out, perhaps the most useful activity of military operations research in peacetime will be the organization and study of such tactical experiments

Although operational experiments usually deal with simplified components of an operation, this is not to say that such experiments have little value, though it is an argument that such experiments must be designed very carefully in order to produce useful quantitative results As a matter of fact, operational experiments have already proved to be a most valuable source of quantitative data concerning operations, and it is highly important that such experiments be continued in greater numbers in the future There is great need, in particular, for further study in the techniques of planning these tactical experiments and in methods of measuring the results. These matters are discussed in detail in Chapter 8

1 3 6 Analytical Methods

Finally, operations research must also use purely theoretical methods in its development. In fact, if it is to progress as any other branch of science, its aim must be to transform as rapidly as possible the empirical data that it collects into generalized theories which can then be manipulated by mathematical methods to obtain other results This aim is just as true of the "life sciences" (of which operational research is a minor member) as it is of the physical sciences, although the progress is more difficult The work of J B S Haldane,[2] R A Fisher,[3] and others is a good example of the power of theoretical methods in genetics A certain amount of analogous theoretical work has been done in operations research on the effect of various strategic distributions of forces This is reviewed in Chapter 4

An important element which enters into the theoretical treatment of tactics and strategy and, indeed, in business and industry, is competition between the opposing forces The system as a whole cannot be considered as a purely mechanical one with single responses to specific situations The recent work of Von Neumann and Morgenstern[4] indicates that even this element of competition can be handled mathematically in an adequate manner Some aspects of their work are discussed in Chapter 5

The fact that at present purely theoretical analyses of strategy and tactics confine themselves to extremely simplified components of operations must not blind us to the importance of such studies and to their eventual practical utility The theoretical aspects of every science must start with the study of extremely simplified special cases When these simple cases are fully understood and are then compared with the actualities, further complexities can be introduced, and cases of practical importance can eventually be studied As has been cogently said,[4] "The mechanical problem of the free fall of bodies is a very trivial physical phenomenon, but it was the study of this exceedingly simple fact, and its comparison with the astronomical material, which brought forth mechanics "

1 3 7 Summary of Methods

The general procedure for operations research is, therefore, quite similar to that used in scientific research in general, the subject matter being the chief difference Data concerning past operations of a given sort are collected Variations in results are correlated statistically with variations in details of the operation to find the rough dependence of these results on the various operational parameters involved Various measures of effectiveness of the operation as a whole are devised in order to discover which displays most fully the dependence of the outcome on these parameters and which measures the properties of the outcome that are most desirable Research then concentrates on those parameters that produce the measures of effectiveness most critically

At this stage preliminary predictions can sometimes be made, which may immediately produce improvements Trial changes in procedure may be made, data from which will broaden the interrelations and make them more definite Already the research is beginning to "pay off"

The research cannot be considered satisfactorily completed, however, until the dependence of the results on the various operational parameters is satisfactorily explained in terms of the elements involved the personnel, equipment, and organization of the operation At this point any of the techniques of science, mathematics, physics, or biology, may be used to aid in arriving at this explanation Subsidiary experiments, detailed mathematical analyses and laboratory measurements are often needed From this broader study one should then be able to make broader predictions concerning results under changing conditions These should be checked wherever possible by new operational experiments under controlled conditions If all of them are successful, one can begin to say that the operation is understood and that the optimum operation can be designed for various conditions

In many cases also the complete theory will indicate that certain equipment involved in the operation could be improved These findings can then be turned over to a development laboratory for implementation From the point of view of operations research, of course, such results are in the nature of by-products, since usually the problem is to improve the operations, using the equipment available at the time

In some cases several different measures of effectiveness of the operation will turn up, and the choice of optimum operation will depend on the choice of measure In this event the report must include an examination of the several alternatives, clearly enough stated so that the executive department can make a decision concerning which criterion should be used

Finally, it must be emphasized that the problem is not completed when the details of the operation are understood by the operations research worker alone Since the purpose of the analysis is to provide the executive department with a basis for decision, the problem is successfully completed only when the executive department understands the essential parts of the conclusions of the analysis Consequently, an important part of operations research is the presentation of the result, sometimes by an oral briefing, but usually by a written report

The purpose of the report is to set forth clearly and distinctly the quantitative picture of the operation, to point out the sensitive items, and to predict changes that might bring improvements The report should contain conclusions but usually *should not contain recommendations* It should be designed to serve as a basis for decision but should not itself make the decisions Sometimes this distinction is a fine one, it is nevertheless an important one It should be apparent by now that the operations research group would lose some of its freedom of action if it usurped the duties of the executive and the executive would lose his effectiveness if he permitted such usurpation

1 3 8   General Comments

It must be emphasized again that the operations research worker is *not* a "gadgeteer," spending most of his time devising new equipment or modifying old equipment Such activity is important and also requires technically trained men to help the services, but it is an activity that should be carried on primarily by scientists attached to the service commands or bureaus rather than by men attached to the operational commands, as are the operations research men The operations research worker must often resist the urge to turn from the refractory problems of strategy and tactics, which are primarily his job, to the more congenial task of "playing" with a piece of new equipment True, there are times when the operations research man is the only technical man with an operational command, and equipment modifications must be done by him or they do not get done In this case, of course, the necessary "gadgeteering" is carried through However, the operations research man must keep in mind, in these cases, that he is stepping out of his own field and that such activity should not be allowed to keep him long from his proper studies of operations It is possible to call in technical men from the service commands to do the gadgeteering, but there is no one else to do the operations research if he does not do it

An important difference between operations research and other scientific work is the sense of *urgency* involved In this field a preliminary analysis based on incomplete data may often be much more valuable than a more thorough study using adequate data, simply because the crucial decisions cannot wait on the slower study but must be based on the preliminary analysis The big improvements often come from the first quick survey of a new field, later detailed study may only gain small additional factors The worker cannot afford to scorn superficial work, for wars (and, ofttimes, industry) do not wait for exhaustive study (although the exhaustive study should also be made, to back up the preliminary work) This is an additional reason for divesting the operations research worker of extraneous responsibilities and duties, so that he can have as much leisure time as possible to make as thorough a study as possible before the crucial decision must be made

14 PERSONNEL AND ORGANIZATION

It should be apparent by now that the operations research worker does not need to be a specialist in any particular branch of science He does, however, need to be a person with considerable experience in *research* of a scientific nature, whether he is a biologist, a physicist, a mathematician, or a worker in some other science The important requisite is that impersonal curiosity concerning new subjects that is the very essence of research ability

141 Choice of Personnel

The research scientist is trained to reject unsupported statements and has come to have the habit of desiring to rest his decisions on some quantitative basis, even if the basis is only a rough estimate This makes the research worker good at detecting the existence of problems and questions of which the regular executive staff may be unaware Research scientists also are trained to get down to the fundamentals of a question, to seek out broad underlying principles through a mass of sometimes conflicting and irrelevant data They know how to handle data and how to guard against fallacious interpretations of statistics

The particular type of mentality that is a success in operations research appears to be found most frequently in physics and biology and their associated borderline sciences, the special outlook seems to be found somewhat less commonly in mathematics, engineering, and economics, although there are some brilliant exceptions A tendency to look at an operation as a whole, common to theoretical research, is needed The gadgeteer, whose solution to any problem is more equipment, is definitely not desired

The operations research worker must be chosen for his personality as well as for his research ability, since part of his job is the presentation of results to nonscientific executive staffs He should be able to express himself easily and clearly Since many executive decisions, both in war and in peace, must be made in an atmosphere of secrecy, the operations research worker must be "security-minded" as discussed in 1 2 7 He must be capable of resisting the tendency toward "secrecy for secrecy's sake," but he must at the same time appreciate the need for security in some aspects of his work and he must be capable of understanding and implementing the necessary details involved in maintaining security

142 Importance of Mutual Understanding between Administrator and Scientist

The reaching of a working understanding on "terms of reference" between the operations research worker and the administrative head to whom he is assigned is one of the most important organizational problems encountered in entering a new field of operations research Scientist and administrator perform different functions and often must take opposite points of view The scientist must always be skeptical and is often impatient at arbitrary decisions, the administrator must eventually make decisions which are in part arbitrary and is often impatient at skepticism It takes a great deal of understanding and mutual trust for the two to work closely enough together to realize to the fullest the potentialities of the partnership

The foregoing psychological difficulties are pointed out here so they can be foreseen and allowed for in the future During World War II they often caused confusion and inefficiency because they were not appreciated Fundamentally, the problem is to convince the administrator that the scientist can help him make his decisions more effectively and wisely, and to convince the scientist that the executive is still the one to make the basic decisions

The first reaction of the executive to operations research is usually that the scientists are welcome but that there seems to be no important problem suitable for them to attack Next comes a reaction of suspicion and impatience, when the usual scientific procedure of scrutinizing critically all assumptions is commenced Considerable tact must be employed to persuade the administrator that measures of value and estimates of results are not called in question simply from a desire to criticize

At this stage in the proceedings great care must be exercised to keep the initial doubts and questionings (necessary for the scientific analysis) from spreading to other parts of the organization. Once a few successful solutions have been obtained and the executive realizes that all this critical questioning does produce results, the worst of the opposition is over In time the executive comes to recognize the sort of problems that operations research can handle and comes to refer these problems to the group without prodding from the group itself (at least until the normal rotation brings a new set of officers who must be indoctrinated anew)

Occasionally there is some suspicion that the operations research worker wishes to take over the command function of the executive This may come up if the findings of the operations research worker are considerably at variance with the preconceived opinion of the officer This suspicion can only be overcome if both the worker and the officer realize that the results of operations research are *only a part* of the material from which final decision must be made In any administrative decision there enter a great number of considerations that cannot be put into quantitative form (or at least cannot yet be put into this form) Knowledge of these qualitative aspects and ability to handle them are the proper function of the administrator, and *not* the prerogative of operations research

The operations research worker must work out those aspects of the problem that are amenable to quantitative analysis and report his findings to the executive The administrator must then combine these findings with the qualitative aspects mentioned previously, to form a basis for the final decision This decision must be made by the executive officer If his decision runs counter to the scientific findings at times, the scientist must not consider that this is necessarily a repudiation of his work These questions of organization and relationships are discussed more fully in Chapter 8. The particular example chosen for discussion there is a military one, but the translation to other situations should be obvious

1.4.3   Possible Peacetime Applications

Very much the same sort of initial opposition can be expected from governmental and industrial ad-

ministrators Once this is overcome, however, there is no reason why operations research should not be as fruitful in aiding in the solution of these problems as it was in helping solve military problems Just as with problems of war, of course, some operations will be much more fruitful of results than others Traffic problems, for instance, are highly amenable, for data are easy to obtain, and changes in conditions (if not too drastic) can be produced to study the effects

On the other hand, the design of city housing and municipal facilities requires data that are difficult to obtain, the solution is strongly dependent on terrain and other individual circumstances, and operational experiments are difficult if not impossible The field of housing and of city planning is an extremely important one, however, and operations research in this field could be started whenever an adequate administrative authority is set up to whom the scientist could report and which could insure that the research is more than idle academic exercise

Operations research in telephone operation is not difficult because the whole system is under a more or less unified control (In fact, operations research in this field has been going on for a number of years under the name of systems engineering) Operations research in house heating, however, might well be fruitless, because the fragmented nature of the industry makes the gathering of data difficult and makes any action on proposed solutions well-nigh impossible (A question that might be important, but that would be difficult to answer, would be. If another war is likely to occur in the near future, should coal heating, oil heating, or electric heating be encouraged in the homes in northeastern United States?) Operations research on traffic might well result in suggestions for change in design of automobiles, but the competitive nature of this industry would make it extremely difficult for the suggestions to be put into practice.

All these comments serve to emphasize the obvious fact that operations research is fruitful *only* when it studies *actual operations* and that a partnership between administrator and scientist, which is fundamental in the process, requires an administrator *with authority* for the scientist to work with Operations research done separately from an administrator in charge of operations becomes an empty exercise To be valuable it must be toughened by the repeated impact of hard operational facts and pressing day-by-day demands, and its scale of values must be repeatedly tested in the acid of use. Otherwise it may be philosophy, but it is hardly science

Chapter 2

PROBABILITY

THE THEORY OF PROBABILITY is the branch of mathematics which is most useful in operations research Nearly all results of operations of war involve elements of chance, usually to a large extent, so that only when the results of a number of similar operations are examined does any regularity evidence itself It is nearly as important to know the degree by which individual operations may differ from some expected average, as it is to know how the average depends on the variables involved In analyzing operational data, which are often meager and fragmentary, it is necessary to be able to estimate how likely it is that the next operations will display characteristics similar to those analyzed Probability enters into many analytical problems as well as all the statistical problems

The present chapter will sketch those parts of the theory of probability which are of greatest use in operations research, and will illustrate the theory with a few examples Section 5 1 will deal in detail with specific methods of handling statistical problems, and Chapters 6 and 7 will deal with some of the applications of probability theory to analytical problems For further details of the theory, the reader is referred to texts on probability theory [*]

2 1   FUNDAMENTAL CONCEPTS

In many situations the system of causes which lead to particular results is so complex that it is impossible, or at least impracticable, to predict exactly which of a number of possible results will arise from a given cause If a penny is tossed, it is possible in principle to analyze the forces acting on the penny and the motions they produce, and so to predict whether the penny will come to rest with heads or tails showing, however, no one has ever taken the effort to carry out the analysis When a gun is fired at a target, it should again be possible to predict exactly where the shell will hit, but the prediction would involve a knowledge of the characteristics of the gun, shell, propellant, and atmosphere far more exact than has yet been obtained.

With a perfect penny, tossed at random, there is no more reason to expect heads than tails to appear. We say then that heads and tails are *equally likely* to appear In throwing a symmetrical die the numbers 1, 2, 3, 4, 5, and 6 are equally likely. This notion of equal likelihood is basic to the theory of probability It does not seem to be possible to give it an exact definition, but we accept it as a self-evident intuitive concept At times (as with a coin or die) we reach the conclusion that two results are equally likely from considerations of symmetry In other cases the conclusion is made on the basis of past experience Thus, for example, if a gun is fired a great number of times, and right and left deflections appear an equal number of times, we reach the conclusion that right and left deflections are equally likely.

From the notion of equal likelihood we can derive the idea of randomness Suppose that we have a chance method by which a point is chosen on a line of finite length. If the method is such that the point is equally likely to fall in any of a number of parts of the line of equal length, we say that the point is chosen *at random* For example, if a perfectly balanced wheel is spun hard and allowed to come to rest under the action of a small amount of friction, the point of the circumference which comes to rest under a stationary index pointer is a random point of the circumference Or a random point may be chosen by drawing a series of numbers from a hat containing slips of paper with the digits 0, 1, 2,   9 (replacing the slip after each drawing), and writing the result as a fraction in decimal notation This fraction is then the coordinate of a random point on a line of unit length Examples of random sequences of numbers are given in Tables I and II on pages 153 to 155

We may also speak of points chosen at random in spaces of more than one dimension. Thus, for example, we may say that a point is chosen at random in a given area if, given two parts of the area of equal size, the chosen point is equally likely to be in either one of them.

2 1 1   Probability

If we now consider a situation in which any one of a number of results may occur (but not necessarily with equal likelihood), we may compare the likelihoods of these results with the likelihood that a point chosen at random on a line falls within a given inter-

11

val on that line In fact, the line may be divided into a set of intervals in such a way that each interval corresponds to one of the possible results, and so that the likelihood of each result and the likelihood of a random point of the line falling in the corresponding interval are equal

Thus, in the case of the tossed penny, we may compare the chances of heads and tails with the chance that a point chosen at random on a line falls in the right or left half of the line The situation is shown in

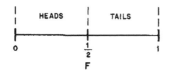

FIGURE 1   Comparison of randomly chosen points on a line with throws of a coin

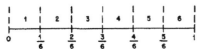

FIGURE 2   Comparison of randomly chosen points on a line with throws of a die. Each ⅙ portion of the line corresponds to a face of the die

Figure 1 For the rolls of a die, the intervals for the possible results may be chosen as in Figure 2

When the process has been carried out, the length of the interval corresponding to each result, measured in terms of the total length of the line as a unit, is defined as the *probability* of that result Thus the probability of throwing heads with a coin is ½, and the probability of rolling a 3 with a die is ⅙

Several theorems concerning probabilities are obvious from this definition the probability that one or another of a set of possible results will be obtained is the sum of the probabilities of the individual results, the sum of the probabilities of all the results is unity, if p is the probability of any result, the probability that the result does not happen is $1 - p$, and so on

2 1 2   Distribution Functions

This same definition can be applied when the possible results consist of values of a continuous variable Consider the following example A long rod is pivoted at its center and spun We wish to know the probability that when it comes to rest, the rod (or its extension) will intersect a given line within any given interval (Figure 3A) Let XY be the line, and let AB

be the rod, pivoted at the point O, a perpendicular distance a from XY Let x be the distance of the point of intersection from the foot of the perpendicular from O to XY If θ is the angle made between the rod and a line parallel to XY, then the effect of the

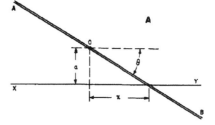

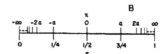

FIGURE 3   A Rod AB is spun about pivot O and comes to rest at angle θ, intersecting line XY at point x B Shows relation between x and $F = 1 - \theta/\pi$

spinning is to choose a value of θ at random between 0 and π The value of x is then determined by

$$x = a \cot \theta \tag{1}$$

Since θ has a random value between 0 and π, then $F = (\pi - \theta)/\pi$ has a random value between 0 and 1, and

$$x = -a \cot (\pi F) \tag{2}$$

We may now represent the situation by a diagram of the type of Figures 1 and 2 if we take a line of unit length and mark it with a uniform scale for the variable F, and another scale for the corresponding values of x This is shown in Figure 3B The probability that x lies between any two values x_1 and x_2 is equal to the length of the corresponding interval on this scale Arithmetically this is equal to $F_2 - F_1$, so that this probability is

$$P = F_2 - F_1 = -\frac{1}{\pi}\cot^{-1}\left(\frac{x_2}{a}\right) + \frac{1}{\pi}\cot^{-1}\left(\frac{x_1}{a}\right) \tag{3}$$

---

*The expression $(\pi - \theta)/\pi$ is chosen instead of the more obvious θ/π in order to make x an increasing, rather than a decreasing, function of F

We see from the previous problem that we have two basic types of variables This will also hold true in the general case.

The fundamental variable, from the theoretical point of view, we will call the *random variable* ξ, which will have any value (within its allowed range) with *equal probability* The mechanics of the problem must be analyzed sufficiently to say that a random trial corresponds to a random choice of ξ

The second type of variable, the *stochastic variable* x will be dependent upon the random variable, that is, a random choice of ξ will define some value of x The stochastic variable is the quantity we measure experimentally We may write x as some function of ξ such that the proper relationship holds for all values of ξ and x

For convenience in analyzing the problem, we make a choice of origin and scale for the random variable such that the values of ξ will occur between zero and unity We may do this by suitably combining the random variable with the (constant) values it takes at the ends of its allowed range When this is done, the values found for ξ in the course of many trials will be distributed more or less uniformly over the interval (0, 1) (In the limit, as the number of trials goes to infinity, all possible values of ξ from zero to unity will occur)

If ξ, which is now defined from zero to unity, is represented as a function of x, we may write

$$\xi = F(x), \qquad 0 \leqq \xi \leqq 1 \qquad (1)$$

This function, $F(x)$, is such that the process of choosing a value of x is the same as choosing a value of ξ *at random* in the interval (0, 1) $F(x)$ is then called the *distribution function* of the variable x The probability that x lies between x_1 and x_2 is $F(x_2) - F(x_1)$

For an infinitesimal interval dx, located at x, the probability that the stochastic variable lies in this interval is $F(x + dx) - F(x) = (dF/dx)dx$ (by a Taylor's series expansion). The function $f(x) = dF/dx$ is known as the *probability density* at x The traditional treatment of probabilities in a continuum takes the probability density as fundamental In dealing with statistical data, however, working with $f(x)$ involves the difficulties and inaccuracies inherent in numerical differentiation This can largely be avoided by using $F(x)$ instead of $f(x)$ [In addition, if $F(x)$ is discontinuous, the probability density has no simple meaning]

We see how this applies to the previous problem There, θ is the random variable, with its allowed values going from 0 to π, and x is the stochastic variable, where $x = a \cot \theta$ The scale and origin of θ are then redefined, so that we form the new random variable with a range from zero to unity, that is,

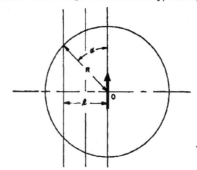

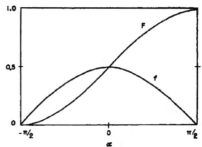

FIGURE 4 Probability of sighting an object at relative bearing α. The distribution function is F, and f is the probability density

$(\pi - \theta)/\pi$ This new random variable, when taken as a function of the stochastic variable x, is then the distribution function for x

$$F(x) = -\frac{1}{\pi} \cot^{-1}\left(\frac{x}{a}\right)$$

The probability density is therefore

$$f(x) = \frac{1}{\pi}\left(\frac{a}{x^2 + a^2}\right)$$

Another example, corresponding to a more immediately useful problem, comes from the theory of search (see Division 6, Volume 2B for further details) Suppose a search vessel, at O in Figure 4, is moving with constant velocity in the direction indicated by the arrow The object searched for (life raft, enemy vessel, etc) is likely to be anywhere on the ocean, and is assumed at rest for simplicity. We make the simplifying assumption (which is not a bad one for some cases) that if the object comes within a radius R of the vessel it will be discovered The question to be answered here is the probability that the object, if it is discovered, comes into view at a relative bearing α.

Relative to the search vessel, the ocean is moving along the parallel paths shown in the figure The object will also move along one of these relative paths, say the one coming a nearest distance l from the search vessel It is not difficult to see that, if the object is placed at random, and if it is to be discovered, the value of l will *occur at random* between the limits $-R$ and $+R$.

We see, therefore, that since all values of l (between $-R$ and $+R$) have equal probability, l is the random variable The angle α, which is to be measured experimentally, is the stochastic variable, and is related to the random variable by $l = R \sin \alpha$. We now redefine the random variable so that it takes on values between zero and unity, that is,

$$\xi = \frac{R + l}{2R}, \quad 0 \leqq \xi \leqq 1 \text{ when } -R \leqq l \leqq R.$$

We may therefore write for the distribution function

$$F(\alpha) = \frac{R + R \sin \alpha}{2R}$$

$$= \tfrac{1}{2}(1 + \sin \alpha).$$

The probability that the object will be sighted between the bearings α_1 and α_2 $(-\pi/2 < \alpha_1, \alpha_2 < \pi/2)$ is

$$F(\alpha_2) - F(\alpha_1) = \tfrac{1}{2}(\sin \alpha_2 - \sin \alpha_1)$$

In particular, the probability that the object will be sighted between the bearings α and $\alpha + d\alpha$ (i e , will be sighted "at the bearing α" in the element $d\alpha$) is

$$f(\alpha)d\alpha = \tfrac{1}{2} \cos \alpha d\alpha$$

The quantity $f(\alpha) = \tfrac{1}{2} \cos \alpha$ is the probability density. Both F and f are plotted in Figure 4.

We see that, as long as our assumptions hold (efficiency of lookouts equal in all directions), all objects

sighted at range R), then the object is more likely to be sighted in the forward quarter than on either beam, since $f(\alpha)$ is largest in this region Moreover, a restriction of the lookouts to searching over the forward quarter will only reduce the probability of sighting by approximately 30 per cent (In the example considered here, this might be the wrong restriction to make, for two lookouts facing in opposite directions and looking out on either beam will eventually sight *all* the targets which all-round-looking lookouts could discover Why? Which restriction is best must be decided on other grounds)

The distribution function may be applied to discrete as well as to continuous stochastic variables The rolling of a die, for example, may be thought of in terms of a variable x, the number appearing on the die, and a distribution function F, related by the equations

$$
\begin{array}{ll}
x = 1 & 0 \leqq F < 1/6 \\
x = 2 & 1/6 \leqq F < 2/6 \\
x = 3 & 2/6 \leqq F < 3/6 \\
x = 4 & 3/6 \leqq F < 4/6 \\
x = 5 & 4/6 \leqq F < 5/6 \\
x = 6 & 5/6 \leqq F \leqq 1
\end{array}
$$

It should be noted that x is a single-valued function of F (although discontinuous), but F is not a single-valued function of x To try to express the probability density $f = dF/dx$ in such cases involves mathematical difficulties which cannot be discussed here

In each problem dealt with in the theory of probability we are dealing with one or more trials A gun is shot, or a depth charge is tested, or a fighter plane encounters an enemy, or a search plane tries to find an enemy vessel. In each case we are interested in the outcome of the trial or trials, which usually takes the form of a numerical result The range of the shell shot from the gun may be the interesting quantity, or the depth at which the depth charge exploded, or the length of time required to find the enemy vessel Sometimes the answer can be a discrete one, we may be interested only in whether the fighter plane was shot down or whether it shot down the enemy, or whether neither was shot down This numerical result, which may differ from trial to trial, is what is called the stochastic variable, x We are usually interested in determining the probability of occurrence of different values of this variable for different trials, or else we are interested in determining its average value for a large number of trials

In a great number of cases these probabilities and average values can only be determined experimentally by making a large number of trials In some other cases, such as the ones considered previously in this chapter, it is possible to analyze the situation completely and to work out mathematically the expected behavior of the stochastic variable at future trials It is possible to make this analysis in a much larger number of cases than might be expected, and in a great many more cases it is possible to make an approximate analysis of the situation which will be satisfactory for most requirements

2 1 3 Distribution Functions in Several Variables

In more complicated situations, the result of a chance process requires more than a single variable for its expression Such cases can be handled in a way

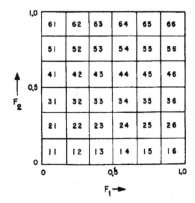

FIGURE 5 Representation of probability distribution in two variables Two dice

entirely similar to those of the previous section, but the distribution function, instead of corresponding to points chosen at random on a line, now corresponds to points chosen at random in an area, a solid, or a figure of a higher number of dimensions

As an illustration, consider the throws of a pair of dice The result of each throw can be thought of as determined by a random variable, F_1 for the first die, and F_2 for the second, in the way described in the preceding section For the two together we may combine the choosing of F_1 and F_2 into the process of choosing a point at random in a square, in which F_1

and F_2 are the two coordinates of the point. Figure 5 shows such a square It divides into 36 small squares, each corresponding to a single result of the throw Since each of these has an area equal to $\frac{1}{36}$ (the area of the large square being unity), the probability of any one throw is $\frac{1}{36}$ It is also easy to see the probability of obtaining any given total There are just six squares in which the total is 7, so the probability of throwing 7 is $\frac{6}{36}$ or $\frac{1}{6}$

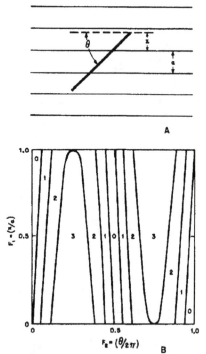

A

B

FIGURE 6 Needle on ruled paper (Buffon's problem) Plot of distribution functions versus numbers of lines crossed

As a second illustration, we may consider the following problem (Buffon's needle problem) A sheet of paper is ruled with parallel lines a distance a apart A needle of length l is thrown on the sheet at random. We wish to find the probability that the needle crosses 0, 1, 2, of the rulings Figure 6A shows a typical result of a trial Let x be the perpendicular

distance from the point of the needle to the first rul-
ing that the needle touches, and let θ be the angle
made by the needle with a line parallel to the rulings.
The number of rulings crossed by the needle is shown
in the following table:

If $l \sin \theta$ lies between			The number of rulings crossed is
$x + a$	and	$x + 2a$	2
x	and	$x + a$	1
$x - a$	and	x	0
$x - 2a$	and	$x - a$	1
$x - 3a$	and	$x - 2a$	2

Now by "throwing the needle at random" is meant
simply that all values of x between 0 and a are
equally likely, and all values of θ between 0 and 2π are
equally likely The distribution functions for x and θ
are therefore simply

$$F_1 = \frac{x}{a}, \qquad F_2 = \frac{\theta}{2\pi},$$

The throwing of the needle is equivalent to choosing
a point at random in a unit square whose coordinates
are F_1 and F_2 The regions of the square corresponding to 0, 1, 2, ·   rulings crossed are separated by
the curves

$$x + na = l \sin \theta \ (n = \quad , -2, -1, 0, 1, 2 \quad) \quad (5)$$

The structure of the square for the special case
$l = 3a$ is shown in Figure 6B The probabilities of
obtaining 0, 1, 2, or 3 crossings may be found analytically by integration or graphically by measuring the
areas on the square distribution diagram The results
are shown in the following table

No crossings	Probability
0	0 107
1	0 227
2	0 314
3	0 352

2.1 4   Compound Probabilities

If there are two results, A and B, either or both of
which may arise from a given set of causes, there are
a number of probabilities which require expression
We shall use the following notation ·

$P(A)$ = probability that A occurs if nothing is
known about B

$P(B)$ = probability that B occurs if nothing is
known about A

$P(AB)$ = probability that both A and B occur.

$P(A|B)$ = probability that A occurs if B is known
to have occurred.

$P(B|A)$ = probability that B occurs if A is known
to have occurred

We shall also use the expressions $\bar{A}$ and $\bar{B}$ for "not A"
and "not B," so that, for example, $P(\bar{A}|B)$ is the
probability that A does not occur, if B does occur

Such a system can be represented generally by the
choice of a random point in a plane area (Figure 7).

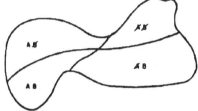

FIGURE 7   Graphical representation of compound probabilities

This area may be divided *into four regions*[b] *corre-
sponding to the four possible results: AB, $\bar{A}B$, $A\bar{B}$, $\bar{A}\bar{B}$*
The ratios of the areas of these regions to the total
area are the four fundamental probabilities $P(AB)$,
$P(\bar{A}B)$, $P(A\bar{B})$, and $P(\bar{A}\bar{B})$ Obviously we have

$$P(A) = P(AB) + P(A\bar{B}), \qquad (6)$$
$$P(B) = P(AB) + P(\bar{A}B)$$

We must now consider the *conditional* probabilities
$P(A|B)$, $P(B|A)$, etc If B is known to have happened, the random point is known to have fallen in
the combined area $AB + \bar{A}B$, but is equally likely
to be anywhere in this area, while the result A occurs
if, and only if, the point falls in AB The probability
$P(A|B)$ is therefore the ratio of the area AB to the
area $AB + \bar{A}B$, or

$$P(A|B) = \frac{P(AB)}{P(AB) + P(\bar{A}B)} = \frac{P(AB)}{P(B)}$$

Hence

$$P(AB) = P(B) \ P(A|B). \qquad (7)$$

[b] These are drawn as connected regions in Figure 7, but
this is not always the case

That is, the probability that A and B both happen is the product of the probability that B occurs if nothing is known about A, and the probability that A occurs if B is known to have happened

In some cases $P(A|B) = P(A)$ In this case we say that A is *independent* of B In terms of the fundamental probabilities $P(AB)$, etc, A is independent of B if

$$P(A|B) = \frac{P(AB)}{P(AB)+P(\bar{A}B)} = P(A)$$
$$= P(AB) + P(A\bar{B}),$$

or

$$P(AB) = [P(AB)]^2 + P(\bar{A}B)P(AB)$$
$$+ P(AB)P(A\bar{B}) + P(A\bar{B})P(\bar{A}B)$$
$$= P(AB)[P(AB) + P(\bar{A}B) + P(A\bar{B})]$$
$$+ P(A\bar{B})P(\bar{A}B)$$
$$= P(AB)[1 - P(\bar{A}\bar{B})] + P(A\bar{B})P(\bar{A}B)$$

This simplifies to

$$\frac{P(AB)}{P(\bar{A}B)} = \frac{P(A\bar{B})}{P(\bar{A}\bar{B})} \quad \text{(when } A \text{ is independent of } B\text{)}. \quad (8)$$

It will be noted that the condition that B is independent of A reduces to the same form, i e, that B is independent of A if A is independent of B.

Interesting and nontrivial examples illustrating the general principles of probability theory are very difficult to obtain this early in the discussion. Examples with tossed coins or dice are simple enough to satisfy fairly well the simple mathematical concepts we are discussing, but they are a far cry from the practical problems we hope to discuss later On the other hand, these practical problems require concepts and methods we have not yet discussed in order to solve them, or else must be hedged about by so many restrictions, in order to fit them to the mathematical principles being discussed, that they seem quite artificial The example given next will illustrate the principles of compound probability, but will also illustrate the difficulties in obtaining examples

We suppose a point P_1 placed at random somewhere within a strip of width $10d$ In order to make the example illustrate the principles we have discussed heretofore, we must imagine that the distance x_1 of P_1 from one side of the strip is chosen at random As a partial connection with practical problems which we shall discuss in more detail later, we might

imagine P_1 to be the position of a bomb crater produced by a bomber during area bombing (It would be difficult to imagine the sort of area bombing which would exactly satisfy the requirements of P_1 falling exactly inside the strip and being completely at random inside the strip, but it would not be difficult to imagine a type of area bombing which would *approximately* satisfy these requirements) Inside this strip are a series of six strips of width d (railroad tracks, perhaps) which we are interested in bombing This is shown in Figure 8 The random variable for point P_1 will then be $(x_1/10d)$ We can say that, when the value of this variable is between 0 3 and 0.4, track 2 will be destroyed The probability that this track will be destroyed will therefore be the difference between these two quantities, which is equal to one-tenth

Now suppose another bomb is dropped within the strip The situation relating to the position of this point P_2 will depend upon the relationship between the two bombs dropped The second bomb might be dropped by a different plane coming over at a different time and having no relation to the first plane In this case we can probably say that the dropping of the second bomb is independent of the dropping of the first bomb, and the second random variable $(x_2/10d)$ is independent of the first random variable The square area representing probabilities will then be as shown on the left side of Figure 8 The numbers in the various small squares indicate the particular strip within which the two bombs fall Since the two variables are completely random, the probabilities of occurrence are proportional to the areas involved. For instance, the probability that the first bomb fall on track 2 is one-tenth The probability that one or the other of the bombs fall on track 2 is the area of all those rectangles which have a number two inside them, i e, 0 19

The definitions discussed earlier in this section can also be illustrated For instance, the probability that track 5 will be hit by the second bomb, if we know that the first bomb has hit track 2, will be

$$P(5|2) = \frac{P(25)}{P(2)} = \frac{0\ 01}{0\ 10} = 0\ 1$$

This is equal to the probability $P(5)$ that track 5 is hit by the second bomb when we do not know what happened to the first bomb On further analysis it will be seen that this simple relationship comes about due to the fact that the areas involved in the present case are all rectangular, with boundaries parallel to the

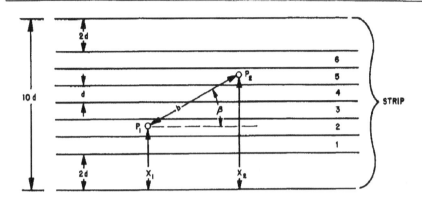

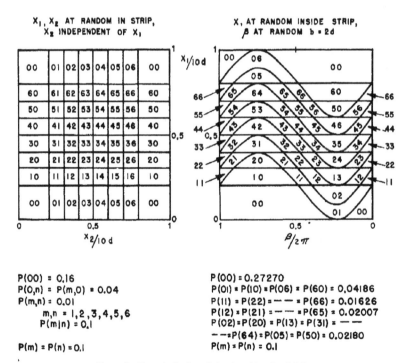

X₁, X₂ AT RANDOM IN STRIP,
X₂ INDEPENDENT OF X₁

X, AT RANDOM INSIDE STRIP,
β AT RANDOM b = 2d

$P(00) = 0.16$
$P(0,n) = P(m,0) = 0.04$
$P(m,n) = 0.01$
$\quad m,n = 1,2,3,4,5,6$
$P(m|n) = 0.1$

$P(m) = P(n) = 0.1$

$P(00) = 0.27270$
$P(01) = P(10) = P(06) = P(60) = 0.04186$
$P(11) = P(22) = —— = P(66) = 0.01626$
$P(12) = P(21) = —— = P(65) = 0.02007$
$P(02) = P(20) = P(13) = P(31) = ——$
$\quad —— = P(64) = P(05) = P(50) = 0.02180$
$P(m) = P(n) = 0.1$

FIGURE 8   Example of independent and conditional probabilities

edges of the probability square. This has occurred because the two random variables are independent of each other. Equation (8) can also be verified in this case, and again it is not difficult to see that the equation is satisfied because the subareas are rectangular in shape with their edges parallel to the main square.

In contrast, let us consider next that the second bomb is dropped a given distance $b = 2d$ away from the first bomb in a random direction (this case is related to the Buffon needle problem). This is perhaps a simplified picture of what happens when two bombs are dropped in train. In the actual case, of course, the distance is not exactly determined; however, this would mean introducing another random variable, and so, for the present example, we shall assume that the distance between points P_1 and P_2 is exactly $2d$. The two random variables are therefore $(x_1/10d)$ and $(\beta/2\pi)$ (shown in Figure 8). We note that, since we have required that P_1 fall at random within the full strip, in this example it sometimes occurs that P_2 will fall outside the strip. According to our assumptions, however, it can never fall more than a distance $2d$ beyond the edges.

The probability square for this second case is shown at the right in Figure 8. Since the two variables are not independent, we see that the areas corresponding to the different tracks being hit are not rectangles and, in fact, that a good many of them are missing entirely. For instance, according to our assumptions, it is impossible for track 5 to be hit by the second bomb if track 2 is hit by the first bomb. The probability of the first bomb hitting one of the tracks is still one-tenth, and, as might be expected, the probability of the second bomb hitting one of the tracks, if we do not know what has happened to the first bomb, is also equal to one-tenth. The probability that two adjacent tracks be hit, such as $P(1,2)$, is greater in this case than it was in the previous case, and the probability that two tracks a distance $2d$ apart be hit is somewhat larger still.

The probability that the second bomb will land on track 4 if we know that the first bomb has landed on track 2 is given by the following equation.

$$P(4|2) = \frac{P(24)}{P(2)} = \frac{0.02180}{0.1} = 0.2180$$

We see in this case that the result is not equal to $P(4)$. To check equation (8) we compute the following quantities.

$$P(2\mathcal{A}) = 1 - [P(20) + P(21) + P(22) + P(23)$$
$$+ P(24) + P(25) + P(26) + P(04)$$
$$+ P(14) + P(34) + P(44) + P(54)$$
$$+ P(64)]$$

$$= 1 - P(20) - P(21) - P(22) - P(23)$$
$$- P(24) - P(34) - P(44) - P(54)$$
$$- P(64)$$

$$= 0.82180 ;$$

$$P(24) = P(04) + P(14) + P(34) + P(44)$$
$$+ P(54) + P(64)$$

$$= P(34) + P(44) + P(54) + P(64)$$
$$= 0.07820$$
$$= P(2\mathcal{A}) .$$

A similar computation indicates that equation (8) does not hold, and therefore that the position of bomb one cannot be independent of the position of bomb two.

$$\frac{P(24)}{P(2\mathcal{A})} = 0.279 , \qquad \frac{P(2\mathcal{A})}{P(2\mathcal{A})} = 0.095$$

This is only natural, since our assumption regarding the fixed value of b makes independence impossible. The fact that the position of the second bomb is not independent of the position of the first bomb shows up in the nonrectangular division of the various areas in the probability square and in the corresponding impossibility to satisfy equation (8).

A number of conclusions which have an approximate application to certain practical problems in train bombing might be deduced from this example. For instance, we see that the probability $P(00)$ is larger when the bombs are dropped in train than when they are dropped independently. This is natural, of course, since if the first bomb misses, the second bomb is more likely to miss when it is in train than when it is not. However, we will discuss the train bombing problem in more detail later.

2.1.5 Expected Values

Suppose we have decided on the stochastic variable for the problem we are interested in, and suppose our analysis has made it possible to determine the functional relationship between this stochastic variable x and the random variable ξ which has equal probability of being anywhere in the range from zero to unity In addition to knowing the relative probabilities for the occurrence of different values of x, we will often wish to put our expectation of the results of a large number of trials in terms of *average*, or *expected*, values.

In practice the average value would be obtained by making a large number of trials at random and computing the average value of x from these trials If we have analyzed our problem correctly, we should be able to predict the value of this average with more or

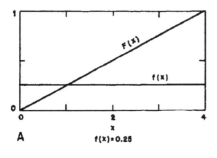

A $f(x)=0.25$

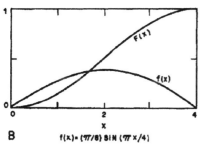

B $f(x) = (\pi/8) \sin (\pi x/4)$

FIGURE 9   Examples of distribution functions and probability densities with equal expected values of x Values of $\xi = F$ occur at random

less accuracy The predicted or idealized value of the average will be called the *expected value* of the stochastic variable x The actual average value obtained by making a series of trials would differ from this expected value by an amount which we would expect usually to diminish as the number of trials increases More will be said concerning this later

As an example of these general statements, let us consider the distribution functions and probability densities given in Figure 9 In the first case, the probability density is constant, independent of x, so that

x is directly proportional to the random variable $F = \xi$. Consequently, x is equally likely to have a value anywhere in the range 0 to 4. In a large number of trials one would expect to find a value of x larger than 2 just as often as a value of x smaller than 2; one can see intuitively that the expected value of x, which should correspond closely to the average of a large number of tries, would equal 2

Glancing at the second figure, we note that the probability density has a maximum near the center of the range for x, and therefore x does not vary linearly with the random variable $F = \xi$. Nevertheless, in this case also, due to the symmetry of the figure, one would intuitively see that the expected value of x is again 2

What then is the difference in the behavior of the two cases? How could we most easily distinguish between the two if we did not have the curves for probability density in front of us? One sees that in case A the value of x, taken from an individual trial, is more likely to differ widely from the expected value than is the case B In the first case the probability density is uniform, whereas in the second case the probability density is largest near $x = 2$, and falls off to zero at the two ends of the range

It would be a useful thing to have a numerical measure of this chance of large discrepancy of an individual trial away from the expected value The average value of the difference between an individual trial and the expected value is not a satisfactory measure because this, by definition, has positive values as often as negative values, and the final average should cancel out to zero If we remove the algebraic sign of the difference, however, by squaring, we can obtain a numerical measure Specifically we compute the average (or rather, the expected value) of the square of the difference between the result of an individual trial and the expected value of the result. The square root of this average square deviation will be called the *standard deviation*

Let us now try to state these concepts in a little more precise manner

If a very large number of choices of a random variable is made, we feel intuitively that if the range of the variable is divided into any number of equal intervals, we will choose values equally often in each of the equal intervals. In fact, this is essentially what we mean by our definition of a random variable This does not mean that this will be the actual result of a trial—on this we shall have more to say later Nevertheless, we shall call this the *expected* result.

In particular, if we may make N choices of a random variable ξ whose range is 0 to 1, the expected number of values in any infinitesimal interval $d\xi$ is $Nd\xi$

If x is a stochastic variable determined by ξ, the average value of x, if the expected result is obtained, is called the *expected value* of x, $E(x)$ This is obviously given by

$$E(x) = \int_0^1 xd\xi$$

$$= \int xf(x)dx \quad \text{(if } f \text{ exists)}$$

(9)

If there are only a discrete set of values x_i possible for x, with probabilities p_i, this reduces to

$$E(x) = \sum_i x_i p_i$$

(10)

The continuous case may be evaluated graphically by plotting x as a function of ξ $E(x)$ is then the area between the curve and the ξ axis

It should be noted that the expected value of a sum $x + y$ is the sum $E(x) + E(y)$ Naturally the expected value of ax is $aE(x)$, if a is a constant.

According to our previous discussion, we will define the *standard deviation* σ of a stochastic variable to be the square root of the expected value of the square of the difference between x and $E(x)$

$$\sigma^2(x) = E\{[x - E(x)]^2\}$$

$$= E\{x^2 - 2xE(x) + [E(x)]^2\}$$

(11)

$$= E(x^2) - 2E(x)E(x) + [E(x)]^2$$

$$= E(x^2) - [E(x)]^2$$

In the case shown in Figure 9A, $x = 4\xi$,

$$E(4\xi) = 4\int_0^1 \xi d\xi = 2 ,$$

$$E(16\xi^2) = \int_0^1 (16\xi^2)d\xi = \frac{16}{3} ,$$

(12)

$$\sigma^2(4\xi) = \frac{16}{3} - \frac{12}{3} = \frac{4}{3}; \quad \sigma = 1155 .$$

The standard deviation indicates that the result of a single trial differs on the average by a little more than a unit on either side of the average value, 2. This is often written as $E(x) \pm \sigma(x)$, in this case 2 ± 1 16

For the case of Figure 9B the expected value and the standard deviation turn out to be

$$f(x) = \frac{\pi}{8} \sin \frac{\pi x}{4} , \quad F(x) = \frac{1}{2} - \frac{1}{2} \cos \frac{\pi x}{4} ;$$

$$E(x) = \frac{\pi}{8} \int_0^4 x \sin \frac{\pi x}{4} dx = 2 ,$$

(13)

$$E(x^2) = \frac{\pi}{8} \int_0^4 x^2 \sin \frac{\pi x}{4} dx = 4\,7578 ;$$

$$\sigma^2 = 0\,7578 , \quad \sigma = 0\,8705 .$$

We notice that the standard deviation σ is less for this case than for the case of Figure 9A given in equation (12) This is to be expected, since the probability density of Figure 9B shows a more pronounced clustering of values around the expected value 2

If a point is chosen at random within a circle of radius a, we may find the expected value of the distance from the point to the center For, in this case, if x and y are coordinates with origin at the center of the circle,

$$E(r) = \frac{1}{\pi a^2} \iint r dx dy ,$$

when the integration is over the circle Transforming to polar coordinates,

$$E(r) = \frac{1}{\pi a^2} \iint r^2 dr d\theta$$

$$= \frac{2}{3} a$$

We also have

$$E(r^2) = \frac{1}{\pi a^2} \iint r^3 \cdot r dr d\theta$$

$$= \frac{1}{2} a^2 ,$$

$$\sigma^2(r) = \frac{1}{2} a^2 - \frac{4}{9} a^2 = \frac{1}{18} a^2$$

2.2   THE SIMPLE DISTRIBUTION LAWS

With a trial or series of trials involving random elements, such as operations of war often turn out to be, the result of an individual trial cannot be predicted exactly in advance What can be predicted, if we can analyze the problem thoroughly, is the probability of certain events occurring, which can be expressed in terms of the distribution function or the probability density If the probability of a certain event occurring is large, then we can reasonably expect that for most of the trials this event will occur, unless the probability is unity, however, there is always the chance that we will be unlucky in the first or succeeding tries

When a large number of trials can be carried out, a knowledge of the distribution function enables one to predict average values with more or less precision As more and more trials are made, we can expect the average value of the result to correspond closer and closer to the expected value which has been discussed in the previous section One can also compute the chance that the average result of many trials will differ by a specified amount from the computed expected value If the general form of the distribution function is known, one can even compute the probability that the average results of a second series of trials will differ by a specified amount from the average result of a first series of trials

Such calculations are extremely important in studying operations which are repeated many times, such as bombing runs or submarine attacks If the first 50 antishipping strikes result in 10 enemy vessels sunk, it might be important to compute the probability that the next 50 strikes would sink at least 8 enemy ships This can be done if the distribution corresponding to the attack is known at least approximately

Consequently, it is important to compute the distribution functions for a number of very general statistical situations, which correspond more or less accurately to actual situations often encountered In a great number of cases this correspondence is not exact, but is close enough so that statistical predictions can be made with reasonable success The more useful cases will be discussed in this section It should be emphasized again that there are many situations encountered in practice where none of the common distribution laws apply, so that it is not wise to apply the results of this section blindly to a new problem

2 2 1   Binomial Distribution

The simplest case is where the result of the trial can be called either a success or a failure, such as the trial of tossing a coin to get heads, or the firing of a torpedo at an enemy vessel. In some of these cases it is possible to determine the probability of success at each trial, we can call this p The probability of failure in a given trial is therefore $q = 1 - p$

A typical random sequence of successes, S, and failures, F, is shown in Table 1 where the probability of success $p = 0\ 5$ This sequence is typical of random

TABLE 1 Random sequence of successes (S) and failures (F), when the probability of success is 0 5

FFFSS	*FFSSS*	*FSSSS*	*SFFSF*	*SSSSF*
SFFFF	*SSFSF*	*SFFFS*	*SFFSS*	*FFSFF*
SFFFF	*FSFSF*	*FSFFS*	*FSSSS*	*FFSSS*
SFSSF	*SSSSS*	*SSSFF*	*FFSFF*	*SFFFF*

events and illustrates a number of their properties Other sequences can be obtained from Table I at the back of the book

In the first place, the average result of a small number of trials may give a completely erroneous picture of the probability of success of the rest of the trials In this case the first three trials were all failures, which might discourage one if it were not known that the probability of success is 50 per cent We notice also that the seventeenth set of five trials is all successes If this were the first set of five trials, it might lead to overconfidence

In the twenty sets of five tries each, there is one with all five successes, there are three with four successes and one failure, six with three successes and two failures, five with two successes and three failures, five with one success and four failures, and there is none with five failures It is often useful to be able to compute the expected values of the frequency of occurrence of such cases The expected value of the fraction of times a given proportion of successes and failures occur in a set of trials is, of course, the probability of occurrence of the proportion We shall compute the probability of occurrence of s successes and $n - s$ failures in a set of n trials, when the probability of success in a single trial is p

Fully as important is the inverse problem where we have made a series of trials and wish to deduce from them the probability of success p for an individual trial An examination of Table 1 will indicate that

TABLE 2 Comparison of results of Table 1 with expected values $(n = 5, p = 0.5)$

	$s = 5$	$s = 4$	$s = 3$	$s = 2$	$s = 1$	$s = 0$
Per cent success in five trials	100	80	60	40	20	0
Fraction of times combination observed	0 05	0 15	0 30	0 25	0 25	0
Expected value of fraction, $P(s, 5)$	0 03	0 16	0 31	0 31	0 16	0 03

Observed mean square deviation $(s - 2.5)_{avg}^2 = 1.35$

we cannot compute exactly the value of p from the results of a finite number of trials (unless, of course, we can analyze the situation completely by mathematics and predict the value of p). What we can do is to compute the most probable value of p and compute the probability that p has other values However, this knowledge is sufficient to enable us to compute expected values for another similar series of trials. This problem will also be discussed later in the section

By the law of compound probabilities, if each trial is independent the probability of a given sequence of s successes and $n - s$ failures in a given order (such as $FSFFF$, for instance, or else $FFFFS$) is

$$p^s q^{n-s}, \quad \text{where } q = 1 - p$$

Corresponding to any given values of s and n there are

$$\frac{n!}{s!(n-s)!}$$

different orders[6] in which the s successes and $n - s$ failures can occur (for instance one success and four failures is either $SFFFF$, $FSFFF$, $FFSFF$, $FFFSF$, or $FFFFS$) It follows that the total probability of obtaining s successes and $n - s$ failures in n trials is

$$P(s, n) = \frac{n!}{s!(n-s)!} p^s q^{n-s}. \quad (14)$$

If we expand $(p + q)^n$ by the binomial theorem, we see that $P(s, n)$ is just the value of the term containing $p^s q^{n-s}$ in the expansion For this reason the distribution of the probability of obtaining s successes in n trials is known as the *binomial distribution*.

The expected number of successes is, by equation (10),

[6] For a discussion of the laws of permutations and combinations, see Fry[1]

$$E(s) = \sum_{s=0}^{n} s P(s, n)$$

$$= \sum_{s=0}^{n} s \frac{n!}{s!(n-s)!} p^s q^{n-s}$$

$$= p \frac{\partial}{\partial p} \sum_{s=0}^{n} \frac{n!}{s!(n-s)!} p^s q^{n-s}$$

$$= p \frac{\partial}{\partial p} (p + q)^n$$

$$= np(p + q)^{n-1},$$

or, since $p + q = 1$,

$$E(s) = np. \quad (15)$$

In other words, the expected number of successes is equal to the number of trials times the probability of success per trial, which is as it should be In the case given in Table 1 the expected number of successes in five tries would be 2 5 In the sequence of twenty sets shown in Table 1, all possible values of s except $s = 0$ occurred The fractional number of times a particular value of s occurred in the sequence of tests is given in Table 2 These fractions are also compared with their expected values $P(s, 5)$ The correspondence is fairly close

The observed value of s, the number of successes in five trials, may differ considerably from the expected value 2 5 For instance, in five cases out of twenty the value is $s = 1$ This is reflected in the value of the mean square deviation computed from the actual results given in Table 1 This comes out to be 1 35, having a square root approximately equal to 1 2 We can express the observations given in Table 1 by saying that the number of successes in five trials is 2.5 ± 1.2 The value of the root-mean-square deviation gives a measure of how widely an individual series of trials will deviate from the expected value

To find the standard deviation,

$$E(s^2) = \sum_{s=0}^{n} s^2 \frac{n!}{s!(n-s)!} p^s q^{n-s}$$

$$= p\frac{\partial}{\partial p}\left[p\frac{\partial}{\partial p}(p+q)^n \right]$$

$$= np + n(n-1)p^2$$

Hence

$$\sigma^2(s) = E(s^2) - [E(s)]^2$$
$$= np(1-p)$$
$$= npq. \tag{16}$$

The standard deviation is, of course, the expected value of the root-mean-square deviation For Table 1 we have found that the root-mean-square deviation was $\sqrt{1\,35}$ The standard deviation for this case turns out to be $\sqrt{1\,25}$, which is a reasonable check Theoretical calculations would therefore have indicated that the number of successes in five trials would be $2\,5 \pm 1\,1$, which corresponds fairly closely to the actual results of the sequence given in Table 1

As an example for the reader, it might be instructive to analyze the following random sequence of successes and failures for the probability of success equal to 0 3

FFFFF	*SSFFF*	*FFFFF*	*FFSFF*	*SFFFF*
SFFFF	*SFSFS*	*FSSFS*	*SSSFF*	*FFFFS*
SFFSF	*FFFFF*	*FSSSS*	*SFFSF*	*FFFSS*
FFSFS	*FFFFF*	*FSFSF*	*FFFFF*	*SFFFF*

Now, suppose we are given the sequence of results of Table 1, and are asked to find the value of p, the probability of success of an individual trial This question will be discussed more completely in the section on sampling, but it is instructive to commence the discussion here. The most probable value of p would be obtained by dividing the number of successes actually observed by the total number of trials, which for any single set of five trials may differ widely from the true value A crude measure of how widely the true value may differ from the observed value can be computed by assuming that the value of p actually equals the observed value of s/n and computing a mean square deviation from this assumed value of p

$$\text{Rough estimate}\cdot \sigma^2 = s\left(1 - \frac{s}{n}\right), \tag{17}$$

where s is the observed number of successes in n

trials For example, if we performed only the first set of five trials in Table 1, we would then estimate that the expected number of successes in five future trials would be $2 \pm 1\,1$ where the figure after the plus-or-minus sign is computed from the expression above·

$$\sqrt{2(1 - 0\,4)} = 1\,1 .\,.$$

Our estimated value of p from the first set of five trials is therefore $0\,4 \pm 0.2$ If we wish to make this estimate more accurate, we must perform a larger number of trials than five

The formula given above for obtaining a rough estimate of σ^2 breaks down completely in certain cases For instance, in the seventeenth set of trials (which turned out to be all successes) the rough estimate turns out to be zero, since $s = n$ A more satisfactory way of estimating the likely range of p can be obtained from equation (14) For an observed number of successes s in n trials, we can find out over what range of assumed values of p the probability of occurrence of this result, $P(s, n)$ is greater than one chance in three (or perhaps one chance in ten if one wishes to be finicky) If we had been unlucky enough to obtain five successes in five trials when the "actual" value of p was 0 5, we would not have been able to obtain a very good estimate of the value of p from only these five trials All we could have said from this one sequence of trials was that there was less than one chance in three that the true value of p was smaller than 0 8, and that the chances were less than one in ten that the true value of p was less than 0 6 The difficulties are inherent in the situation, five trials are too few to yield a dependable value of p

An instructive illustration of these general statements lies in the criticism of an occasionally used procedure for determining the percentage of duds in a batch of shells (or torpedoes or grenades). to fire the shells until one dud appears, and then to stop the test Suppose $n - 1$ shells were fired before a dud appeared and then the nth shell was a dud The predicted fraction of duds, based on such a test, would be $1/n$ and the predicted number of duds in N shells would be N/n

But it is rather dangerous to base predictions on the observation of only one failure, we could be quite seriously off in our prediction of how many duds would be in the next n shells From equation (14), the probability of finding one dud in n trials, when the expected fraction of duds is q is

$$P(n - 1, n) = nq(1 - q)^{n-1},$$

which approaches nqe^{-nq} when q is small In this case we do not know q, but we wish to determine the range of values of q over which the probability nqe^{-nq} has reasonably large values (is larger than 0.1 for instance)

The maximum value of $P(n-1, n)$ is e^{-1}, corresponding to the most probable value for q of $1/n$ In other words, the most probable prediction from our series of n trials is that there is one dud in every n shells. But, if we assume that q is twice this (2 duds per n shells), $P(n-1, n)$ is $2e^{-2}$, which is still larger than 0 1 In fact, the range of values of q for which $P(n-1, n)$ is larger than 0 1 (i e , for which the result of our trials would be reasonably probable) is from approximately 0 11/n to 3 5/n Therefore, it is reasonably probable that the "most probable" value of the fraction of duds, $1/n$, is *nine times* larger than the "correct" value, or is too small by a *factor of nearly 4* In other words, it is fairly likely that the next n shells would have four duds instead of one, it is also likely that there would be only one dud in the next $9n$ shells

The moral of this analysis is that, if we wish to be "reasonably certain" of the fraction of duds in a lot of shells, we must fire enough shells so that more than one dud appears (in practice, enough trials so that at least ten duds appear is adequate).

A much more thoroughgoing analysis of these questions is given later in this chapter

We are frequently interested in not the probability of obtaining exactly s successes, but rather a number of successes between two limits, s_1 and s_2 When n, s_1, and s_2 are large, the calculation of the individual probabilities for all the values of s between s_1 and s_2 becomes very laborious These calculations can be simplified by the use of summation formulas based on the beta function, which we shall now derive

The probability that in n trials we obtain s or fewer successes is

$$P(\leq s, n) = \sum_{k=0}^{s} \frac{n!}{k!(n-k)!} p^k q^{n-k}$$

$$= q^n + \frac{n}{1!} pq^{n-1} + \frac{n(n-1)}{2!} p^2 q^{n-2} \cdots$$

$$+ \frac{n(n-1)\cdots(n-s+1)}{s!} p^s q^{n-s}$$

(18)

The derivative of $P(\leq s, n)$ with respect to p (remembering $q = 1 - p$) is easily seen to be

$$\frac{dP(\leq s, n)}{dp} = -\frac{n(n-1)\cdots(n-s)}{s!} p^s q^{n-s-1}$$

$$= -\frac{n!}{s!(n-s-1)!} p^s q^{n-s-1}$$

The other terms in the sum all cancel Hence

$$P(\leq s, n) = -\int_0^p \frac{n!}{s!(n-s-1)!} p^s (1-p)^{n-s-1} dp + c.$$

But, if $p = 1$, obviously $P(\leq s, n) = 0$ Hence

$$c = +\int_0^1 \frac{n!}{s!(n-s-1)!} p^s (1-p)^{n-s-1} dp,$$

and

$$P(\leq s, n) = \int_p^1 \frac{n!}{s!(n-s-1)!} p^s (1-p)^{n-s-1} dp$$

Now the incomplete beta function is defined as

$$B_x(a, b) = \int_0^x p^{a-1} (1-p)^{b-1} dp, \qquad (19)$$

and the complete beta function as

$$B(a, b) = \int_0^1 p^{a-1} (1-p)^{b-1} dp = \frac{(a-1)!(b-1)!}{(a+b-1)!} \quad (20)$$

We therefore see that the distribution function for this case is

$$F_b(s, n) = P(\leq s, n)$$

$$= 1 - \frac{B_p(s+1, n-s)}{B(s+1, n-s)}$$

$$= 1 - I_p(s+1, n-s), \qquad (21)$$

where $F_b(s, n)$ is the binomial distribution function, that is, the probability of obtaining s or fewer successes in n trials

Tables of the ratio

$$I_x(a, b) = \frac{B_x(a, b)}{B(a, b)}$$

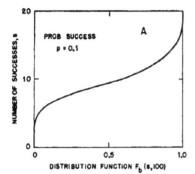

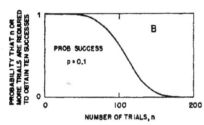

FIGURE 10   A Binomial distribution function $F_b(s, n)$ for $n = 100$, $p = 0.1$ B Probability $F_b(s - 1, n - 1)$ that n or more tries are required to obtain 10 hits, for $s = 10$, $p = 0.1$

have been published[6] and serve as the most convenient method of evaluating $F_b(s, n)$ A short table of $F_b(s, n)$ is given at the back of the book (Table IV)

With $F_b(s, n)$ known, the probability that the number of successes in n trials is between s_1 and s_2 is easily found   In fact

$$P(s_1 \leqq s \leqq s_2, n) = \sum_{k=s}^{n} \frac{n!}{k!(n-k)!} p^k q^{n-k}$$

$$= P(\leqq s_2, n) - P(\leqq s_1 - 1, n)$$

$$= F_b(s_2, n) - F_b(s_1 - 1, n)$$

$$= I_p(s_1, n-s_1+1) - I_p(s_2+1, n-s_2)$$

$$(22)$$

To illustrate these results, suppose that a gun has a probability of 1/10 of hitting a target on each shot If 100 rounds are fired, the expected number of hits

is $1/10 \times 100 = 10$ The standard deviation is given by

$$\sigma^2 = 100 \times \frac{1}{10} \times \frac{9}{10} = 9,$$

or

$$\sigma = 3$$

These two results are sometimes summarized by saying that the expected number of hits is 10 ± 3 The probability $P(\leqq s, 100)$, or $F_b(s, 100)$, of obtaining s or fewer hits is shown in Figure 10A

We may also use these same results to determine how many trials will be needed to obtain a given number of successes, for the probability that n or more trials will be needed to obtain s successes is exactly the same as the probability that $n - 1$ trials produce $s - 1$ or less successes   Hence, using obvious notation,

$$P(s, \geqq n) = P(\leqq s - 1, n - 1)$$

$$= F_b(s - 1, n - 1)$$

$$= 1 - I_p(s, n - s - 1) \qquad (23)$$

In the example of the gun, if 10 hits are required, the probability that n or more shots are required is shown in Figure 10B

2.2.2   The Normal Distribution

When the number of trials is large, the frequency of successes in a series of repeated trials becomes practically a continuous variable   Instead of s, it then becomes more convenient to use $x = s/n$ as a new variable   The expected value of x is then p, and its standard deviation is given by

$$\sigma^2(x) = \frac{pq}{n}.$$

The probability that the fraction of trials resulting in success is less than x is of course equal to the probability that the number of successes is less than xn, so that

$$P(< x, n) = 1 - I_p[nx, n(1 - x)],$$

if we neglect terms of the order of unity in comparison with n

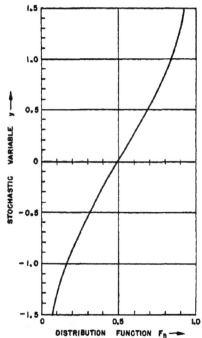

FIGURE 11. Normal distribution function $F_n(y)$ Expected value of y is $E(y) = 0$, and standard deviation $\sigma(y) = 1$ See Table V at back of book

It is sometimes convenient to use still another variable y, defined by

$$y = \frac{x - p}{\sqrt{\dfrac{pq}{n}}} = \sqrt{\frac{n}{pq}}\left(\frac{s}{n} - p\right),$$

whose expected value is 0, and whose standard deviation is 1 In terms of y

$$P(<y, n) = 1 - I_p\left[n\left(p + \sqrt{\frac{pq}{n}}\, y\right), n\left(q - \sqrt{\frac{pq}{n}}\, y\right)\right]$$

As n becomes larger and larger, the curves of $P(<y, n)$ against y approach a limiting curve, which is generally known as the *normal distribution curve*

It is shown in standard works on probability that the limiting curve has for its equation·

$$F_n(y) = P(<y, \infty)$$

$$= \frac{1}{\sqrt{2\pi}} \int_{-\infty}^{y} e^{-u^2/2} du ,$$

$$F_n(-y) = 1 - F_n(y) \tag{24}$$

The curve of y as a function of F is shown in Figure 11, and a table of values is given in Table V at the back of the book By its definition, F is the random variable corresponding to the stochastic variable y

The normal distribution law is much used (in fact *too* much used) as an approximation to other distribution laws It is applied, for example, not only to long series of repeated trials, but also to fairly short series, and also to represent the distribution of unanalyzed errors which occur in physical measurements Its advantage is that if x is any stochastic variable whose expected value is m and standard deviation is σ, we may define a variable

$$y = \frac{x - m}{\sigma}, \tag{25}$$

and assume for better or worse that y follows the normal distribution law We thus set up a distribution law on the scanty basis of only the two constants m and σ This procedure, however, is dangerous and can lead to very erroneous conclusions unless tests are applied to verify the normality of the distribution Nevertheless, the normal distribution is most valuable because of its simplicity

A number of features of the normal law are obvious from Figure 11 The distribution is symmetrical in the sense that the probability that the value of y lies between y_1 and y_2 is the same as the probability that it lies between $-y_2$ and $-y_1$ Small values of y are more likely than large values. In fact, there is a 50 per cent probability that y lies between $-0\,67$ and $+0\,67$ and a 90 per cent probability that y lies between $-1\,64$ and $+1\,64$ By definition, for a normal distribution

$$E(y) = 0 ; \qquad \sigma^2(y) = 1 \tag{26}$$

Table III at the back of the book gives typical sequences of random values of y and of y^2. They have been obtained by considering the random numbers of Table I as five-digit decimal fractions, equal to random values of $F_n(y)$ From these, by use of tables of y as a function of F_n, we obtain corresponding values of y, the stochastic variable A constant amount has been added to each group of values of y so that the average value of y for each group is exactly zero This would not be strictly true for random values of y, but it makes the table more useful for some of the applications discussed in a later chapter Nor is it true that the actual values of the mean square deviation, $\overline{(y^2)}$, for each group are equal to unity, the standard deviation The larger the sample, however, the nearer will this be true (for instance, the mean square deviation for the whole of Table III is 1 015)

A glance at Table III shows that magnitudes of y smaller than unity are fairly common, magnitudes larger than two are quite uncommon This is typical of normal distributions Some interesting and useful applications of Table III will be given in Chapter 6

Deviations from the point-of-aim of aircraft bombs usually follow the normal distribution, with a standard deviation in range (along the track of the plane) greater than the standard deviation in deflection (perpendicular to the track of the plane). Therefore, a simple example would be the case of the bombing of a carrier, when the plane approaches on the beam In this case the length of the carrier is considerably larger than the deflection error, so that misses are over or under (i e , in range) rather than right or left, and the problem becomes a one-dimensional case. If the standard error of the bombardier and bomb in range is σ, and if the width of the carrier is a, then the probability of hitting the carrier with a single-bomb drop is

$$F_n\left(\frac{a}{2\sigma}\right) - F_n\left(-\frac{a}{2\sigma}\right)$$

$$= 2F_n\left(\frac{a}{2\sigma}\right) - 1 \xrightarrow{\sigma \to \infty} \left(\frac{a}{2\sigma}\right)\sqrt{1/2\pi}$$

$$= 0\ 40\left(\frac{a}{2\sigma}\right) \xrightarrow{\sigma \to 0} 1 - 1\ 60\left(\frac{\sigma}{a}\right)e^{-(a^2/8\sigma^2)}$$

If the bombardier is poorly trained (i e , the error σ is much larger than a) then halving the error will double the expected number of hits On the other hand, if the bombardier is good (i e , σ is much smaller than a), then a further reduction of error will not produce a proportional increase in the number of hits This is another illustration of the general rule that it pays more to improve the accuracy of the poorest in the team rather than to improve still further that of the best

The case where more than one bomb is dropped is discussed in Chapter 6

2 2.3 The Poisson Distribution

In our discussions so far of random points on a line, we have considered only the case in which the length of the line is finite. If the line is allowed to increase in length without limit, the probability that a given point falls in any fixed interval obviously approaches zero If, however, we choose not one, but a number of points, and let this number grow larger in proportion to the length of the line, then the probability of finding any given number of points in any fixed interval may be expected to approach a finite limit

Suppose that on a line of length L, kL points are chosen on the line independently and at random This probability that any one of these points lies in a given interval of length x is

$$\frac{x}{L},$$

and, by the binomial distribution law, the probability that exactly m of the kL points will be found in the interval x is

$$\frac{(kL)\ !}{m\ !(kL - m)\ !}\left(\frac{x}{L}\right)^m\left(1 - \frac{x}{L}\right)^{kL-m},$$

as L approaches infinity it is easily seen that this approaches

$$\frac{(kx)^m e^{-kx}}{m\ !}$$

The expected value of m is

$$E = E(m) = \sum_{m=0}^{\infty}\frac{m(kx)^m e^{-kx}}{m\ !}$$

$$= kx. \tag{27}$$

In view of this result we may write the probability of obtaining m points as

$$P(m, E) = \frac{E^m e^{-E}}{m\ !}. \tag{28}$$

The Poisson distribution occurs under more general conditions than the foregoing derivation would indicate It may be, for example, that points are not distributed uniformly along a line, but with a density $\rho(x)$, where x is now a coordinate measured along the line. In this case the expected number of points falling in the interval (x_1, x_2) is

$$E = \int_{x_1}^{x_2} \rho(x)dx$$

With this value of E, the probability that m points fall in this interval is still given by (28) To show this, let us introduce a new coordinate y, defined by

$$y = \int_0^x \rho(x)dx,$$

and change the scale along the line so that y is uniform instead of x Then on this distorted line the points are also distributed uniformly, so that the expected number in the interval (y_1, y_2) is equal to $y_2 - y_1$, that is, to the length of the interval Hence the Poisson law holds on the distorted line, and since the transformation from x to y is single valued, it must have held on the original line

It is not even necessary to confine the Poisson law to the distribution of points on a line If points are independently distributed over a plane, or through a volume, in such a way that the probability of any particular point falling in any given region is small, then the Poisson distribution holds in the form of equation (28) This result shows that the probability of m points being in an interval depends only on the expected number, and nothing else This equation is the basis of the *Poisson distribution*

The expected value of m^2 is

$$E(m^2) = \sum_{m=0}^{\infty} m^2 \frac{E^m e^{-E}}{m!} = E^2 + E,$$

TABLE 3 Random sequence of one hundred numbers between 000 and 999, typical of the behavior of a random variable. From Table I (page 153)

577	131	608	360	359	716	352	423	386	032
737	646	257	939	736	701	646	934	337	661
170	680	634	089	318	533	398	720	077	228
432	338	255	586	415	263	806	838	393	745
059	699	586	193	784	863	983	274	171	141
355	327	648	592	760	094	129	790	187	556
303	146	673	734	807	552	669	753	417	110
640	430	737	170	346	205	491	217	187	733
000	182	328	947	028	557	192	510	550	541
870	025	984	851	293	313	557	384	286	960

These same hundred numbers shown in order of increasing size, to show fluctuating behavior of successive differences

value	diff	value	diff	value	diff	value	diff	value	diff
000	25	193	12	359	1	577	9	734	2
025	3	205	12	360	24	586	0	736	1
028	4	217	11	384	2	586	6	737	0
032	27	228	27	386	7	592	16	737	8
059	18	255	2	393	5	608	26	745	8
077	12	257	6	398	17	634	6	753	7
089	5	263	11	415	2	640	6	760	24
094	16	274	12	417	6	646	0	784	6
110	19	286	7	423	7	646	2	790	16
129	2	293	10	430	2	648	13	806	1
131	10	303	10	432	59	661	2	807	31
141	5	313	5	491	19	663	6	838	13
146	24	318	9	510	23	669	7	851	19
170	0	327	1	533	8	673	19	870	64
170	1	328	9	541	9	680	2	934	5
171	11	337	1	550	2	699	15	939	8
182	5	338	8	552	4	701	4	947	13
187	0	346	6	556	1	716	13	960	23
187	5	352	3	557	0	720	1	983	1
192	1	355	4	557	20	733		984	

Mean value of random variable = 471 3
Mean value of difference = 10 00

and the standard deviation is given by

$$\sigma^2 = E(m^2) - E^2(m) = E^2 + E - E^2 = E . \quad (29)$$

An important property of the Poisson distribution is expressed by this equation *the standard deviation equals the square root of the expected number.* If we choose an interval small enough so that the expected number E in the interval is one or two, samples containing zero or $2E$ will be frequent (i e , $\sigma \simeq 1$) If the interval is large enough to expect a hundred, then the usual fluctuations about this expected value will be of the order of ten, the *percentage* fluctuation decreasing as the expected value increases

As an example of the Poisson distribution we can analyze Table 3

One hundred points on a line of one thousand units corresponds to a large enough sample so that the Poisson distribution should hold reasonably well The second part of the table shows the distribution of these points along a line, as discussed in this subsection We note the seeming tendency to "bunching" which is always evidenced by random events

If we count up the number of intervals of ten units length (000 to 009, 010 to 019, , 990 to 999) which contain no point, we find that 34 of them are so characterized (for instance 010 to 019, 040 to 049 · contain no point), we find 44 contain one point, 25 two points, and so on There are one hundred points and one hundred intervals, so the expected number of points in an interval is unity We can therefore compare the fraction of intervals having m points with the probability $P(m, 1)$ given in equation (28)

m, No points in interval	0	1	2	3	4	5
Computed probability, $P(m, 1)$	0 37	0 37	0 18	0 06	0 015	0 003
Observed fraction of cases	0 34	0 44	0 15	0 04	0 01	0 02

which is a fairly satisfactory correspondence

The distribution function for the Poisson distribution is the probability that m points or *fewer* are in the interval.

$$F_p(m, E) = \sum_{n=0}^{m} P(n, E) = \int_E^\infty P(m, x)dx , \quad (30)$$

where $P(m, E)$ is given in equation (28) This interesting relationship shows that the probability that m points or fewer are found in an interval with expected number E is equal to the probability that m points

are found in an interval *equal to or larger* than one which would be expected to have E points This duality between m and E is another peculiar property of the Poisson distribution Values of the function $F_p(m, E)$, for various values of m and E, are given in Table VI at the back of the book

The Poisson distribution will apply in a very large number of important situations It is particularly common when the variable x is time For example, the number of alpha particles emitted by a radium preparation in a given time interval follows the Poisson law, because the particles are emitted independently and at random times The number of telephone calls received at a large exchange is also nearly random over short intervals of time, and the Poisson law again applies

This distribution is also useful in studying problems of aerial search (see Division 6, Volume 2B) If N enemy units are distributed at random over a region of the ocean of area A, and if a plane can search over Q square miles of ocean per hour of flight, then the expected number of units sighted for a flight of T hours is

$$E = \frac{NQT}{A}$$

In actual practice the enemy units are not usually distributed at random, each independent of the position of the other, but in many cases (such as for the search for submarines) the results are sufficiently similar to those for the Poisson distribution to make a study of this distribution profitable

For instance, suppose that the expected number of enemy units sighted is S per hour of flight, and suppose that the maximum range of the plane used is 6 hours, with maximum load of gasoline For purposes of illustration of the method of analysis, we will assume that the plane is supposed to attack each unit it sees with one bomb, and that each bomb weighs the equivalent of an hour's worth of gasoline (i e , the plane with 5 bombs could only fly for 1 hour, and a plane with 2 bombs could fly for 4 hours, etc) Once this extremely simplified case has been discussed, it will not be difficult to find methods for handling more complicated cases which accord more closely with real conditions

If the plane carries M bombs, the expected number of sightings per flight is $E = S(6 - M)$, and the probability that the plane sights m units per flight is

$$\frac{1}{m!} [S(6 - M)]^m e^{S(M-6)} = P[m, S(6 - M)]$$

If m is less than M, all m units are bombed, but if m is larger than M, only M units are bombed because the plane has only M bombs along The problem is to determine the value of M so that, on the average, the greatest number of enemy units will be bombed per flight

One could approach the problem from a naive point of view, assuming that the plane *always* made the expected number of sightings per flight In this case the number of bombs M should equal the expected number of sightings $S(6 - M)$, so that M should be the nearest integer to $[6S/(1 + S)]$ This result turns out to be nearly the correct one, *except when S is small* When the expected number of sightings per 6-hour flight is less than 2 $(S < 1/3)$ the simple formula would indicate that only *one* bomb should be carried This naive reasoning, however, neglects the fact that there is a chance that more than one unit will be seen during a flight, and, if only one bomb is carried, this extra chance will be lost

To appraise this possibility in a quantitative manner, we use the Poisson distribution to compute the average, or expected, value of the number of bombs dropped per flight

$$B = \sum_{n=0}^{M} nP[n, S(6-M)] + M \sum_{n=M+1}^{\infty} P[n, S(6-M)]$$
$$= M - \sum_{n=0}^{M} (M - n)P[n, S(6 - M)]$$

Values of B for different values of S and M are given in Table 4

TABLE 4 Expected number of enemy units bombed per flight B for different values of S and of M

$S =$	2	1	0 6	0 3
$M = 1$	1 00	0 99	0 95	0 78
2	2 00	1 89	1 60	1 04
3	2 92	2 33	1 64	0 88
4	3 22	1 92	1 19	0 60
5	1 98	1 01	0 60	0 30

We see that the naive reasoning discussed above is good enough for $S = 2$ or 1, for the values of M giving the largest expected value of B are 4 and 3, respectively, which are the values given by the simple formula $[6S/(1 + S)]$. But for S less than unity the effect mentioned above comes more strongly into play, and it often turns out that it is best to carry more bombs than the simple formula would require, just to take advantage of the occasional times the plane encounters more enemy units than the expected number For $S = 0.6$ we should carry 3 bombs instead of 2, and for $S = 0.3$ we should carry 2 bombs instead of 1

As a somewhat more complicated example, let us consider the case of a newsboy who is required to buy his papers at 2 cents and sell them at 3 cents, and is not allowed to return his unsold papers He has found by experience that he has on the average 10 customers a day, and that customers appear at random How many papers should he buy?

By "at random," it is here meant that, in the first place, the newsboy has no regular customers, who can be counted on to appear regularly, and, secondly, that, as people pass him on the street, one person is as likely to buy as the next. Under these conditions we may expect the Poisson law to hold

Now suppose that the newsboy buys k papers, and that m customers appear If m is equal to or less than k, m papers are sold The newsboy's profit is then $3m - 2k$ If m is greater than k, only k papers can be sold, and his profit is exactly k His expected profit then is

$$E_k = \sum_{m=0}^{k} (3m - 2k) \frac{10^m e^{-10}}{m!} + \sum_{m=k+1}^{\infty} k \frac{10^m e^{-10}}{m!}$$

It is easily seen that

$$E_{k+1} - E_k = \sum_{m=0}^{k} (-2) \frac{10^m e^{-10}}{m!} + \sum_{m=k+1}^{\infty} \frac{10^m e^{-10}}{m!}.$$

But, since

$$\sum_{m=0}^{\infty} \frac{10^m e^{-10}}{m!} = 1,$$

this may be written

$$E_{k+1} - E_k = 1 - 3 \sum_{m=0}^{k} \frac{10^m e^{-10}}{m!}.$$

If we imagine the newsboy buying his papers one by one, then if he has already bought k papers, he should buy the $(k + 1)$st only if $E_{k+1} - E_k$ is positive. The number he should buy is therefore the lowest number k for which $E_{k+1} - E_k$ is negative. Table 5 shows the calculation in detail.

TABLE 5 The newsboy problem

k	$\dfrac{10^k e^{-10}}{k!}$	$\displaystyle\sum_{m=0}^{k} \dfrac{10^m e^{-10}}{m!}$	$E_{k+1} - E_k$	E_k
0	0 00005	0 00005	0 99985	0
1	0 0005	0 0005	0 9985	0 9999
2	0 0023	0 0028	0 9916	1 9984
3	0 0076	0 0104	0 9688	2 9900
4	0 0189	0 0293	0 9124	3 9589
5	0 0378	0 0671	0 7987	4 8715
6	0 0631	0 1302	0 6094	5 6697
7	0 0901	0 2203	0 3394	6 2784
8	0 1126	0 3329	0 0013	6 6088
9	0 1251	0 4580	−0 3737	6 6195
10	0 1251	0 5831	−0 7490	6 2485
11	0 1137	0 6968	−1 0904	5 4962
12	0 0948	0 7916	−1 3748	4 4058
13	0 0729	0 8645	−1 5935	3 0310

The first column gives the values of k, the second, the values of $\dfrac{10^m e^{-10}}{m!}$ for $m = k$, the third, the values of $\displaystyle\sum_{m=0}^{k} \dfrac{10^m e^{-10}}{m!}$, the fourth, the values of $E_{k+1} - E_k$, and the last column, the values of E_k. The table shows clearly that the newsboy should buy only 9 papers, and that his expected profit is 6 6 cents. If he made the obvious purchase of 10 papers, his expected profit would be 6 per cent less. In this, the losses he would incur when fewer than the expected 10 customers buy more than offset his gains if 10 or more customers come along. The two examples show the possible errors of the "naive" point of view, and indicate how the distribution function can be used to obtain a better answer.

2.3   SAMPLING

Suppose that a gun has been fired at a target 100 times, and that 40 hits were obtained. We wish to make the "best estimate" of the probability p that another shot fired from this gun under the same conditions will be a hit. We commenced discussing this question earlier in this chapter. Now we are better equipped to treat it in detail.

The crux of this problem lies in the interpretation of the expression "best estimate." The difficulty arises because of the fact that no matter what the value of p may be (except 0 or 1) it is possible that 40 hits will result in 100 shots. It is therefore impossible from the given facts to deduce the exact value of p. Any formula which expresses the value of p in terms of the number of hits and misses is subject to error. All we can calculate is the probability that p will have some given value.

In spite of this difficulty, we feel intuitively that the value of p is "probably somewhere around" 0 40. That is to say, we are quite sure that p is not 0 01 or 0 99, although we wouldn't be prepared to deny that the value is not 0 39 or 0 41. In other words, we might say that 0 01 and 0 99 are "unreasonable" values of p, while 0 39 and 0 41 are "reasonable" values. If we are asked why we feel that 0 01 is an unreasonable value of p, we might point out that the probability of getting 40 hits in 100 shots with $p = 0\ 01$ is, from equation (14),

$$\frac{100!}{40!\,60!}\,(0\ 01)^{40}\,(0\ 99)^{60},$$

which is about 10^{-52}, and is so small that we can "reasonably" assume that such an improbable event has not taken place. But, even if we take $p = 0\ 40$, the probability of obtaining exactly 40 hits in 100 shots is

$$\frac{100!}{40!\,60!}\,(0\ 40)^{40}\,(0\ 60)^{60},$$

which is only 0 08. It is not immediately obvious that this is large enough to make 0 40 a "reasonable" value of p.

In order to obtain a better criterion of "reasonableness," or "goodness of fit," it has become usual to adopt a method suggested by Pearson. This method does not aim at obtaining a definite value of p from the trials (as we have seen, this is not possible), but rather seeks to determine a range of values of p within which it is "reasonable" to find its real value. To test an assumed value of p, we compute just the consequent expected result of the experiment (in this case the expected number of hits, 100 p). The agreement between the actual result and the expected result is measured by the absolute value of the difference between the two, in this case $|40 - (100p)|$. We now compute the probability that in a second experiment, similar to the original, we would obtain a result which is as far or farther from agreeing with the expected result as the actual result of the first experiment differs from this expected result We thus get a number which is equal to 1 if the first experiment gave exactly the expected result, but otherwise is less than 1 This number is taken as a measure of the "reasonableness" of the value of p tested, and, if it is too small (usually less than 0 05), the value is called "unreasonable "

When the sample is fairly large, this calculation may be simplified by using the normal law as an approximation to the binomial law To illustrate the process, let us calculate the "reasonableness" of any value p in the case of the gun The expected number of hits is then $100p$, and the difference between the observed and expected hits is $|100p - 40|$. If we shot another 100 rounds, the agreement with the expected number of hits would be as bad or worse if the number of hits was equal to or more than $100p + |100p - 40|$, or if it was equal to or less than $100p - |100p - 40|$ If we approximate the actual distribution of the number of hits in the second 100 rounds by a normal distribution with a mean $100p$ and a standard deviation

$$\sigma = \sqrt{100p(1 - p)}, \quad \text{[see equation (16)]}$$

then the probability that the second series gives a worse agreement than the first series is

$$\sqrt{\frac{2}{\pi}} \int_{|40-100p|/\sigma}^{\infty} e^{-\frac{1}{2}x^2} \, dx \quad \text{[see equation (24)]}$$

The values of this integral are easily obtained from Table V in the back of the book or in standard reference books [7][8] In the general case where m successes have been obtained in n trials this becomes

$$\sqrt{\frac{2}{\pi}} \int_{|m-np|/\sigma}^{\infty} e^{-\frac{1}{2}x^2} \, dx, \quad (31)$$

where σ is equal to $\sqrt{np(1 - p)}$

Plots of this "goodness of fit" against the assumed value of p for the cases $n = 100$, $m = 40$ and $n = 10$, $m = 4$ are shown in Figure 12. If we take 0 05 as the limit of reasonableness, then, for the case $n = 100$, $m = 40$, the values of p between 0 31 and 0 50 are "reasonable" values In the case $n = 10$, $m = 4$, the values between 0 16 and 0 69 are "reasonable" values of p It may be pointed out here that for such a small sample the normal law is a poor approximation to the

binomial distribution Nevertheless, in this case the range of "reasonable" values of p is so large that for most purposes it would be necessary to make further trials before acting on this result, while, in the few cases where even the vague knowledge given by the small sample is sufficient, the additional vagueness added by the use of the normal law can hardly be enough to influence the result Thus the best answer to our original question is that the probability p that

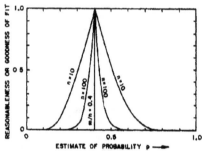

FIGURE 12 Reasonableness of estimate of probability of success p when 10 trials have resulted in 4 successes, and when 100 trials have resulted in 40 successes

the next shot fired from the gun hit the target is most likely equal to 0 40, but it could reasonably have a value between 0 31 and 0 5

There is one serious disadvantage to this method of testing trial values of a probability: the method affords no way of taking into account any knowledge we may have possessed before the trials which might have made one value of p more likely than another. If, for example, we knew that the gun being fired was one of a lot all manufactured together in exactly the same way, and that previous trials on the other guns of the lot had all given values of p near 0 3, then it is obvious that in the situation of Figure 12 the value 0 3 is more "reasonable" than the value 0 5, even though the curves show these values as equally reasonable In most applications, however, we have no such information, and, although there exists a real logical difficulty with the method, it is ordinarily safe to ignore it

2.3 1 The χ^2 (Chi-Squared) Test

A great number of trials result in more than just success or failure. For instance, a shot from a gun may hit the bull's-eye or the first or second ring as well as miss the target entirely. Similarly, a torpedo may miss the ship, may damage it, or may sink it If we know the geometry of the problem completely, we sometimes may be able to compute the *a priori* probability p_i that the ith possibility occur when a trial is made, for instance, p_1 could be the probability of hitting the bull's-eye, whereas p_2 would be the probability of hitting inside the first ring, and so on Or, to take another example, probability p_1 could be the probability of shooting down an incoming plane with a 5-inch antiaircraft battery when the plane is between 6,000 and 4,000 yards away from the battery (the guns opened up at 6,000 yards' range), p_2 the probability that the plane is shot down when the range is between 4,000 and 2,000 yards, and p_3 is the probability of shooting the plane down when the range is less than 2,000 yards

To generalize from these examples, we can say that a given trial may result in a number of different specific events, such as hitting the bull's-eye or the first ring, and so forth Suppose there are s different specific possibilities We can usually choose these possibilities in a number of different ways so that the value of the integer s will vary according to the nature of the trial and the degree of detail with which we wish to study the results The quantity s is usually called the "number of degrees of freedom" of the trials In order to complete the enumeration of the results, we must always include the negative results in addition to the s different specific results which may come from a trial, that is, we may also obtain *none* of these specified results In other words, it is always possible for the bullet to hit neither the bull's-eye nor any of the rings, but to miss the target entirely. In the case of a die, not only may the faces 1, 2, 3, 4, or 5 turn up, but none of these (i e , the face 6) may turn up In other words, the total number of possible results for the trial turn out to be 1 plus the number of degrees of freedom, that is, $s + 1$.

Corresponding to each possible result there is an a priori probability $p_1, p_2, \cdots, p_s, \ldots, p_{s+1}$, where the sum of all these probabilities must equal unity. If now we make n trials, the expected number of trials which result in condition 1 will be np_1, and so forth The sum of all these expected values must equal n

But the case we are considering at present is the reverse of this We have just made n trials and we wish to find from them "reasonable" values for the probability of occurrence of each of the different results. In the n trials, m_1 trials have resulted in

occurrence 1, m_2 have resulted in occurrence 2, etc The sum of all the m's must equal n. From this we wish to deduce reasonable values of the probabilities p_i.

To be more precise, we wish to know whether the observed result is reasonable on the hypothesis that the probability that a single trial falls into the ith group is $p_i (\Sigma p_i = 1)$ This judgment can be made by calculating the probability that a series of n trials with the given probabilities would give a result which deviates as much or more from the expected result as does the observed result The principal difficulty here is in the question of when one result deviates more from the expected result than another For example, consider the following results

TABLE 6

Group	1	2	3
Expected No	3	12	4
Trial 1	4	10	5
Trial 2	5	12	2

Is trial 1 or trial 2 in better agreement with the expected result? For the moment, however, we leave this question aside

The probability of getting a particular set of numbers m_i in a given series of n trials is found from the multinomial expansion of $(p_1 + p_2 + \cdots + p_r)^n$, where the p_i contain the probability of failure as well as of success

$$P = \frac{n!}{m_1! m_2! \cdots m_r!} p_1{}^{m_1} p_2{}^{m_2} \cdots p_r{}^{m_r}, \quad (32)$$

where $\nu = s + 1$ and where $\Sigma m_i = n$ It is easily shown that (treating m_i as a continuous variable) this is a maximum for $m_i = np_i$ Putting

$$P_{\max} = \frac{n!}{(np_1)! (np_2)! \cdots (np_r)!} p_1{}^{np_1} p_2{}^{np_1} \cdots p_r{}^{np_r},$$

we have

$$\frac{P}{P_{\max}} = \frac{(np_1)! (np_2)! \cdots (np_r)!}{m_1! m_2! \cdots m_r!} p_1{}^{m_1 - np_1} p_2{}^{m_2 - np_1} \cdots$$

This is a product of terms of the form

$$\frac{(np)!}{m!} p^{m - np}.$$

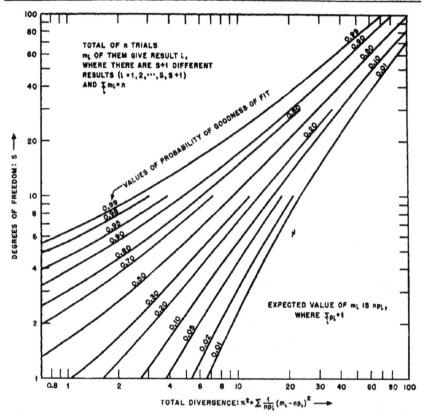

FIGURE 13   Pearson's criterion for goodness of fit $P(>\chi^2)$ Contours of probability $P(>\chi^2)$ that fit is good, plotted against degrees of freedom s and against squared divergence χ^2

Now if m and np are reasonably large, we may put $(np)! = (np/e)^{np}$ and $m! = (m/e)^m$ Our typical term then becomes, after suitable expansions and approximations,[5]

$$e^{-(m-np)^2/2np},$$

a result valid when m and np are not too small   The quantity

$$\delta_i^2 = \frac{(m_i - np_i)^2}{np_i} \qquad (33)$$

is called the *divergence* of the ith group from its expected value   In the following equation we see that

$$\frac{P}{P_{max}} = e^{-\frac{1}{2}\Sigma \delta_i^2} = e^{-\frac{1}{2}\chi^2},$$

where

$$\chi^2 = \sum \delta_i^2 = \sum \frac{1}{np_i} (m_i - np_i)^2 \qquad (34)$$

is the *total divergence* of the series of trials.

We therefore see that except for the constant factor P_{max} the probability of getting a given result is a function only of χ^2, and rapidly decreases as χ^2 increases   We may use this result to settle the question of which of two results deviates more from the expected result we shall state (by definition) that of two given results, the one with the greater value of x^2 deviates the more from the expected result.

The probability of obtaining a result which deviates more than a given result from the expected result may now be calculated by direct summation Approximating this sum by an integral leads to the answer [5]

$$P(>x^2) = \frac{1}{2^{s/2-1}\Gamma(s/2)} \int_x^\infty u^{s-1} e^{-\frac{1}{2}u^2} du, \quad (35)$$

where s, the "number of degrees of freedom," is equal to $\nu - 1$ Tables of this function are given in Fry[5] and other works on statistics For rough work it may be pointed out that $P(>x^2)$ is small when x^2 is greater than s, and large (near 1) when x^2 is much smaller than s A contour plot of this function is given in Figure 13

We can now return to Table 6, to point out that the trial fits the computed or expected values best which gives smallest values of x^2 In Table 6 we have $s = 2$, $np_1 = 3$, $np_2 = 12$, and $np_3 = 4$ In trial 1, $m_1 = 4$, $m_2 = 10$, and $m_3 = 5$ Therefore,

$$x^2 = \frac{1}{3}(4-3)^2 + \frac{1}{12}(10-12)^2 + \frac{1}{4}(5-4)^2 = \frac{11}{12},$$

whereas, for trial 2,

$$x^2 = \frac{1}{3}(5-3)^2 + \frac{1}{12}(12-12)^2 + \frac{1}{4}(2-4)^2 = \frac{7}{3}.$$

Therefore, trial 1 agrees more closely with the expected values than does trial 2 In fact, comparing these results with Figure 13, we see that the chance that the results of trial 1 "really" correspond to the expected case (the discrepancy being simply chance fluctuation) is 2 in 3, whereas the probability that trial 2 corresponds to the expected case is only half as great, 1 in 3

Usually only the results of a trial are known; we have to assume values for the p's, and compute the chance that the true state of things is no farther afield than the assumed state The assumption which gives the smallest value of x^2 is the most probable assumption.

2.3 2 **Some Examples**

In a rocket-firing test, the target consists of two concentric rings, one 10 feet in radius, the other 20

feet in radius. In a trial, 25 rockets are fired Of these 10 hit inside the smaller ring, 10 between the rings, and 5 outside the rings We expect from previous experience that the hits are distributed according to the circular normal law, whose probability density is

$$\frac{1}{2\pi\sigma^2} e^{-r^2/2\sigma^2}.$$

We wish to test the validity of this law, and to determine a value of σ

Our method of procedure is to apply the x^2 test to these results using various values of σ If $P(>x^2)$ is always small for all values of σ, we have an indication that the assumed distribution does not hold. If $P(>x^2)$ is large for some values of σ, we then know that the results are reasonable for those values, and the data are not inconsistent with the normal distribution.

It is easily seen that the probability of a shot hitting inside a ring of radius r is (assuming the probability density given above)

$$1 - e^{-r^2/2\sigma^2}$$

Hence the probabilities p_1, p_2, and p_3 of hitting inside the inner ring, between the rings, and outside the outer ring are

$$p_1 = 1 - e^{-50/\sigma^2},$$
$$p_2 = e^{-50/\sigma^2} - e^{-200/\sigma^2},$$
$$p_3 = e^{-200/\sigma^2}$$

These must be compared with $m_1 = 10$, $m_2 = 10$, $m_3 = 5$

Suppose that we begin with the hypothesis that $\sigma = 10$ feet Then

$$p_1 = 0\,394,$$
$$p_2 = 0\,471,$$
$$p_3 = 0\,135$$

We now proceed as in the following table.

| | | $\sigma = 10$ feet | | |
Group	Actual Hits	Expected Hits	Difference	Divergence
1	10	9 84	+0 16	0 003
2	10	11 80	−1 80	0 274
3	5	3 36	+1 64	0 800
Total	25	25 00	$x^2 = 1\,077$	
			$P(>x^2) = 0\,58$	

Since $s = 2$, we look up $P(>x^2)$ in the table for two degrees of freedom. It is seen that $\sigma = 10$ ft gives a

σ (feet)	8 6	8 7	8 8		10 8	10 9	11 0		14 2	14 3	14 4
$P(>\chi^2)$	0 03	0 04	0 07		0 77	0 775	0 76	.	0 06	0 05	0 04

reasonable result which means that the normal law is reasonable

We may proceed in this way and find values of $P(>\chi^2)$ for other values of σ The table above shows some results It shows that the most reasonable value of σ is 10 9 feet, but that all values between 8 8 feet and 14 3 feet are reasonable $[P(>\chi^2)>0\ 05]$

Statistical data on antisubmarine flying for three months give the following figures

Month	Hours flown	Contacts	Hours per contact
1	2,600	5	520
2	3,500	6	583
3	4,000	6	667
Total	10,100	17	Avg 595

The hours per contact seem to be rising, and we wish to know if the increase is significant.

To test this, let us test the hypothesis that the hours per contact has remained constant at the average value 595 We may then calculate $P(>\chi^2)$ as in the following table

Month	Contacts	Expected contacts	Difference	Divergence
1	5	4 4	0 6	0 08
2	6	6 0	0 0	0 00
3	6	6 8	0 8	0 09
				$\chi^2=0\ 17$
	$S=2$			$P(>\chi^2)=0\ 98$

Obviously, the difference may very well be due to chance

Chapter 3

THE USE OF MEASURES OF EFFECTIVENESS

THE MATERIAL in the preceding chapter, and much that is included in the following chapters, is in the nature of tools which the operations research worker finds useful A familiarity with these techniques is necessary for the worker, but it is not in itself a guarantee that the worker will be successful in operations research Just as with every other field of applied science, the improvement of operations of war by the application of scientific analysis requires a certain flair which comes with practice, but which is difficult to put into words

It is important first to obtain an overall quantitative picture of the operation under study One must first see what is similar in operations of a given kind before it will be worthwhile seeing how they differ from each other In order to make a start in so complex a subject, one must ruthlessly strip away details (which can be taken into account later), and arrive at a few broad, very approximate "constants of the operation " By studying the variations of these constants, one can then perhaps begin to see how to improve the operation

It is well to emphasize that these constants which measure the operation are useful even though they are extremely approximate, it might almost be said that they are more valuable *because* they are very approximate This is because successful application of operations research usually results in improvements by factors of 3 or 10 or more Many operations are ineffectively compared to their theoretical optimum because of a single faulty component inadequate training of crews, or incorrect use of equipment, or inadequate equipment Usually, when the "bottleneck" has been discovered and removed, the improvements in effectiveness are measured in hundreds or even thousands of per cent In our first study of any operation we are looking for these large factors of possible improvement They can be discovered if the constants of the operation are given only to one significant figure, and any greater accuracy simply adds unessential detail

One might term this type of thinking "hemibel thinking " A bel is defined as a unit in a logarithmic scale* corresponding to a factor of 10 Consequently,

a hemibel corresponds to a factor of the square root of 10, or approximately 3 Ordinarily, in the preliminary analysis of an operation, it is sufficient to locate the value of the constant to within a factor of 3 Hemibel thinking is extremely useful in any branch of science, and most successful scientists employ it habitually It is particularly useful in operations research

Having obtained the constants of the operation under study in units of hemibels (or to one significant figure), we take our next step by comparing these constants We first compare the value of the constants obtained in actual operations with the optimum theoretical value, if this can be computed If the actual value is within a hemibel (i e, within a factor of 3) of the theoretical value, then it is extremely unlikely that any improvement in the details of the operation will result in significant improvement In the usual case, however, there is a wide gap between the actual and theoretical results In these cases a hint as to the possible means of improvement can usually be obtained by a crude sorting of the operational data to see whether changes in personnel, equipment, or tactics produce a significant change in the constants In many cases a theoretical study of the optimum values of the constants will indicate possibilities of improvement

The present chapter will give a few examples of the sort of constants which can be looked for, and the sort of conclusions which may be drawn from their study

3 1   SWEEP RATES

An important function for some naval forces, particularly for some naval aircraft, is that of scouting or patrol, that is, search for the enemy In submarine warfare search is particularly important The submarine must find the enemy shipping before it can fire its torpedoes, and the antisubmarine craft must find the enemy submarine in order to attack it, or to route its convoys evasively, and so on

Patrol or search is an operation which is peculiarly amenable to operations research The action is simple, and repeated often enough under conditions sufficiently similar to enable satisfactory data to be accumulated From these data measures of effectiveness can be computed periodically from which a great deal can be deduced By comparing the opera-

---

* This suggests the advantage of using logarithmic graph paper in plotting data Unity is zero hemibels, 3 is 1 hemibel, 10 is 2 hemibels, 30 is 3 hemibels, and 10,000 is 8 hemibels A hemibel is 5 decibels An appropriate abbreviation would be hb, corresponding to db for decibel

tional values of the constants with the theoretically optimum values, one can obtain an overall picture as to the efficiency of our own forces Sudden changes in the constants without change in our own tactics will usually mean a change in enemy tactics which, of course, needs investigation and usually counteraction

3 1 1   Calculation of Constants

In the simplest case a number of search units (e g , aircraft or submarine) are sent into a certain area A of the ocean to search for enemy craft. A total of T units of time (hours or days) is spent by one or another of the search craft in the area, and a number of contacts C with an enemy unit are reported It is obvious that the total number of contacts obtained in a month is not a significant measure of the effectiveness of the searching craft because it depends on the length of time spent in searching A more useful constant would be the average number of contacts made in the area per unit of time spent in searching (C divided by T)

The number of contacts per unit of searching time is a simple measure which is useful for some purposes and not useful for others As long as the scene of the search remains the same, the quantity (C/T) depends on the efficiency of the individual searching craft and also on the number N of enemy craft which are in the area on the average Consequently, any sudden change in this quantity would indicate a change in enemy concealment tactics, or else a change in the number of enemy craft present Since this quantity depends so strongly on the enemy's actions, it is not a satisfactory one to compare against theoretically optimum values in order to see whether the searching effort can be appreciably improved or not Nor is it an expedient quantity to use in comparing the search efforts in two different areas

A large area is more difficult to search over than a small one since it takes more time to cover the larger area with the same density of search Consequently, the number of contacts per unit searching time should be multiplied by the area searched over in order to compensate for this area effect, and so that the searching effort in two different areas can be compared on a more or less equal basis

3 1 2   Operational Sweep Rate

One further particularly profitable step can be taken, if other sources of intelligence allow one to estimate (to within a factor of 3) the average number of enemy craft in the area while the search was going on

The quantity which can then be computed is the number of contacts per unit search time, multiplied by the area searched over and divided by the estimated number of enemy units in the area Since the dimensions of this quantity are square miles per hour, it is usually called the effective, or operational, *sweep rate*

Operational sweep rate

$$Q_{op} = \left(\frac{C A}{NT}\right) \frac{\text{square miles}}{\text{hour (or day)}} \qquad (1)$$

C = number of contacts,
A = area searched over in square miles,
T = total searching time in hours (or days);
N = probable number of enemy craft in area

This quantity is a measure of the ability of a single search craft to find a single enemy unit under actual operational conditions It equals the effective area of ocean swept over by a single search craft in an hour (or day)

Another way of looking at this constant is taken by remembering that (N/A) is the *average density* of target craft, in number per square mile Since (C/T) is the number of contacts produced per hour (or day) $Q_{op} = (C/T) \div (N/A)$ is the number of contacts which would be obtained per hour (or day) if the density of target craft were one per square mile

3.1 3   Theoretical Sweep Rate

Sweep rates can be compared from area to area and from time to time, since the effects of different size of areas and of different numbers of enemy craft are already balanced out Sweep rates can also be compared with the theoretical optimum for the craft in question In Division 6, Volume 2B it is shown that the sweep rate is equal to twice the "effective lateral range of detection" of the search craft equipment, multiplied by the speed of the search craft

Theoretical sweep rate

$$Q_{th} = 2Rv \frac{\text{square miles}}{\text{hour (or day)}} \qquad (2)$$

R = effective lateral range of detection in miles,

v = average speed of search craft in miles per hour (or day)

A comparison of this sweep rate with the operational value will provide us with the criterion for excellence which we need

The ratio between Q_{op} and Q_{th} is a factor which depends both on the effectiveness of our side in using the search equipment available, and on the effectiveness of the enemy in evading detection For instance, if the search craft is a plane equipped with radar, and if the radar is in poor operational condition on the average, this ratio will be correspondingly diminished Similarly, if the enemy craft is a submarine, then a reduction of the average time it spent on the surface would reduce the ratio for search planes using radar or visual sighting. The ratio also would be reduced if the area were covered by the searching craft in a nonuniform manner, and if the enemy craft tended to congregate in those regions which were searched least Correspondingly, the ratio (Q_{op}/Q_{th}) will be increased (and may even be greater than unity) if the enemy craft tend to congregate in one region of the area, and if the searching effort is also concentrated there It can be seen that a comparison of the two sweep rates constitutes a very powerful means of following the fluctuations in efficacy of the search operation as the warfare develops

3.1 4   Submarine Patrol

A few examples will show the usefulness of the quantities mentioned here The first example comes from data on the sighting of merchant vessels by submarines on patrol Typical figures are given in Table 1 All numbers are rounded off to one or two

TABLE 1 Contacts on merchant vessels by submarines

Region	B	D	E
Area, sq miles, A	80,000	250,000	400,000
Avg No ships present, N	20	20	25
Ship flow through area per day, F	6	3	4
Sub-days in area, T	800	250	700
Contacts, C	400	140	200
Sweep rate, Q_{op}	2,000	7,000	4,500
Fraction of ship flow sighted by a sub, $\dfrac{C}{FT}$	0 08	0 2	0 07
Sightings per sub per day	0 5	0 6	0 3

significant figures, since the estimate of the number of ships present in the area is uncertain, and there is no need of having the accuracy of the other figures any larger The operational sweep rate (computed from

the data) is also tabulated Since the ratio of the values of Q for regions B and E is less than 1 hemibel, the difference in the sweep rates for those regions is probably due to the rather wide limits of error of the values of N. The difference in sweep rate between areas B and D is probably significant however (it corresponds to a ratio of more than a hemibel) Investigation of this difference shows that the antisubmarine activity in region B was considerably more effective than in D, and, consequently, the submarines in region B had to spend more time submerged and had correspondingly less time to make sightings The obvious suggestion (unless there are other strategic reasons to the contrary) is to transfer some of the effort from region B to region D, since the yield per submarine per day is as good, and since the danger to the submarine is considerably less

For purposes of comparison, we compute the theoretical sweep rate A submarine on patrol covers about 200 miles a day on the average, and the average range of visibility for a merchant vessel is between 15 and 20 miles The theoretical sweep rate, therefore, is about 6,000 to 8,000 square miles per day This corresponds remarkably closely with the operational sweep rate in regions D and E The close correspondence indicates that the submarines are seeing all the shipping they could be expected to see (i e , with detection equipment having a range of 15 to 20 miles) It also indicates that the enemy has not been at all successful in evading the patrolling submarines, for such evasion would have shown up as a relative diminution in Q_{op} The reduced value of sweep rate in region B has already been explained

Therefore, a study of the sweep rate for submarines against merchant vessels has indicated (for the case tabulated) that no important amount of shipping is missed because of poor training of lookouts or of failure of detection equipment. It has also indicated that one of the three regions is less productive than the other two, further investigation has revealed the reason The fact that each submarine in region D sighted one ship in every five that passed through the region is a further indication of the extraordinary effectiveness of the submarines patrolling these areas

3 1 5   Aircraft Search for Submarines

Another example, not quite so impressive, but perhaps more instructive, can be taken from data on search for submarines by antisubmarine aircraft Typical values are shown in Table 2, for three successive months, for three contiguous areas Here the quantity T represents the total time spent by aircraft over the ocean on antisubmarine patrol of all sorts in the region during the month in question The quantity C represents the total number of verified sightings of a surfaced submarine in the area and during the month in question From these data the value of the operational sweep rate, Q_{op}, can be computed and is expressed also on a hemibel scale From these figures a number of interesting conclusions can be drawn, and a number of useful suggestions can be made for the improving of the operational results.

rines. During the latter month the submarines carried on an all-out attack, coming closer to shore than before or since, and staying longer on the surface, in order to sight more shipping This bolder policy exposed the submarines to too many attacks, so they returned to more cautious tactics in June The episode serves to indicate that at least one-half of the 2 hemibel discrepancy between operational and theoretically maximum sweep rates is probably due to the submergence tactics of the submarine

The other factor of 3 is partially attributable to a deficiency in operational training and practice in

TABLE 2 Sightings of submarines by antisubmarine aircraft

Region	A			B			C		
Area, sq miles, A	300,000			600,000			900,000		
Month	A	M	J	A	M	J	A	M	J
Avg No subs, N	7	7	6	1	4	3	3	7	5
Total plane time (in thousands of hours), T	20	25	24	6	7	9	5	5	6
Contacts, C	39	37	30	2	35	14	4	11	9
Sweep rate, Q_{op}	80	60	60	200	750	300	240	280	270
Sweep rate in hemibels	4	4	4	5	6	5	5	5	5

We first compare the operational sweep rate with the theoretically optimum rate The usual antisubmarine patrol plane flies at a speed of about 150 knots The average range of visibility of a surfaced U-boat in flyable weather is about 10 miles Therefore, if the submarines were on the surface all of the time during which the planes were searching, we should expect the theoretical search rate to be 3,000 square miles per hour, according to equation (2) On the hemibel scale this is a value of 7 If the submarines on the average spent a certain fraction of the time submerged, then Q_{th} would be proportionally diminished We see that the average value of the sweep rate in regions B and C is about one-tenth (2 hemibels) smaller than the maximum theoretical value of 3,000

Part of this discrepancy is undoubtedly due to the submergence tactics of the submarines In fact, the sudden rise in the sweep rate in region B from April to May was later discovered to be almost entirely due to a change in tactics on the part of the subma-

antisubmarine lookout keeping Antisubmarine patrol is a monotonous duty The average plane can fly for hundreds of hours (representing an elapsed time of six months or more) before a sighting is made Experience has shown that, unless special competitive practice exercises are used continuously, performance of such tasks can easily fall below one-third of their maximum effectiveness Data in similar circumstances, mentioned later in this chapter, show that a diversion of 10 per cent of the operational effort into carefully planned practice can increase the overall effectiveness by factors of two to four

We have thus partially explained the discrepancy between the operational sweep rate in regions B and C and the theoretically optimum sweep rate; we have seen the reason for the sudden increase for one month in region B We must now investigate the result of region A which displays a consistently low score in spite of (or perhaps because of) the large number of antisubmarine flying hours in the region. Search in region A is consistently 1 hemibel worse (a factor of

3) than in the other two regions Study of the details of the attacks indicates that the submarines were not more wary in this region, the factor of 3 could thus not be explained by assuming that the submarines spent one-third as much time on the surface in region A. Nor could training entirely account for the difference. A number of new squadrons were "broken in" in region A, but even the more experienced squadrons turned in the lower average

3.1 6　　Distribution of Flying Effort

In this case the actual track plans of the antisubmarine patrols in region A were studied in order to see whether the patrol perhaps concentrated the

effort in region A. Flying in the inner zone, where three-quarters of the flying was done, is only one-tenth as effective as flying in the outer zone, where less than 1 per cent of the flying was done Due perhaps to the large amount of flying in the inner zone, the submarines did not come this close to shore very often, and, when they came, kept well submerged In the outer zones, however, they appeared to have been as unwary as in region B in the month of May

If a redistribution of flying effort would not have changed submarine tactics, then a shift of 2,000 hours of flying per month from the inner zone to the outer (which would have made practically no change in the density of flying in the inner zone, but which would have increased the density of flying in the outer

TABLE 3　Sightings of submarines by antisubmarine planes, offshore effect

Distance from shore in miles	0 to 60	60 to 120	120 to 180	180 to 240
Flying time in sub-region, T (in thousands of hours)	15 50	3 70	0 60	0 17
Contacts made in sub-region, C	21	11	5	2
Contacts per 1,000 hours flown, (C/T)	1 3	3	8	12
Contacts per 1,000 hours flown, in hemibels	0	1	2	2

flying effort in regions where the submarines were not likely to be This indeed proved to be the case, for it was found that a disproportionately large fraction of the total antisubmarine flying in region A was too close to shore to have a very large chance of finding a submarine on the surface The data for the month of April (and also for other months) was broken down according to the amount of patrol time spent a given distance off shore The results for the one month are given in Table 3 In this analysis it was not necessary to compute the sweep rate, but only to compare the number of contacts per thousand hours flown in various strips at different distances from the shore This simplification is possible since different strips of the same region are being compared for the same periods of time, consequently, the areas are equal and the average distribution of submarines is the same The simplification is desirable since it is not known, even approximately, where the seven submarines, which were present in that region in that month, were distributed among the offshore zones

A comparison of the different values of contacts per 1,000 hours flown for the different offshore bands, immediately explains the ineffectiveness of the search

zone by a factor of 13) would have approximately doubled the number of contacts made in the whole region during that month Actually, of course, when a more uniform distribution of flying effort was inaugurated in this region, the submarines in the outer zones soon became more wary and the number of contacts per thousand hours flown in the outer region soon dropped to about 4 or 5 This still represented a factor of 3, however, over the inshore flying yield We therefore can conclude that the discrepancy of one hemibel in sweep rate between region A and regions B and C is primarily due to a maldistribution of patrol flying in region A, the great preponderance of flying in that region being in localities where the submarines were not When these facts were pointed out, a certain amount of redistribution of flying was made (within the limitations imposed by other factors), and a certain amount of improvement was observed

The case described here is not a unique one, in fact, it is a good illustration of a situation often encountered in operations research The planning officials did not have the time to make the detailed analysis necessary for the filling in of Table 3 They saw that many more contacts were being made on submarines close inshore than farther out, and they did not have at hand the data to show that this was entirely due to the fact that nearly all the flying was close to shore The data on contacts, which is more conspicuous, might have actually persuaded the operations officer to increase still further the proportion of flying close to shore Only a detailed analysis of the amount of flying time in each zone, resulting in a tabulation of the sort given in Table 3, was able to give the officer a true picture of the situation When this had been done, it was possible for the officer to balance the discernible gains to be obtained by increasing the offshore flying against other possible detriments In this case, as with most others encountered in this field, other factors enter, the usefulness of the patrol planes could not be measured solely by their collection of contacts, and the other factors favored inshore flying

3 1 7   Antisubmarine Flying in the Bay of Biscay

An example of the use of sweep rate for following tactical changes in a phase of warfare will be taken from the RAF Coastal Command struggle against German U-boats in the Bay of Biscay After the Germans had captured France, the Bay of Biscay ports were the principal operational bases for U-boats Nearly all of the German submarines operating in the Atlantic went out and came back through the Bay of Biscay About the beginning of 1942, when the RAF began to have enough long range planes, a number of them were assigned to antisubmarine duty in the Bay to harass these transit U-boats Since the submarines had to be discovered before they could be attacked, and since these planes were out only to attack submarines, a measure of the success of the campaign was the number of U-boat sightings made by the aircraft

The relevant data for this part of the operation are shown in Figure 1 for the years 1942 and 1943 The number of hours of antisubmarine patrol flying in the Bay per month, the number of sightings of U-boats resulting, and the estimated average number of U-boats in the Bay area during the month are plotted in the upper part of the figure From these values and from the area of the Bay searched over (130,000 square miles), one can compute the values of the operational sweep rate which are shown in the lower half of the figure

The graph for Q_{op} indicates that two complete cycles of events have occurred during the two years shown The first half of 1942 and the first half of 1943 gave sweep rates of the order of 300 square miles per hour, which correspond favorably with the sweep rates obtained in regions B and C in Table 2 The factor of 10 difference between these values and the theoretically maximum value of 3,000 square miles per hour can be explained, as before, partly by the known discrepancy between lookout practice in actual operation and theoretically optimum lookout effectiveness, and mainly by submarine evasive tactics It was known at the beginning of 1942 that the submarines came to the surface for the most part at night, and stayed submerged during a good part of the day Since most of the antisubmarine patrols were during daylight, these tactics could account for a possible factor of 5, leaving a factor of 2 to be accounted for (perhaps) by lookout fatigue, etc.

During the early part of 1942, the air cover over the Bay of Biscay increased, and the transit submarines began to experience a serious number of attacks In the spring a few squadrons of radar planes were equipped for night-flying, with searchlights to enable them to make attacks at night on the submarines When these went into operation, the effective search rate for all types of planes increased at first. The night-flying planes caught a large number of submarines on the surface at night These night attacks caused the submarines to submerge more at night and surface more in the daytime, therefore the day-flying planes also found more submarines on the surface

The consequent additional hazard to the U-boats forced a countermeasure from the Germans, for even though the night-flying was a small percentage of the total air effort in the Bay, the effects of night attack on morale were quite serious The Germans started equipping their submarines with radar receivers capable of hearing the L-band radar set carried in the British planes When these sets were operating properly, they would give the submarine adequate warning of the approach of a radar plane, so that it could submerge before the plane could make a sighting or attack Despite difficulties in getting the sets to work effectively, they became more and more successful, and the operational sweep rate for the British planes dropped abruptly in the late summer of 1942, reaching a value about one-fifth of that previously attained

When this low value of sweep rate continued for

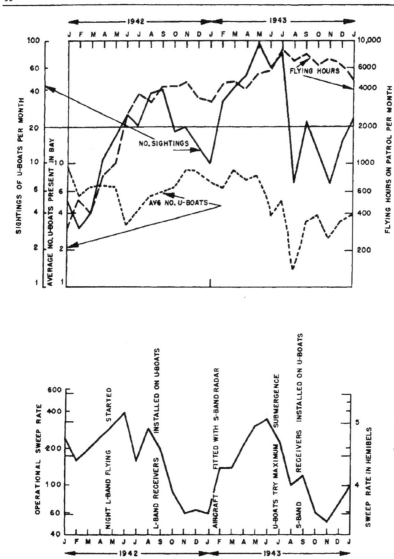

FIGURE 1 Sightings of U-boats by antisubmarine aircraft in the Bay of Biscay in 1942-1943

*

several months, it was obviously necessary for the British to introduce a new measure. This was done by fitting the antisubmarine aircraft with S-band radar which could not be detected by the L-band receivers on the German submarines at that time Commencing with the first of 1943, the sweep rate accordingly rose again as more and more planes were fitted with the shorter wave radar sets Again the U-boats proved particularly susceptible to the attacks of night-flying planes equipped with the new radar sets and with searchlights By midsummer of 1943, the sweep rate was back as high as it had been a year before.

The obvious German countermeasure was to equip the submarines with S-band receivers This, however, involved a great many design and manufacturing difficulties, and these receivers were not to be available until the fall of 1943. In the interim the Germans sharply reduced the number of submarines sent out, and instructed those which did go out to stay submerged as much as possible in the Bay region This reduced the operational sweep rate for the RAF planes to some extent, and, by the time the U-boats had been equipped with S-band receivers in the fall, the sweep rate reached the same low values it had reached in the previous fall The later cycle, which occurred in 1944, involved other factors which we will not have time to discuss here

This last example shows how it is sometimes possible to watch the overall course of a part of warfare by watching the fluctuations of a measure of effectiveness One can at the same time see the actual benefits accruing from a new measure and also see how effective are the countermeasures By keeping a month-to-month chart of the quantity, one can time the introduction of new measures, and also can assess the danger of an enemy measure A number of other examples of this sort will be given later in this chapter

3 2   EXCHANGE RATES

A useful measure of effectiveness for all forms of warfare is the exchange rate, the ratio between enemy loss and own loss Knowledge of its value enables one to estimate the cost of any given operation and to balance this cost against other benefits accruing from the operation Here again a great deal of insight can be obtained into the tactical trends by comparing exchange rates, in particular, by determining how the rate depends on the relative strength of the forces involved.

When the engagement is between similar units, as in a battle between tanks or between fighter planes, the units of strength on each side are the same, and the problem is fairly straightforward Data are needed on a large number of engagements involving a range of sizes of forces involved Data on the strength of the opposed forces at the beginning of each engagement and on the resulting losses to both sides are needed These can then be subjected to statistical analysis to determine the dependence of the losses on the other factors involved

Suppose m and n are the number of own and enemy units involved, and suppose k and l are the respective losses in the single engagements In general, k and l will depend on m and n, and the nature of the dependence is determined by the tactics involved in the engagement For instance, if the engagement consists of a sequence of individual combats between single opposed units, then both k and l are proportional to either m or n (whichever is smaller), and the exchange rate (l/k) is independent of the size of the opposing forces On the other hand, if each unit on one side gets about an equal chance to shoot at each unit on the other side, then the losses on one side will be proportional to the number of opposing units (that is, k will be proportional to n, and l will be proportional to m) These matters will be discussed in further detail and from a somewhat different point of view in the next chapter.

3 2 1   Air-to-Air Combat

The engagements between American and Japanese fighter aircraft in the Pacific in 1943–44 seem to have corresponded more closely to the individual-combat type of engagements The data which have been analyzed indicate that the exchange rate for Japanese against U S fighters (l/k) was approximately independent of the size of the forces in the engagement. The percentage of Japanese fighters lost per engagement seems to have been independent of the numbers involved (i e , k was proportional to n), whereas the percentage of U S fighters lost per engagement seemed to increase with an increase of Japanese fighters, and decrease with an increase of U. S. fighters (i e , l was also proportional to n)

The exchange rate for U. S. fighters in the Pacific during the years 1943 and 1944 remained at the surprisingly high value of approximately 10 This circumstance contributed to a very high degree to the success of the U S Navy in the Pacific It was, therefore, of importance to analyze as far as possible the reasons for this high exchange rate in order to see the importance of the various contributing factors, such as training and combat experience, the effect of the characteristics of planes, etc The problem is naturally very complex, and it is possible here only to give an indication of the relative importance of the contributing factors

Certainly a very considerable factor has been the longer training which the U S pilots underwent compared to the Japanese pilots A thoroughgoing study of the results of training and of the proper balance between primary training and operational practice training has not yet been made, so that a quantitative appraisal of the effects of training is as yet impossible Later in this chapter we shall give an example which indicates that it sometimes is worth while even to withdraw aircraft from operations for a short time in order to give the pilots increased training There is considerable need for further operational research in such problems. It is suspected that, in general, the total effectiveness of many forces would be increased if somewhat more time were given to refresher training in the field, and slightly less to operations

The combat experience of the pilot involved has also had its part in the high exchange rate The RAF Fighter Command Operations Research Group has studied the chance of a pilot being shot down as a function of the number of combats the pilot has been in. This chance decreases by about a factor of 3 from the first to the sixth combat A study made by the Operations Research Group, U S. Army Air Forces, indicates that the chance of shooting down the enemy when once in a combat increases by 50 per cent or more with increasing experience

The exchange rate will also depend on the types of planes entering the engagement An analysis of British-German engagements indicates that Spitfire 9 has an exchange rate about twice that of Spitfire 5 The difference is probably mostly due to the difference in speed, about 40 knots There are indications that the exchange rate for F6F-5 is considerably larger than that for the F6F-3 Since the factors of training, experience, and plane type all appear to have been in the favor of the United States, it is not surprising that the exchange rate turned out to be as large as 10 Nevertheless, it would be of interest to carry out further analysis to determine which of these factors is the most important

3 2.2 Convoys versus Submarines

When the engagement is between units of different sorts, the problem becomes more complicated For one thing, a complete balance of gain and loss can only be obtained when it is possible to compare the value of one unit with one of a different type The question of the relative values of different units in an engagement will be taken up later in this chapter In some cases of mixed engagements, however, it is possible to gain a considerable insight into the dynamics of the warfare without having to go into the vexing question of comparative values

An interesting example of a mixed engagement is the attack on convoys by submarines Here an additional factor enters the picture, the number of escort vessels Therefore there are three forces entering each engagement, the number of merchant vessels in the convoy, m, the number of escort vessels, c, and the number of U-boats in the attacking pack, n The two losses during the engagement which are of interest here are k, the number of merchant vessels sunk per pack attack, and l, the number of U-boats sunk per engagement The exchange rate of interest here is (l/k), the number of submarines sunk per merchant vessel sunk

As an example we will consider the data on the attacks on North Atlantic convoys during the years 1941 and 1942 The time is chosen after the Germans had introduced their wolf-pack tactics, and before the introduction of the escort carriers, so that the

TABLE 4 U-boat attacks on convoys in North Atlantic, 1941 1942 m = no M/V in convoy, c = no escorts, n = no U/B in pack, k = M/V sunk per engagement, l = U/B sunk per engagement

Independence of M/V sunk on convoy size

| m { | large | 15–24 | 25–34 | 35–44 | 45–54 |
	mean	20	30	39	48
No engagements		8	11	13	7
k, mean		5	6	6	5
c, mean		7	7	6	7
n, mean		7	5	6	5

period was one of comparative stability The first, and perhaps the most important aspect of the data, is that the number of merchant vessels sunk per pack attack turned out to be independent of the number of merchant vessels in convoy This is shown in Table 4 Here the data are sorted out according to size of

convoy, and spreads over a range of nearly 1 hemibel
Nevertheless the mean value of k for each value of m
is independent of m within the accuracy of the data
The mean values of c and n are also given for the data
chosen, to show that their averages are fairly constant, and therefore that the results are not due to a
counterbalancing trend in these quantities As far as
the data show, no more vessels are sunk on the average from a large convoy than are sunk from a small
convoy when attacked In other words, the *percentage*
of vessels sunk from a large convoy is smaller than the
percentage of vessels sunk from a small convoy This
is the fundamental fact which makes convoying
profitable

The number of merchant vessels sunk per engagement does depend upon the number of escort vessels
and on the number of U-boats in the pack, however
The dependence of k on U-boat pack size is shown in
Table 5 Here the data are sorted out according to n

TABLE 5 Dependence of M/V sunk on U/B pack size

| n { range | 1 | 2–5 | 6–9 | 10–15 | Averages |
n { mean	1	3 6	7	14	(weighted)
No engage-ments	29	32	22	5	88 total
k, mean	0 9	3	4	6	6 7
c, mean	6	7	7	8	6 7
(kc/n)	5 4	5 8	4 0	3 4	5 1

over a range of more than two hemibels The quantity k itself changes by a factor of two hemibels over
this range, but the quantity (k/n) stays constant
within the accuracy of the data

The dependence of the quantity k on the number
of escort vessels in the convoy is shown in Table 6

TABLE 6 Dependence of M/V sunk on no escorts

| c { range | 1–3 | 4–6 | 7–9 | 10–12 | 13–15 | Averages |
c { mean	2	5	8	11	14	(weighted)
No engage-ments	6	42	25	13	2	88 total
k, mean	4 5	3 4	3 0	1 1	2 0	
n, mean	3	4	4	2	10	3 8
(kc/n)	3 0	4 2	6 0	6 0	2 8	4 9

Here the data are sorted out according to c over a
range of nearly 2 hemibels Unfortunately a sorting
according to c has also meant a partial sorting according to n, so that the value of k fluctuates rather
widely It is perhaps allowable to say that k is inversely proportional to c, although this inverse de-

pendence does not seem to hold for c as small as
unity We are here looking for major changes, however, and fine points should first be set aside

Consequently we can say that, within the accuracy
which we are considering here, and over the intermediate range of values of escort size and U-boat
size, the number of merchant vessels lost per pack
attack is proportional to the number of U-boats in
the pack, and is roughly inversely proportional to
the number of escorts

3 2 3   Resulting Exchange Rates

A similar analysis of the submarines sunk during
these pack attacks shows that l, the number of U-
boats sunk per attack, is proportional to the number
of U-boats in the pack, n, and also proportional to
the number of escorts protecting the convoy, c To
the approximation considered here, then, the two
quantities turn out to be dependent on the forces
involved in the manner shown in equation (3) The
corresponding exchange rate is also given in this
equation

$$k \sim 5\left(\frac{n}{c}\right), \qquad l \sim \left(\frac{nc}{100}\right), \qquad (3)$$

$$\left(\frac{l}{k}\right) \simeq \left(\frac{c^2}{500}\right)$$

As pointed out before, the dependence of k and l on
n and c does not extend to the limits of very small or
very large values Nevertheless the equations seem
to be reasonably valid in the ranges of practical
interest

The important facts to be deduced from this set of
equations seem to be (1) the number of ships lost
per attack is independent of the size of the convoy,
and (2) the exchange rate seems to be proportional
to the square of the number of escort vessels per
convoy This squared effect comes about due to the
fact that the number of merchant vessels lost is
reduced, and at the same time the number of U-boats
lost per attack is *increased*, when the escorts are increased, the effect coming in twice in the exchange
rate The effect of pack size cancels out in the exchange rate From any point of view, therefore, the
case for large convoys is a persuasive one

When the figures quoted here were presented to
the appropriate authorities, action was taken to increase the average size of convoys, thereby also in-

creasing the average number of escort vessels per
convoy As often occurs in cases of this sort, the
eventual gain was much *greater* than that predicted
by the above reasoning, because by increasing convoy
and escort size the exchange rate (U/B sunk)/(M/V
sunk) was increased to a point where it became un-
profitable for the Germans to attack North Atlantic
convoys, and the U-boats went elsewhere This defeat in the North Atlantic contributed to the turning
point in the "Battle of the Atlantic "

3.3   COMPARATIVE EFFECTIVENESS

In many cases of importance it is necessary to
compare the relative effectiveness of two different
weapons or tactics in gaining some strategic end It is
possible to destroy enemy shipping, for instance, by
using submarines or by using aircraft, it is possible to
combat enemy submarines by attacking them on the
high seas or while they are in harbor, refueling, it is
possible to use aircraft in attacking enemy front-line
troops or in destroying munitions factories Such
comparisons are always difficult It is often hard to
find a common unit of measure, and frequently po-
litical and other nonquantitative aspects must enter
into the decision Nevertheless, in these cases it is
important and useful that the operations research
worker be able to make as objective and quantitative
a comparison as possible in order to insure that emotional and personal arguments do not carry the decision by default

In such cases an important part of the problem lies
in the choice of an equitable and usable unit of comparison Care must be taken lest the choice of units
prejudice the results by omitting important aspects
of the problem In fact, it is sometimes almost impossible to find a practicable unit of measure which
does not prejudge the problem to some extent It is
therefore important for the operations research
worker to estimate as objectively as possible what
aspects of the problem must be measured and what
can be neglected without vitiating the results Some
important imponderables must be left out because
they cannot be expressed in quantitative terms
These omissions must be recognized, so that they
may be given their proper weight in the final decision For instance, the effects of bombing or of area
gunfire on morale are matters which cannot be adequately expressed in numbers It is best, therefore,
when discussing the effects of bombing or area fire,
to confine the numbers to physical results and to

point out that the resulting numbers do not include
the effect on morale.

Where disparate tactics are to be compared, it is
not to be expected that the quantitative comparison
will be at all accurate Hence, unless the results for
the alternative methods differ by factors of a hembel
or more, one should conclude that the alternatives
are effectively equivalent. One might say that the
nonquantitative aspects of the decision would often
be able to counterbalance differences of factors of two
or less, but should not outweigh order-of-magnitude
differences

3 3 1   Effectiveness of Anti-Ship Weapons

In many naval problems it is important to be able
to assess the relative importance of ship damage to
ship sinking In such cases a profitable measure of
comparison is the amount of time a dockyard will
take to make up a loss A damaged ship requires so
much dockyard time for repair, and a ship sunk requires so much time to build a replacement Until
this time is made up, the ship will not be back in
service, and no amount of money or trained personnel
can provide its equivalent meanwhile A comparison
of the various methods of attacking shipping can
therefore be given in terms of the number of shipmonths lost by the enemy, and a comparison of different defensive methods can be given in terms of the
number of shipmonths gained by our side

An interesting example of this type of comparison
is given by a study by the Director of Naval Operations Research, Admiralty, on the relative importance of different types of protective armor on British
cruisers In World War II England had a number of
her cruisers damaged or lost by various causes shells
from enemy naval vessels, bombs, mines, and torpedoes The purpose of the study was to assess the
relative importance of the damage due to these four
causes and thereby to show what it was most important to defend against

In this study the effects of the damage were measured by giving the number of months the cruiser was
out of service for repairs The equivalent value of a
cruiser sunk was taken to be 36 cruiser-months since
it takes about this time to build a new cruiser In
addition to giving an indication of the cost of repairing or replacing the casualties, the cruiser-month loss
measure reflects the degree to which the Navy was
immobilized as a result of the attack.

The data in Table 7 show a number of interesting

TABLE 7. Casualties to cruisers by enemy action

Cause		Shell	Bomb	Mine	Tor-pedo	Total
Ships sunk		3	9	1	11	24
Ships damaged		18	56	9	19	102
Total casualties		21	65	10	30	126
Cruiser-months lost	by sinking	110	320	40	400	870
	by damage	30	90	60	180	360
	Total	140	410	100	580	1,230
	Per cent	11	34	8	47	100
Cruiser-months per casualty		7	6	10	19	10

points In the first place, the number of cruiser casualties (sunk and damaged) as a result of bombing attacks were more than 50 per cent of all casualties, but the number of cruiser-months lost per casualty due to bombing attacks was less than for the other types of attack In fact in terms of cruiser-months lost, torpedo attacks were considerably more important, a torpedo casualty turns out to be about three times as serious as a bomb casualty A further study of the bombing casualties indicated that most of the cruisers sunk by this means, corresponding to more than half of the cruiser-months lost by bombing, were sunk by the effect of underwater damage caused by near misses Consequently, a great deal more than half of the total cruiser-months lost due to enemy action has come from underwater damage to the ship's structure Most of the rest of the cruiser-months lost due to bombing were the result of fires started by direct hits of bombs

The conclusions indicated from this table are not difficult to reach. more attention should be given to fire control equipment and training, and new cruisers should be designed with better underwater protection, even if it means the sacrifice of some above-water armor

3 3 2 Bombing U-Boat Pens versus Escorting Convoys

A similar, though more complicated, analysis was used in studying the question of the relative value of using aircraft to escort convoys, to bomb submarine base facilities, or to hunt down submarines in the Bay of Biscay In this case the unit of effort is the sortie, an individual flight by a plane The unit of gain is,

of course, the reduction in the number of ships sunk The time chosen for the example is the last six months of 1942, and the place is the waters within aerial range of Great Britain

During this time convoys from England were attacked or threatened with attack about one-tenth of the time Some of the threatened convoys were given air escort protection, and others were not Those not protected had a higher loss rate than those which were protected by aircraft, so that the aircraft actually saved ships from being sunk The data for the last six months of 1942 for Coastal Command aircraft show that every hundred sorties flown to protect threatened convoys saved about 30 ships from being sunk Consequently, if the aircraft were used only to protect threatened convoys, their anti-submarine (or "shipping-protective") efficiency was extremely high, for they saved about 30 ships per hundred sorties flown. If, however, all convoys have to be protected all the time in order to insure protection when the convoy is threatened, then the plane's effectiveness is diluted, and only about 3 ships are saved per hundred sorties of ordinary escort flying

Turning now to the use of aircraft in bombing the U-boat repair and refitting bases in the Bay of Biscay, we must rely on the assessments of damage obtained from photographic reconnaissance after each bombing raid No submarines were sunk in port, but there was enough damage to the bases to slow down the refitting of the submarines and therefore to keep them off the high seas It was estimated that about 15 U-boat months were lost due to the damaging effect of the raids At that time each submarine on the average sank about 0.8 ship per month on patrol Consequently a loss of 15 U-boat months due to damage of repair facilities represented a gain to our side of about 12 ships which were not sunk This was accomplished by a series of raids which totaled about 1,100 sorties Consequently the gain to our side was about one ship saved per hundred sorties of effort against the U-boat bases This effort is not as effective as escorting convoy and is far less effective than protecting convoys which are threatened with attack.

The use of aircraft for antisubmarine patrol in the Bay of Biscay is an example of the use of offensive tactics for a defensive strategical task The immediate result of the patrols is a number of submarines sunk plus a number more delayed in passage through the Bay The final result, however, is in saving our ships from being sunk The average life of a submarine on patrol at that time was about ten months

If it were on patrol in the North Atlantic convoy region at that time, it sank about eight ships before it was sunk. From this point of view, therefore, each submarine sunk in the Bay of Biscay represented a net saving of about eight ships From another point of view, however, it is perhaps better to estimate the equivalent amount of time lost by the Germans in replacing the sunk submarines In 1942 there were enough submarines being constructed so that the bottleneck was in the training of the crews This training period (done in the Baltic) took about six months, so that one could say that a submarine sunk was equivalent to about six submarine-months lost Therefore, from this point of view, a submarine sunk was equivalent to about six ships saved, which corresponds fairly well with the other estimate of eight ships saved

In the last half of 1942, aircraft patrol in the Bay of Biscay sighted about six U-boats per hundred sorties and sank about one-half a U-boat per hundred sorties In addition, it is estimated that a hundred sorties produced a net delaying effect on the submarines in transit of about one U-boat month, corresponding to one ship saved Therefore, the net effect of offensive patrol in the Bay of Biscay area corresponded to between four and five ships saved per hundred sorties, an effectiveness which is somewhat larger than continuous escort of convoy, is considerably larger than the effectiveness of bombing the U-boat bases, but which is considerably smaller than the effectiveness of protecting threatened convoys Naturally, these relative effectiveness values changed as the war progressed.

The above comparative figures are not the whole basis upon which a decision as to employment of aircraft should be reached Nevertheless, they are a part of the material which must be considered, and the decision would be less likely to be correct if these figures were not available Presumably, if there were a very small amount of flying effort which could be expended in antisubmarine work, then the planes should be assigned to the protection of threatened convoys With a somewhat greater number of planes available, it probably would be advisable to spend part of that effort in the Bay of Biscay Another consideration also enters into the problem the fact that it might be possible to divert bombers from other missions to bomb the U-boat bases from time to time, whereas it would not be possible to use these same bombers to escort convoys or patrol the Bay of Biscay.

3 3 3 Submarine versus Aircraft as Anti-Ship Weapons

A comparison between submarines and aircraft in sinking enemy shipping is another question of considerable interest, but one which raises still more non-quantitative considerations. We can attempt to compute, however, the expected number of enemy ships sunk by the average operational submarine and compare it with the number of ships sunk by an aircraft used as efficiently as possible in the same region The problem in both cases divides itself into two questions the number of ships sighted per operational month, and the average number of ships sunk per sighting The first question involves the values of sweep rate which have been discussed in Section 3 1 For instance, the average commissioned submarine spends about one-third of its time in the patrol area, so that on the average ten days are spent there out of each month During this time the submarine can search over an area of 60,000 square miles (assuming a sweep rate of 6,000 square miles per day) unless the enemy antisubmarine effort is too severe In U S submarine attacks against Japanese merchant vessels, one ship out of eight sighted was sunk Therefore in an area with an average density of shipping of one merchant vessel per thousand square miles, an operational submarine would sink about eight ships, on the average, per operational month

Long range aircraft suitable for antishipping work average about eighty hours in the air per month If the patrol courses were well laid-out, it would be possible to spend a half of this airborne time in the shipping area, so that each plane might be expected to spend about forty hours per month searching for ships According to Table 2 a reasonable sweep rate for merchant vessels might be 500 square miles per hour, since merchant vessels are more easily sighted than submarines, so that each plane could search over about 20,000 square miles each month of operation In an area where there were on the average one ship per thousand square miles this plane would sight 20 ships per month on the average Data from Coastal Command antishipping planes indicate that, with adequate equipment and training, a plane sinks about one ship out of every 40 sighted (using bombs or rockets) Therefore, in the area under question each plane would sink about a half a ship a month Comparing the two, one sees that a *single submarine* is equivalent, as far as sinking enemy shipping goes, to a *squadron* of long range antishipping planes.

A great deal more than this numerical comparison must be gone into before it is possible to decide whether to use planes or submarines against enemy shipping in any given area In addition to the question of cost of outfitting a submarine as compared to the cost of outfitting a squadron of planes, there is also the point that the plane can be used for other purposes besides sinking ships The exchange rate for the two types of effort must also be taken into account

3.3 4   Anti-Ship versus Anti-City Bombing

The quantitative analysis of the relative effectiveness of aircraft in bombing the enemy's factories or in sinking his ships takes one still further into questions of economics A possible unit of measure would be the monetary value of the destruction caused There is some danger in this, however, for the monetary value of a building or a ship may be very different from its value to a nation at war The important factors in the bombed cities are the destroyed munitions or munitions factories, the destruction of housing is perhaps not as important, unless it reduces the efficiency of the munitions workers Perhaps a better unit of measure would be the number of man-months required to replace the munitions, rebuild the factories, or rebuild the ships sunk If this could be estimated, then it would be possible to compare quantitatively an antishipping sortie and a bombing sortie over an enemy city, for the relative effectiveness in man-months cost to the enemy

Work on this general strategic level can only be done adequately if the operations research worker has access to a great variety of records and intelligence reports In fact it is often impossible to obtain adequate data on all the important factors from the records of one service alone Unless the worker is operating at a high command level, it is usually futile to attempt such broad-scale quantitative comparisons.

3.4   EVALUATION OF EQUIPMENT PERFORMANCE

It has often been said that modern wars are technical wars If this statement has any meaning at all, it indicates that new, specialized weapons are developed and introduced into operations during the war, that we end the war fighting with different weapons than we started with Indeed, in the last war there were many cases where the fighting forces had not yet learned to use effectively the new weapon before that weapon became obsolete. This does not mean that an effort should have been made to slow down the introduction of new weapons. It means that technical thought in learning how and where a new weapon should be used, and in teaching the armed forces the best use of new equipment, is as important as is technical effort in the design and production of the new weapons Here again the quantitative approach of operations research can speed up the overall learning time and make it possible to use the new weapons effectively before they become obsolete A good bit of this work is not operations research in the strict sense of the word; but operations research workers should know how to evaluate weapons and judge where they are useful, because they are often the only technical men on the spot, and must do it

3.4 1   First Use of New Equipment

A great deal of thought must usually be spent on the possible tactical use of new equipment before this equipment gets into operation Someone with technical knowledge, either in the armed forces, or in an operations research group, or in the laboratory, sees the tactical need for a new weapon and sees the technical means by which this need can be satisfied. If this analysis appears to be reasonable a laboratory commences development work, production designs are gradually worked out and, eventually, production commences Unfortunately, there are many slips between the initial idea and its final confirmation in battle The initial tactical analysis may have been faulty, or its embodiment in the new weapon may be unworkable, or the tactical situation may have changed by the time the new equipment gets into operation It is extremely important therefore, that operations research workers, who are in touch with the changing tactical situation, take an active part in evaluating each stage in the development and production and use of new equipment It is particularly important that the first few operational results with the new gear be scrutinized closely to see whether it is necessary to improve on the original idea for use of the gear Detailed analysis of the working of the equipment must be made so as to devise adequate measures of effectiveness for future force requirements, and special action reports must be laid out so as to have the operating forces provide data with which to compare the operational measures with the theoretical ones In order to make these comparisons and in order to suggest changes in use for improving results as rapidly as possible, it is often important to send operations research workers near to the front to observe as closely as possible the working of the new equipment

3 4.2 Devising Operational Practice Training

It usually turns out that the operational forces at first have not the necessary training or understanding in the use of the new weapon The operations research worker must therefore devise methods whereby the fighting forces can learn to use the new weapon while they are fighting with it Practice on the battlefield is usually not the most efficient way of learning to use a new piece of gear For rapidity in learning, it is necessary that the pupil be scored as rapidly as he performs the operation, otherwise he will not remember what he has done wrong if his score turns out to be low Such scoring can seldom be provided on the field of battle, where usually the operator cannot see the results of his actions Consequently, a practice routine must be set up with means of scoring These scores, of course, are measures of effectiveness which can be used to check equipment performance as well as rapidity of learning

3 4.3   Equipment Evaluation

At each stage in the development of the new weapon from the first idea to its final operational embodiment, the operations research worker must evaluate its overall usefulness in terms of the following general questions

1 Is the new weapon worth while using at all? Is it better than some alternative weapon already in use? In what way is it better, and is this a different and important way? Does the cost of the change pay for itself?

2 When and where should the new weapon be used? What are the best tactics for its use, and how is this likely to modify the enemy's tactics? Is the weapon easy to counter and if so, what can we do about it? How can we find whether the enemy is countering or not?

3 Is the new equipment easy to maintain in operation? Are the maintenance crews properly trained, and are there understandable maintenance manuals? What simple operational tests can be devised to insure that the equipment is being kept in good repair?

4. How much training is needed in order that the new weapon be more effective than the old one? Can the results obtained by the weapon be noticed easily in battle, or must operational training, properly scored, be carried on continuously to insure effective use of the gear? What proportion of operational time must be spent in this practice, and how long will it take before the fighting forces can use the new weapon more effectively than they did the old one?

Such evaluation is often extremely difficult, particularly if the new weapon involves radically new principles Experience gathered close behind the front lines is extremely valuable in making such evaluations In many cases the evaluation cannot be complete without supplementing the operational data by data collected from operational experiments performed under controlled conditions This aspect of the problem will be discussed in Chapter 7

In the present section we will give a number of examples of the evaluation of new equipment coming into operation, showing how some of the questions raised above can be answered

3 4 4   Antiaircraft Guns for Merchant Vessels

At the beginning of the war, a great number of British merchant vessels were seriously damaged by aircraft attacks in the Mediterranean The obvious answer was to equip the vessels with antiaircraft guns and crews, and this was done for some ships The program was a somewhat expensive one, however, since antiaircraft guns were needed in many other places also Moreover, experience soon showed that single guns and crews, with the little training which could be spared for merchant vessels, had very little chance of shooting down an attacking plane The argument for and against installation had been going on for nearly a year with no apparent conclusions reached The guns were so ineffective that they hardly seemed worth the expense of installation; on the other hand, they made the merchant vessel crews feel somewhat more safe In the meantime, operational data had been coming in as to the experience of ships with and without gun protection, and it was finally decided to analyze the data in an attempt to settle the question

It was soon found that in only about 4 per cent of the attacks was the enemy plane shot down This was indeed a poor showing, and seemed to indicate that the guns were not worth the price of installation. On second thought, however, it became apparent that the percentage of enemy planes shot down was not the correct measure of effectiveness of the gun The gun was put on to protect the ship, and the proper measure should be whether the ship was less damaged if it had a gun and used it, than if it had no gun or did not use it The important question was whether the antiaircraft fire affects the accuracy of the plane's attack enough to reduce the chance of the ship's being hit Figures for this were collected and the results are shown in Table 8 It is apparent from

TABLE 8 Casualties to merchant vessels from aircraft bombing attacks (low-level attacks)

	AA fired	AA not fired
Bombs dropped	632	304
Bombs which hit	50	39
Per cent hits	8	13
Ships attacked	155	71
Ships sunk	16	18
Per cent sunk	10	25

this table that for low-level horizontal attacks the accuracy of the plane's attack was considerably reduced when antiaircraft guns were firing, and the chance of the ship escaping was considerably better when antiaircraft was used These same results were obtained for enemy dive-bombing attacks. It was obvious therefore that the installation of antiaircraft guns on merchant vessels was something which would definitely increase the ship's chance of survival, even though such guns did not shoot down the attacking planes very often

This numerical analysis finally settled the question For the antiaircraft guns more than paid for themselves if they reduced the chance of the ship being sunk by a factor of more than 2

3 4 5   Antitorpedo Nets

Early in the U-boat war in the Atlantic an attempt was made to save merchant vessels by equipping them with antitorpedo nets which were swung out by booms These nets were capable of stopping some 85 per cent of the German electric torpedo [G7E] but only 20 per cent of the German air-propelled torpedo [G7A] Taking the armament of U-boats as about 60 per cent G7E and 40 per cent G7A gave an average protection against these torpedoes of 59 per cent Since the nets covered only about 75 per cent of the ship, the "net" protection was 44 per cent.

This appears to be a strong argument in favor of equipping all merchant vessels with nets But the

cost was extremely high and the nets slowed down the ships, making an additional cost for fuel and time lost Against some opposition, about 600 ships were fitted with nets before enough operational experience had been obtained to make a reappraisal possible This reappraisal was quite broad in scope, as it involved (1) cost in dollars as against the cost of ships saved by the net, (2) cost in time and in cargo space, (3) cost in manpower to build and maintain the nets The research on the cost in dollars found that the net program did not pay for itself The operational data on the 25 ships which were torpedoed and which were fitted with nets are shown in Table 9 If the 10 ships

TABLE 9

	Sunk	Damaged	Undamaged
12 ships, nets not in use at time of attack	9	3	0
10 ships, nets in use	4	3	3
3 ships, use of nets unknown	3	0	0
	16	6	3

with nets streamed had not had their nets in use, we should expect 7½ to have been sunk and 2½ damaged The nets had thus saved the equivalent of 3½ ships and cargoes But a total of 590 ships had been fitted with nets at an initial cost equal to about twice that of 3½ ships and cargo, not to mention costs of maintenance, etc Thus the program had not paid for itself, and the report of the findings recommended that no further ships be equipped with nets

The previous two examples were cases where the answer was a simple "yes" or "no", the antiaircraft guns were worth the cost of installation, but the antitorpedo nets were not worth the cost In many other cases the answer is not so simple It may turn out that the new weapon has not as general a usefulness as was at first thought, but that it is extremely useful in certain special circumstances Here research on the measures of effectiveness of the weapon can produce a twofold benefit general efficiency is increased because the new weapon is not used in places where it is not efficient, and the effectiveness of special operations is increased considerably by using the new weapon in places where it has a decided advantage

3 4 6   Magnetic Airborne Detector

A clear-cut example of the importance of assigning equipment to tasks commensurate with their abilities is afforded by the case of the *magnetic airborne de-*

tector [MAD], developed to detect submerged submarines from aircraft In addition to being the only airborne means for discovering underwater submarines, MAD offers the advantage of not revealing the presence of the aircraft Although these qualities would seem ideal for antisubmarine search, closer examination reveals certain features limiting the operational effectiveness

The advantage of aircraft for visual or radar search lies in the high speed plus the broad sweep width (roughly twice the detection range) against surfaced submarines (up to several miles) For MAD-equipped aircraft the sweep rate is so reduced by the low MAD detection range (perhaps 100 yards for aircraft at 250 feet altitude and submarine at 250 feet depth), that the expectation of finding a submerged submarine becomes virtually nonexistent, at least for random search over open ocean areas It is comparable to the efforts of a blind man trying to draw a pencil line through a single dot on a large floor.

Although these characteristics place a definite limitation on its usefulness, they do not eliminate MAD as a submarine detection device To the contrary, a full appreciation of the "measures of effectiveness" of MAD, and its peculiarities, point the way to specialized tasks for which it is most effective One such opportunity was exploited during the Italian campaign in helping close off the Gibraltar Straits to Nazi U-boats enroute to the Mediterranean

U-boats had been making submerged passage of the Straits by daylight, utilizing underwater currents for propulsion to reduce noise In the meantime, thousands of hours of fruitless MAD search had been invested in the North Atlantic, while on the other hand, radar search within the Straits was ineffective due to the submerged nature of the passages Finally, it was recognized that here was a special case where MAD could redeem its record, and an MAD patrol, designed in accordance with search theory, was instituted across the Straits Within the first two months of operating the MAD barrier across the channel, two contacts resulting in U-boat sinkings were obtained, and a third one came soon later The result so discouraged the U-boats that no more attempted the passage into the Mediterranean for more than six months Thus even though MAD has only between 1/50th and 1/100th the search rate of radar, it was quite capable of providing an effective blockade across a restricted area, and one which did not provide warning, as would surface craft

This is merely one illustration of how the appropriate use of a new device can mean the difference between complete failure and success

3 4 7   Submarine Torpedo Evaluation

During World War II the U S submarine force introduced an electric torpedo, the Mark 18. Previous to this, the torpedoes used were the Mark 14 and the Mark 23, both steam-propelled The steam torpedoes both ran at 46 knots in their high-power setting Thus they had the advantage of high speed, but they left a clearly discernible wake. The electric torpedo ran a shorter distance and at a much slower speed, 29 knots, however, it had the advantage of being wakeless It was considered that this property of invisible travel more than made up for the slower speed, for the ship attacked would have no previous warning, and the enemy escort vessels would have no torpedo track to follow in commencing their counterattack After the new torpedo had been used for some months, an evaluation was made to see whether the steam torpedoes should not be discontinued entirely

In order to answer these questions, a uniform body of data was chosen attacks in a four-month period by submarines under a single command. In order not to give the Mark 18 torpedo an undue advantage (since attacks with it were made at closer range than attacks with the Mark 14 and Mark 23), no attacks made at ranges over 4,000 yards were considered With these limitations, the analysis of the data resulted in the following conclusions

1 The proportion of successful salvos under equal conditions fired against all types of enemy vessels (except large combatant units) is greater for the Mark 14 and Mark 23 (steam) torpedoes than for the Mark 18 (electric)

2 In attacks on merchant vessels, the proportion of successful salvos is greater with the Mark 14 and Mark 23 by a factor of 1 14

3 In attacks on large combatant units, the proportion of successful salvos appears to be greater with the Mark 18 by a factor of about 1 2

4 In attacks on destroyers, escort vessels, and patrol craft, the proportion of successful salvos is greater with the Mark 14 and Mark 23 by a factor of 1 4, in the case of destroyers, to 2 5, in the case of escort vessels and patrol craft

5 The occurrence and accuracy of deliberate counterattacks by enemy escorts show no correlation with the Mark number of the torpedoes fired in

attacks on merchant convoys This holds true for both day and night attacks

6. In the case of attacks on warships, the proportion of enemy counterattacks is, however, somewhat smaller with the Mark 18 (It was suggested that this might have been due to a better lookout system on the large combatant ships)

7 It was estimated that, if all U S submarines in 1944 had carried full loads of Mark 18 torpedoes, the enemy would have lost about 100 fewer merchant ships than if full loads of Mark 14 and Mark 23 had been carried At the same time it was considered probable that the exclusive use of the Mark 18 would not have prevented a single U S submarine casualty It was therefore recommended that submarines use the Mark 14 and Mark 23 torpedoes against merchant vessels, and that they use Mark 18 torpedoes against large combatant units

In this case it turned out that the danger against which the electric torpedoes were provided (the chance that the enemy would see the wake of the steam torpedoes) was not as great as had been apprehended This, of course, could not have been predicted until a wakeless torpedo had been tried in actual operation It turned out in most cases that the reduction in danger to the submarine was negligible, but that the loss in accuracy of firing torpedoes, due to the slow speed of the electric torpedo, was appreciable. Luckily the specialized advantage of the Mark 18 against large enemy naval vessels was important enough to save the whole development program from being a complete waste of effort

3.4.8 Aircraft Antisubmarine Depth Bombs

Sometimes an examination of the operational results of the first use of new equipment indicates clearly that a slight modification of the equipment will make it very much more effective This sort of situation has turned up several times in connection with the development of the use of aircraft as an antisubmarine weapon. The Germans underestimated the value of aircraft against submarines, in the end aircraft played a very important part in the defeat of the U-boat in the Atlantic

Early in World War II the British Coastal Command used ordinary bombs in their attacks against submarines These were obviously not effective, since they exploded on the surface of the water, and, if they did strike the deck of the submarine, they seldom penetrated the pressure hull. Depth charges

were therefore adapted for aircraft dropping These insured an underwater explosion which would be considerably more destructive to the submarine hull At this point arose the argument as to what should be the depth-setting for the bomb's explosion under water. It was not possible to change this depth-setting in the plane just prior to the attacking run, so that an estimate had to be made as to the best average setting for all attacks, and this setting had to be used all the time

A number of squadrons, no doubt feeling that a submarine was most likely to be submerged, set their depth bombs to explode at 150 feet The absurdity of this setting soon became apparent, however, for submarines at 150-foot depth could not be seen (and therefore not attacked), and submarines near the surface which could be seen would only be somewhat shaken by an explosion at 150-foot depth The depth-setting was next reduced to 50 feet, as a compromise between the "deep setters" and the "shallow setters ' After a year of argument, a numerical analysis was made which settled the argument

The fundamental question was the state of submergence of the submarine at the instant the attacking plane dropped its depth charge If a great number of attacks were made when the submarine was on the surface, then the 50-foot depth-setting was too deep, for an explosion at such a depth was too far away from the pressure hull of a surfaced submarine to have a great chance of producing lethal damage On the other hand, if the submarine was in the act of diving or had just dived at the instant of attack, then perhaps the 50-foot setting would be satisfactory

However, attacks after the submarine has dived are much less likely to be accurate than attacks on surfaced submarines. Therefore, even if the majority of attacks were made on submarines which had submerged a minute or more before the depth charge was dropped, it was not sensible to make the setting best for these cases, because the chance of success for such attacks was very low anyway The depth-setting should be determined by the type of attack which had the best chance of success, which was the attack on the surfaced submarine (unless it turned out that this type of attack was a negligible fraction of the total)

An examination of the operational results indicated that in 40 per cent of the cases the attack was made on a surfaced submarine, and in another 10 per cent of the cases a part of the submarine was visible when the depth charge was dropped Therefore in half of the cases (the half for which the attack was most accurate) the 50-foot depth-setting was too deep In the other half of the cases (when the accuracy was considerably less) the 50-foot depth-setting might be more satisfactory A numerical analysis of the chances of success of the attack as a function of the degree of submergence of the submarine indicated that a change in the depth setting from 50 feet to 25 feet would at least triple the chance of success of the average attack

In consequence of this analysis, it was made doctrine to set the depth of explosion for aerial depth bombs at 25 feet, and to instruct the pilots not to drop depth bombs if the submarine had already submerged for more than half a minute Within a few months after this change in doctrine went into effect, the actual effectiveness of aircraft antisubmarine attacks increased by a factor of more than 2

3 4 9   The Importance of Maintenance

Maintenance is a continual problem with modern weapons of war The performance of even the usual weapons must be checked from time to time to make sure that incomplete care does not seriously reduce their effectiveness As a simple example, we can quote (Table 10) from an analysis made of the

TABLE 10 Bomb-release failures

Type of aircraft	Number of incidents	Bombs failed to release	Failed to explode
PV-1	40	4 (10 per cent)	1
PBY-5A	9	1 (11 per cent)	0
PBM	33	3 (9 per cent)	0
PB4Y	177	8 (4 5 per cent)	0
Total	259	16 (6 2 per cent)	1 (0 4 per cent)

mechanical results from bombs dropped by 17 squadrons in the Pacific Evidently the bomb-fusing mechanism was satisfactory, for only one failed to explode The bomb-release mechanism, however, was not satisfactory, for in each 16 attacks there was one attack which failed because the bombs hung up It was soon found that this was due to an inadequate checking of the bomb shackles This was soon remedied and the percentage of bomb-release failures dropped markedly

3 4 10   Height-Finding Radar

During the last year of the war in the Pacific it became extremely important to keep enemy suicide

bombers away from our task forces. Antiaircraft equipment on the ships was quite effective, but this should, of course, be only used as a last resort The primary defense against suicide bombers is the combat air patrol [CAP] When enemy planes are detected by the search radar a CAP unit is vectored to intercept them This interception is extremely difficult unless the unit is given a fairly accurate measure of the elevation of the incoming enemy planes Consequently, an accurate determination of height by the ship's radar system is an important link in the defense of the task force against enemy bombers

A detailed analysis of the action reports indicated that this height determination gave signs of being the weakest link in the defensive pattern Enemy planes were nearly always detected at ranges greater than 75 miles CAP units were nearly always vectored to intercept, but in entirely too large a fraction of the cases no interception resulted The suspicion that this was due to inaccurate height-finding was strengthened by reports that in a number of cases where several height-finding radars were in use in the same task force they gave discordant results Experts were sent out to several ships having height-finding radars installed, and they found a considerable amount of inaccuracy in their readings In a number of these cases it was found that the alignment of the antenna was out of adjustment, and in a number of other cases the operators were not adequately trained In a number of cases the readings were more than 1,000 feet in error in elevation, which could easily explain the lack of interception of the enemy

Here was a difficulty which was a combination of poor maintenance and insufficient training The fundamental error was in not providing a simple and scorable test to check maintenance and training at frequent intervals By consulting with the experts and with the fleet officers a standard calibration test was devised which all ships could conduct in about three hours with the use of utility aircraft (or one of the ship's own aircraft) as a target These tests were authorized by the type commander of the theater and made it possible for the task force commander to test periodically the adequacy of his height-finding equipment and operators

3 4.11   Radar Bomb Sights

Occasionally new equipment gets sent into the field ahead of manuals or trained personnel, so that the theater has little conception of the limitations or possibilities of the gear The operations research worker in the field can be of considerable help in such cases. An example of this occurred when electronic bombing equipment was first installed in Navy patrol planes in the Pacific. Antishipping strikes with radar bombing equipment [APQ-5] in the Pacific areas had not been as successful with Navy patrol planes as it had been with several Army squadrons (as of June 1, 1945). These facts were disclosed by a statistical survey of the attacks against enemy shipping.

A study was made to discover the cause of failure by examining the equipment performance, the training program, and the tactical use of the equipment in combat areas. New facts came to light in all three categories which promised to solve the difficulty. So far as equipment was concerned, it was learned that calibration of the gear needed constant attention to a degree not appreciated by patrol plane commanders. In addition, there was considerable difference in performance between those planes equipped with the auto-pilot (which is connected directly to the radar bombing equipment), and other planes where the pilot followed the *pilot direction indicator* [PDI]. Thus equipment performance accounted for the rather good results of Army (and Navy) Liberator-type bombers [PB4Y-1] as against the poor showing of Navy PBM-type aircraft.

In the line of training, the performance of student crews was investigated. Each crew was given instruction on a ground trainer for four hours and then made a flight in a school plane. On this flight the student crew watched the instructors drop on the target, and then took over and made 3 or 4 drops. The instructors, who were an average patrol plane crew singled out for the job, were averaging 70 per cent hits, after having made 100 bombing runs, whereas the students were consistently averaging 35 per cent hits with their 3 or 4 drops. Clearly the students were only beginning to learn, and the training period was far too short. A better return on the investment would have resulted if a few crews had been really well trained and sent forward to combat areas as specialists.

Finally, tactics were examined. By July 1, 1945 the Japanese shipping was moving through open waters only at night, and during the day was anchored in protected harbors close against land. Our own Navy submarines were prowling in enemy waters and were surfaced at night, so that doctrine required our aircraft to identify positively any vessel attacked as a non-sub. There were also areas (submarine sanc-tuaries) where aircraft were not allowed to bomb, and still other areas where any target could be bombed. It was a matter of simple logic to propose that the radar bombing equipment be used only at night and only in the nonrestricted areas.

3 4.12   The Effects of Supervised Practice

A striking example of the far-reaching effects of continual, well-supervised practice on the effectiveness of operations can be taken from the experience with very long range [VLR] strategic bombing of Japan. An object of strategic bombing is to destroy the enemy's facilities for producing war goods, with special emphasis on those plants engaged in producing equipment which is hardest to replace. Many such plants are small targets, and to knock them out usually requires accurate bombing. Therefore, the value of a unit of a strategic air force depends upon how many such enemy targets it can destroy in a given time. This rate depends on many factors: the number of aircraft available, their maintenance, the bomb-load per plane, the accuracy with which they can drop bombs, etc.

The training of the bomber crews has an important effect on nearly all of these factors. The initial training is of course important, but it appears that continuous practice-training, which should be carried on in the field of operations, is equally important. One might expect that an operational crew could practice bombing over an enemy target just as well as it could practice over a trial target, and it is not obvious that it would be profitable to reduce the number of bombing missions per month in order to allow time for continued practice. It is, of course, true that scoring of practice bombing is more immediate and detailed than the assessment of operational bombing, so that the crews can learn more quickly their mistakes. It is also true that more experience can be gained in ten hours practice over a trial target than in a ten-hour operational mission.

In order to determine how much value operational practice training can be, the data for one VLR command was studied for a period of six months. For the first half of this period practice bombing was not emphasized in this command. During the second three-month period somewhat more than 10 per cent of the operational time of the crews was spent in practice. The curves of Figure 2 show the comparative results.

The topmost of the four curves shows the average number of hours a VLR plane of this command spent in the air per month The dotted curve gives the total average hours, and the solid curve gives the number of hours spent on missions bombing Japan, the difference between the curves giving the average number of hours per month per plane spent on practice One notices a continual increase in the average operational hours per month per plane, indicating

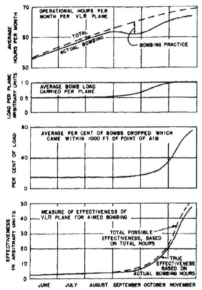

FIGURE 2 Measure of effectiveness of VLR planes for aimed bombing to show effects of operational practice training (Data for one command)

that by November each plane was working approximately 70 per cent more time than the same plane had in June This improvement is only to a small part due to the training of air crews, the principal contributions having been due to increased experience of the maintenance personnel, to modifications in the aircraft, and to cooler weather One sees that during and after September a considerably larger amount of time was spent in practice.

The second curve shows the improvement in load-carrying capacity of the plane A large portion of the phenomenal rise during September and October was due to the standardization of "stripping and weighing" the aircraft. Another contributing factor was the increased experience on the part of pilots, flight engineers, and navigators, so that the cruise-control data were more closely followed and less fuel reserve was required. A detailed analysis indicates that the increase in average bomb-load was in part due to the additional training, that a more experienced crew can, in general, carry a larger load.

The third curve shows a measure of the bombing accuracy of the plane, obtained from assessment of photographs of damage What is plotted is the average per cent of the bombs dropped which come within 1,000 feet of the target It is to be noted that the upward trend in the bombing accuracy begins shortly after the increase in flying training shown in the top curve Other factors affecting the accuracy were changes in formation, permitting the bombings to be controlled by a small number of lead crews, which are given additional training Improved weather, with resulting better physical conditions for the crews, probably also had its effect, though, if this was an important factor, the rise should have occurred in September and early October rather than later One can conclude that the rise in accuracy is due in no small part to increase in training

The product of these three factors (hours per month per plane, bomb-load carried, and accuracy) could be used as an overall measure of effectiveness of an individual VLR plane and crew for the strategic bombing of small targets This product is plotted in the lower curve of Figure 2 The number of hours per month is, of course, the number of hours of actual bombing (i e , the total number of hours per month minus the number of hours used in bombing practice) This is the solid curve, called "true effectiveness " We notice very little change in this measure throughout the first three months From the time the additional training was instituted to the end of the three months' period, there is, however, a phenomenal rise Each plane, by the end of November, is approximately *ten times as effective* as the same plane and crew was the first of September

As has been indicated, some of the rise is due to weather and other causes, but the most important cause seems to have been the additional practice training As a conservative estimate of the cost of this training, we can use the total hours per month per plane instead of the actual bombing hours This gives rise to the dotted curve of the lower graph, which is the measure of effectiveness which a plane would have if it had spent all its operational hours in bombing targets, and if the other improvements (of bomb load carried and of accuracy) had occurred without the training We see that the loss of effectiveness due to the additional time taken out in training is a very small amount compared to the extraordinary rise in bomb-load and accuracy, which the training in part produced

The really large change in effectiveness, as shown in the fourth graph, is of considerable interest It means, in fact, that a VLR plane was *ten times as effective* in destroying enemy installations in November as in August In other words, a squadron of these planes was more effective in November than three groups were in August, though the planes were essentially the same These figures show the futility of numbers compared to quality of performance The results achieved by increased efficiency (by further training) obviously far exceeded those which could have been reached simply by increasing the number of aircraft or the number of missions flown, or by adding more new gadgets This fact is often overlooked in an attempt to win by numbers, with everything being sacrificed simply for more numbers, more aircraft, more sorties, more bombs dropped The curve shows how little mere quantity can count compared to improved quality Furthermore, the biggest improvements, those of plane-loading and accuracy, are largely due to training and continual practice

In other aspects of warfare the effect of practice and training may not be so decisive, but in all cases heretofore analyzed they have turned out to be exceedingly important It would be worth while analyzing other cases in detail, so that in the future one might be able to estimate whether the addition of new equipment or the further training of personnel in the use of the old equipment would be more effective in a given case

3 4 13   Evaluating the Enemy's Countermeasures

In a few cases equipment is misused or discarded because of an exaggerated fear of the vulnerability of the gear to enemy countermeasures Such a possibility must always be prepared for, but it was the experience in World War II that our forces usually credited the enemy with an effective countermeasure long before it actually occurred This subject has

already been mentioned, and will be discussed in some detail in Chapter 5. An example will be given here how a calculation of average effectiveness can serve to answer the fears of enemy countermeasures, and to prolong the use of an effective piece of equipment. The example concerns the use of aircraft-warning radar by U. S. submarines. The advantage of such equipment is that it will detect the aircraft at greater range than will visual lookouts, and thus will give the submarines a better chance of diving before the attack is made The first early-warning set installed on U. S submarines had an average range of detection for Japanese planes only 1 4 times the average range of visual detection for these planes; nevertheless, this added modicum of warning proved of considerable value in a number of cases In fact, our submarines were caught on the surface by the Japanese planes in less than 5 per cent of the attacks, as compared to the 50 per cent chance of surface attack enjoyed by our planes against the U-boat, as mentioned earlier

In the course of radar development, however. the Allies designed and built a radar detector which could pick up the signals from a submarine's early-warning radar It was feared that, if Japanese planes had such a radar receiver on them, the range of detection of submarines using radar, by such planes, would be greatly increased, and that the submarine's radar, instead of being an asset, would become a liability Many submarine skippers became convinced that this had occurred, for they seemed to find that more Japanese planes came into view when their early-warning radar was turned on than when it was off The operational data were analyzed to see if this were so The results of this analysis are given in Table 11

TABLE 11 Aircraft contacts by U S submarines per 100 days stay of submarine in area

	Area A	Area B
Radar early-warning in use	86	67
Radar early-warning not in use	61	51
Ratio	1 4	1 3

These results indicate that submarines with their radar in use saw more planes per hundred days than those submarines with radar not in use At first sight, therefore, it would seem to indicate that the radar-using submarines *were* attracting planes. On second thought, however, one sees that this is not so. The radar-using submarine *should* see more planes because its radius of detection is greater than for submarines where visual sighting is relied upon In fact, the ratio of the numbers of aircraft contacts should be equal to the ratio of the radii of detection, which, as we have seen above, is just the factor 1 4 Consequently the operational data indicate that the radar-using submarines have seen no more planes than they should, compared to the vision-using sub-marines In other words, no more Japanese aircraft congregated over radar-using submarines than congregated over non-radar-using submarines, and, if the Japanese had a radar receiver, it was not doing them any good This analysis helped to kill opposition to the use of radar in U S submarines Since the end of the war, it has been learned that the Japanese had considered installing radar receivers on their planes, but the proposal had been vetoed by the higher command

Chapter 4

STRATEGICAL KINEMATICS

IN CHAPTER 3 we showed that in a great number of cases the approximate constants of warfare are useful without further mathematical analysis, once they have been obtained by theoretical or statistical methods In Section 3.1 we gave an example from the antisubmarine war in the Bay of Biscay, which showed that sometimes the comparison of the value of the constants obtained from operational data with the theoretically possible value will indicate, without further analysis, the modification in tactics necessary to obtain improvement Similarly, we shall see in Section 5 1 that a simple statistical analysis of the constants entering into the effectiveness of suicide bombers against maneuvering surface craft is all that is necessary to indicate the best tactics to be used in avoiding "Kamikazes" Once in a while, a simple comparison of two measures of effectiveness will suffice to answer a strategical question, such as the case discussed in Section 3 3 concerning the relative advantage of aircraft and submarines in sinking enemy shipping Measures of effectiveness, statistically or analytically determined, can be of considerable aid to the strategic planner in working out force requirements for various tasks This chapter will give examples of the strategic usefulness of some of these constants, and will indicate some of the mathematical theory which is basic to strategic applications of the constants

4 1   FORCE REQUIREMENTS

Two examples from the antisubmarine war in the Atlantic will suffice to indicate how measures of effectiveness can aid in determining force requirements The first shows the method of calculating the number of antisubmarine patrol planes needed in a sea frontier, in order adequately to escort the ship-

Miles from base	Average number of units present			
	Convoys	Indepen-dents	Naval vessels	Tugs
0–100	4 3	17 4	2 0	1 4
100–200	2 1	2 3	0 9	0 3
200–300	0 6	1 7	0 7	0 1
300–400	0 3	0 3	0 2	0
400–500	0 1	0 1	0 1	0

ping in the frontier At one period in World War II, a certain frontier had a density of shipping off its coast as shown in the foregoing table

The ocean area in the sea frontier was divided up into zones at different distances from air bases. Shipping charts were then counted, so as to obtain the average number of naval units, convoys, etc , which were to be found each day in each of these zones For instance, on the average, there turns out to be about one and two-thirds independent vessels in the zone between 200 and 300 miles away from an air base, there turns out to be one-tenth of a convoy, on the average, in the zone between 400 and 500 miles from an air base (or, rather, there is a convoy in this region one-tenth of the time)

The region patrolled by the sea frontier planes is divided in this way because it takes more effort to patrol at large distances from a base than it does at short distances Or, to put it another way, it takes more planes to give a convoy adequate coverage when the convoy is far from the air base than when it is close The next part of the problem, therefore, is to determine how many planes of a given type are needed to cover a single unit continuously in a given zone Each plane can fly so many hours a month, the rest of the time it must be at the base in order to rest its crew, and to undergo overhauling. Suppose the average number of hours a month a certain plane can be operational is N Each plane has a maximum number of hours T during which it can stay aloft; this can be called the length of mission. Not all this length of mission is available for escorting vessels, however the plane must fly from the base out to the position of the unit before it can be of use, and it must fly back again to be of use next time This transit time is equal to twice the distance to the center of the zone in question, divided by the speed of the plane

$$L = \text{Transit time} = \frac{1}{V}(100 + 2D),$$

where V is equal to the speed of plane in knots, and D is the distance from the base to the inner edge of the zone in question

4 1 1   Requirements for Air Escort

The length of time which a plane can devote to convoying on each mission is therefore $T - L$ Therefore, the fraction $(T - L)/T$ is the portion of each mission which is actually spent in convoying, so that N times this fraction is the total number of hours a month a single plane can spend in actual escort of a unit in the zone in question Therefore, the number of planes of a given type required to be kept on hand at a base in order to provide continuous escort of a

From this set of tables of force requirements, one can calculate the total number of planes required, as soon as one knows the particular plane which is to cover a given zone, and as soon as one decides what percentage of coverage each unit is to be given For instance, if one wishes to give all convoys complete coverage, naval vessels 50 per cent coverage, and independents and tugs 10 per cent coverage, and if one is to use Liberators for the outer two zones, blimps for the next two zones and for half the coverage in the inner zone, and Kingfishers for the other

		Blimp ZP	Kingfisher OS2U	Liberator PB4Y
N, hours per plane per month		360	80	100
V, speed in knots		50	90	130
T, length of mission, hours		18	4	15
	Distance from bases			
Number of planes required for full escort of one unit	0 100	2 25	12 46	7 58
	100–200	3 00		8 49
	200–300	4 50		9 66
	300–400	9 00		11 22
	400 500			13 38

single unit in a given zone is determined by the equation (assuming 30 days per month)

$$\text{Number of planes required at base} = \frac{720T}{N(T - L)}$$

Typical performance figures for two different types of patrol planes and for navy blimps, together with the number required of each type to give continuous coverage at different distances from the base, are given in the above table

We see from the table that the Kingfishers [OS2U] can only be used for cover in the first zone, and the Liberators are the only planes mentioned in this table which can cover the outer zone We also see that it takes nearly twice as many Liberators to cover a unit in the outermost zone as it does for Liberators to cover a unit in the innermost zone

These two tables can be combined to give the total force requirements for complete coverage of the different units present in the sea frontier in question, as shown in the table on page 63 One multiplies the number of planes required per unit in a given zone by the number of units present in that zone This gives the number of planes or blimps of each kind which would be required to be on hand at bases in order to cover all the units present in the frontier all the time

half of the coverage of the inner zone, then one sees that one needs about 6 Liberators, about 22 blimps, and about 45 Kingfishers on base in order to satisfy these requirements for close coverage against submarines More than this number would need to be on hand in order to provide against simultaneous breakdown, but this is another problem, already touched on in Section 2 2 Other similar requirements must be made up for other antisubmarine duties, such as for general patrols and to take part in submarine hunts after a contact has been made

It should be pointed out that a certain per cent of nonflying weather simply lowers the number of hours per plane per month, but does not affect the aircraft assignments made in the tables above Hours lost due to bad weather are hours lost, and the requisite number of planes must be present to take advantage of the good weather

4 1 2   Expenditure of Depth Charges

Another example of force requirement calculations is given in the determination of the depth charges and ahead-thrown charges used per month in the Atlantic in antisubmarine warfare in 1944 During this time there were approximately 30 enemy submarines on patrol in the Atlantic, and there were

Aircraft Requirements for A/S Escort for Sea Frontier

Day and night cover for convoys

Zone	Avg No units to be covered	Blimps ZP	Kingfishers OS2U	Liberators PB4Y
0–100	4 3	9 7	53 6	32 6
100–200	2 1	6 3	Cannot	17 8
200–300	0 6	2 7	cover	5 8
300–400	0 3	2 7	these	3 3
400–500	0 1		zones	1 3

Day and night cover for naval vessels

Zone	Avg No units to be covered	Blimps ZP	Kingfishers OS2U	Liberators PB4Y
0–100	2 0	4 5	25	15
100–200	0 9	2 7	Cannot	7 6
200–300	0 7	3 1	cover	6 8
300–400	0 2	1 8	these	2 2
400–500	0 1		zones	1 3

Day and night cover for independents and tugs

Zone	Avg No units to be covered	Blimps ZP	Kingfishers OS2U	Liberators PB4Y
0–100	18 8	42	234	142
100–200	2 6	7 8	Cannot	22
200–300	1 8	8 1	cover	17
300–400	0 3	2 7	these	3 3
400–500	0 1		zones	1 3

about 500 antisubmarine ships at sea in the Atlantic, which used 614 depth charges and 700 ahead-thrown charges per month to sink, on the average, 1 25 submarines a month It seems to have turned out that the number of depth charges and ahead-thrown charges used per month is proportional to the number of enemy submarines present at any time For the year 1944, therefore, about 20 depth charges and 23 ahead-thrown charges were used per month per enemy submarine present This figure was used to predict the number of weapons needed in subsequent months once it was possible to estimate the number of enemy submarines which were likely to be on patrol This result was used in determining the production orders for the successive year.

It is possible, on the other hand, that the number of depth charges used was proportional to the number of submarines sunk, this figure for 1944 was about 490 depth charges and 560 ahead-thrown charges per German U-boat sunk. From Intelligence reports, one

can estimate the number of submarines that will be in the Atlantic at some future time, and find the number of submarines expected to be sunk This again gave an alternate estimate of requirements, which turned out to agree with the other estimate approximately

4 2   LANCHESTER'S EQUATIONS

The previous section gave a few simple examples of the use of measures of effectiveness to determine force requirements As usual, the constants of warfare are not very constant, and only approximate forecasts can be obtained In most cases such constants are not known sufficiently accurately to warrant their being used in mathematical equations of any complexity

Occasionally, however, it is useful to insert these constants into differential equations, to see what would happen in the long run if conditions were to remain the same, as far as the constants go These differential equations, in order to be soluble, will have to represent extremely simplified forms of warfare, and therefore their range of applicability will be small We shall point out later in this chapter other serious limitations of such equations Nevertheless, it sometimes happens that considerable insight can be obtained into the interrelationship between measures of effectiveness by studying differential equations involving them Most of these equations compare the losses of the opposing forces, and are obviously related to the corresponding equations for chemical reactions or for the biological increase or decrease of opposing species A great number of different equations of this general sort can be set up, each corresponding to a different tactical or strategical situation, and only a few of them having more than marginal interest A few of the more interesting examples will be given in the present chapter, more as indications for directions of further investigations rather than as descriptions of methods of proven utility

4 2 1   Description of Combat

Some of the simplest and most interesting differential equations relating opposing forces were studied by Lanchester during World War I [9] The following material is taken from his work

One of the great questions at the root of all strategy is that of *concentration*, the concentration of the whole resources of a belligerent on a single purpose or object, and concurrently the concentration of the main strength of his forces, whether naval or military, at one point in the field of operations But the principle of concentration is not in itself a strategic principle, it applies with equal effect to purely tactical operations, it is on its material side based on facts of purely scientific character

There is an important difference between the methods of defence of primitive times and those of the present day which may be used to illustrate the point at issue In olden times, when weapon directly answered weapon, the act of defence was positive and direct, the blow of sword or battleaxe was parried by sword and shield, under modern conditions gun answers gun, the defence from rifle-fire is rifle-fire, and the defence from artillery, artillery But the defence of modern arms is indirect tersely, the enemy is prevented from killing you by your killing him first, and the fighting is essentially collective As a consequence of this difference, the importance of concentration in history has been by no means a constant quantity Under the old conditions it was not possible by any strategic plan or tactical maneuver to bring other than approximately equal numbers of men into the actual fighting line, one man would ordinarily find himself opposed to one man Even were a general to concentrate twice the number of men on any given portion of the field to that of the enemy, the number of men actually wielding their weapons at any given instant (so long

as the fighting line was unbroken) was, roughly speaking, the same on both sides Under present-day conditions all this is changed. With modern long-range weapons—fire-arms, in brief—the concentration of superior numbers gives an immediate superiority in the active combatant ranks, and the numerically inferior force finds itself under a far heavier fire, man for man, than it is able to return The importance of this difference is greater than might casually be supposed, and since it contains the kernel of the whole question, it will be examined in detail

In thus contrasting the ancient conditions with the modern, it is not intended to suggest that the advantages of concentration did not, to some extent, exist under the old order of things For example, when an army broke and fled, undoubtedly any numerical superiority of the victor could be used with telling effect, and, before this, pressure, as distinct from blows, would exercise great influence Also the bow and arrow and the crossbow were weapons that possessed in a lesser degree the properties of fire-arms, inasmuch as they enabled numbers (within limits) to concentrate their attack on the few As here discussed, the conditions are contrasted in their most accentuated form as extremes for the purpose of illustration

Taking, first, the ancient conditions where man is opposed to man, then, assuming the combatants to be of equal fighting value, and other conditions equal, clearly, on an average, as many of the "duels" that go to make up the whole fight will go one way as the other, and there will be about equal numbers killed of the forces engaged, so that if 1,000 men meet 1,000 men, it is of little or no importance whether a "Blue" force of 1,000 men meet a "Red" force of 1,000 men in a single pitched battle, or whether the whole "Blue" force concentrates on 500 of the "Red" force, and, having annihilated them, turns its attention to the other half, there will, presuming the "Reds" stand their ground to the last, be half the "Blue" force wiped out in the annihilation of the Red force [a] in the first battle, and the second battle will start on terms of equality—i e , 500 Blue against 500 Red

4 2 2   The Linear Law

To set the discussion into a mathematical equation, we will let m be the number of combatants in the Red force at any instant and n be the corresponding number in the Blue force The time variable in the equations requires a little explanation, since it is very seldom that warfare goes on continuously In the simplified picture of earlier warfare, each *engagement* (or charge, or battle) was made up of a large number of individual *combats* (or duels) We can label each engagement in sequence and use the ordinal number as the "time" variable t, by the usual extension from discrete to continuous variable Or else we can label the individual combats in sequence and use this index for our time variable T.

---

[a] This is not strictly true, since towards the close of the fight the last few men will be attacked by more than their own number. The main principle is, however, untouched

We will only consider those combats which result in the elimination of one or the other combatant To make the discussion general, we can allow one side or the other a certain superiority in weapons or in training which can be represented in terms of an *exchange rate* As explained before, this is the ratio E between the average number of Blue combatants lost to the average number of Red combatants lost The number of the Red forces lost per combat is equal, on the average, to the ratio of the losses inflicted by the Blue forces on the Red and the total number of combats (which is equal to the total number of losses), and similarly for the Blue losses. Therefore the differential equations for the changes in m and n per combat are

$$\frac{dm}{dT} = -\frac{1}{1+E}, \qquad \frac{dn}{dT} = -\frac{E}{1+E},$$

$$m = m_0 - \frac{T}{1+E}, \qquad n = n_0 - \frac{TE}{1+E};$$

where

$$\frac{dn}{dm} = E, \qquad n_0 - n = E(m_0 - m) \qquad (1)$$

Since the solutions are linear in T and since the relationship between m and n is linear, this set of equations is sometimes called *Lanchester's linear law*

To express the equations in terms of t, we can assume that in the tth engagement there are $F(m, n, t)$ combats The equations in terms of the "engagement variable" t are therefore

$$\frac{dm}{dt} = -\frac{1}{1+E} F(m, n, t),$$

$$\frac{dn}{dt} = -\frac{E}{1+E} F(m, n, t) \qquad (2)$$

Dividing one of these equations by the other, we obtain again $(dn/dm) = E$, as before

The solutions of these two equations represent average or expected values in the sense of probability theory The actual results of any series of engagements will deviate from this average according to the probability analysis given in the next section

We see that the solutions to these equations correspond to the situation discussed above by Lanchester The two opposing forces are equally balanced if the ratio of their initial numbers is equal to the exchange rate E, as has been mentioned above There is consequently no advantage in concentration of forces.

4.2.3 The Square Law

When we turn to the modern case with extended fire power, we find that we cannot break up the individual engagements into unit combats, for each participant in an engagement can fire at every opponent (at least in the ideal case) The time variable must therefore be the indicial number t of the engagement. We will assume that in th tth engagement, a single Red combatant can put out of action $(E/1 + E)G(t)$ Blue combatants, on the average, and an individual Blue combatant can put out of action $(1/1 + E)G(t)$ Red combatants, on the average, where G measures the "intensity of the combat" at the time t The corresponding differential equations for this case are therefore

$$\frac{dm}{dt} = -\frac{n}{1+E}G(t), \qquad \frac{dn}{dt} = -\frac{mE}{1+E}G(t);$$

$$\frac{dm}{dn} = \frac{n}{mE}; \qquad n_0^2 - n^2 = E(m_0^2 - m^2); \qquad (3)$$

where E is again the exchange rate Since the solution of this equation comes out as a relationship between the squares of the numbers of the combatants, this equation is sometimes referred to as *Lanchester's square law*

The advantages of concentration are apparent in the solution of equations (3), for it is apparent that the effective strength of one side is proportional to the first power of its efficiency and proportional to the *square* of the number of combatants entering the engagement Two opposing forces are then equally matched when the exchange rate is equal to the square of the ratio of the number of combatants Consequently, it is more profitable to increase the number of participants in an engagement than it is to increase (by the same amount) the exchange rate (by increasing the effectiveness of the individual weapons) This is not an argument against increased weapon efficiency; it is simply a statement that a tactical or strategical use of concentration may counterbalance any moderate advantage in weapon efficiency

To bring this fact out more clearly, we will return to the engagement mentioned earlier between 1,000 men on the Blue side and 1,000 men on the Red side, each with weapons of equal firepower ($E = 1$) If each side throws in all its manpower into each engagement, the series of battles will end in a draw If, however, the Red general maneuvers so as to bring his 1,000 men into engagement with half of the Blue force, it will be seen that the Blue force is wiped out of existence with a loss of only about 134 men of the Red force, leaving 866 to meet the remaining 500 of the Blue force with an easy and decisive victory The second engagement between 866 Red participants and 500 Blue will result in the annihilation of the second Blue contingent with the loss of about 159 Reds, leaving 707 survivors

4 2 4   Fighting Strength

These equations and their solutions have a great range of approximate application and suggest a number of useful investigations Indeed, an important problem in operations research for any type of warfare is the investigation, both theoretical and statistical, as to how nearly Lanchester's laws apply If it turns out that Lanchester's square law applies, the possibilities of a concentration of forces should at once be studied An obvious application is in aerial warfare It has already been mentioned that an important factor in the large ratio of effectiveness between U S fighting planes and Japanese fighting planes lies in the fact that the U S planes fight in groups of two or three, whereas the Japanese planes usually fight singly

Another quotation from Lanchester[9] is of interest here

It is easy to show that this solution may be interpreted more generally, the "fighting strength" of a force may be broadly defined as proportional to the square of its numerical strength multiplied by the fighting value of its individual units

As an example of the above, let us assume an army of 50,000 giving battle in turn to two armies of 40,000 and 30,000 respectively, equally well armed, then the strengths are equal, since $(50,000)^2 = (40,000)^2 + (30,000)^2$ If, on the other hand, the two smaller armies are given time to effect a junction, then the army of 50,000 will be overwhelmed, for the fighting strength of the opposing force, 70,000 is no longer equal, but is in fact nearly twice as great namely, in the relation of 49 to 25 Superior morale or better tactics or a hundred and one other extraneous causes may intervene in practice to modify the issue but this does not invalidate the mathematical statement

Let us now take an example in which the difference in the fighting value of the unit is a factor We will assume that, as a matter of experiment, one man employing a machine-gun can punish a target to the same extent in a given time as sixteen riflemen What is the number of men armed with the machine-gun necessary to replace a battalion a thousand strong in the field? Taking the fighting value of a rifleman as unity, let $n =$ the number required The fighting strength of the battalion is $(1,000)^2$ or

$$n = \sqrt{\frac{1,000,000}{16}} = \frac{1,000}{4} = 250$$

or one quarter the number of the opposing force

This example is instructive, it exhibits at once the utility and weakness of the method The basic assumption is that the fire of each force is definitely "concentrated" on the opposing force Thus the enemy will concentrate on the one machine-gun operator the fire that would otherwise be distributed over four riflemen, and so on an average he will only last for one quarter the time, and at sixteen times the efficiency during his short life he will only be able to do the work of four riflemen in lieu of sixteen, as one might easily have supposed This is in agreement with the equation The conditions may be regarded as corresponding to those prevalent in the Boer War, when individual-armed firing or sniping was the order of the day

When, on the other hand, the circumstances are such as to preclude the possibility of such concentration, as when searching an area or ridge at long range, or volley firing at a position, or "into the brown," the basic conditions are violated, and the value of the individual machine-gun operator becomes more nearly that of the sixteen riflemen that the power of his weapon represents The same applies when he is opposed by shrapnel fire or any other weapon which is directed at a position rather than the individual It is well thus to call attention to the variations in the conditions and the nature of the resulting departure from the conclusions of theory, such variations are far less common in naval than in military warfare, the individual unit—the ship—is always the gunner's mark

Apart from its connection with the main subject, the present line of treatment has a certain fascination, and leads to results which, though probably correct, are in some degree unexpected If we modify the initial hypothesis to harmonize with the conditions of long-range fire, and assume the fire concentrated on a certain area known to be held by the enemy, and take this area to be independent of the numerical value of the forces, then we have the conditions of equations (1), and the rate of loss is independent of the numbers engaged, being directly as the efficiency of the weapons Under these conditions the fighting strength of the forces is directly proportional to their numerical strength, there is no direct value in concentration, 'gun' concentration, and the advantage of rapid fire is relatively great Thus in effect the conditions approximate more closely to those of ancient warfare

4 2 5   Mathematical Solution

The detailed solution of Lanchester's square law has been studied by Koopman [10] In order to simplify equation (3) one can make a transformation of the time variable into

$$\tau = \frac{\sqrt{E}}{1 + E} \int G(t)dt \qquad (4)$$

Since the time scale is rather arbitrary in any case, the new variable will be just as satisfactory as the other one. In terms of the new variable the equations and their solutions reduce to the following

$$\frac{dm}{d\tau} = - \frac{n}{\sqrt{E}}, \qquad \frac{dn}{d\tau} = - m\sqrt{E},$$

$$m = m_0 \cosh \tau - (n_0/\sqrt{E}) \sinh \tau, \qquad (5)$$

$$n = n_0 \cosh \tau - (m_0 \sqrt{E}) \sinh \tau$$

An interesting property of these hyperbolic solutions is the acceleration of the action toward the end. The last half of the weaker force is annihilated in a shorter time than is the first half. This is, of course, due to the fact that the remaining members of the stronger force are able to concentrate their fire entirely upon the remnant of the weaker force, thus accelerating the destruction. This acceleration is often apparent in actual warfare. One might mention the German collapse in Tunisia, and the Allied-versus-German air struggle in 1943–44.

The next two sections present a detailed discussion of Lanchester's equations and related analyses, which are in the nature of footnotes, indicating possible directions for further investigation, rather than results which have been useful up to the present. They may be by-passed without loss of background for later material.

4 3 PROBABILITY ANALYSIS OF LANCHESTER'S EQUATIONS

Lanchester's equations deal with the average, or expected, values of the number of combatants on each side. Actually probability enters, and the results of Lanchester's equations are simply the most probable results. For the first stages of the battle there is, of course, a certain finite probability of other numbers of combatants surviving, and in the later stages of the battle the solutions to Lanchester's equations may deviate widely from the possible results. This is due to the fact that after a certain length of time there is a certain probability that all of one side will have been eliminated, and the battle will actually have been terminated before the average solution of Lanchester's equations predicts that it would end.

In other words, Lanchester's equations predict that when one side has been completely eliminated, a definite number of the other side always remain. In

the actual case, on the other hand, there is a certain small but nonzero chance that all of one side will be eliminated without the loss of *any* combatants on the other side, and so on, for all possible proportions of losses. The probabilities of the various outcomes can be computed if we assume that the results of each engagement are subject to the laws of probability.

4 3 1 The Linear Law

For instance, for the linear equations, we can say that at each combat, on the average, $(E/E + 1)$ Red units are lost, and, on the average, $(1/E + 1)$ Blue units are lost. Then, after T combats (if T is smaller than n_0 or m_0), the multinomial distribution shows that the probability that there will be α Red units lost and $\beta \, (= T - \alpha)$ Blue units lost is

$$P(\alpha, \beta) = \frac{T!}{\alpha! \, \beta!} \frac{E^\alpha}{(1 + E)^T}, \, T = \alpha + \beta \leqq m_0, n_0, \quad (6)$$

so that a wide range of outcomes are possible, some of them differing widely from the solutions of equations (1). However, for a given time T (less than m_0 or n_0) the *average number* of Red and Blue units lost is just that given in equations (1). Therefore, for the first part of the engagement, the solution to Lanchester's equation is valid, on the average.

When the index T gets large enough, however, there is a chance that all of one force is annihilated. For instance, when $T = n_0$, there is a certain probability $P(0, n_0) = (1 + E)^{-n_0}$ that *all* of the Blue units will have been annihilated and none of the Red units. If this should have occurred, the battle would end then and there. There is also a possibility that the battle will end with one Red unit lost and all of the Blue units lost. The probability of this occurring is $P(1, n_0)$.

It is not difficult to see that the probabilities $P(\alpha, n_0)$ and $P(m_0, \beta)$ are not obtained from the formula (6). Further detailed analysis shows that the correct formulas for these special cases are.

$$P(\alpha, n_0) = \frac{(\alpha + n_0 - 1)!}{\alpha! \, (n_0 - 1)!} \frac{E^\alpha}{(1 + E)^{\alpha + n_0}},$$

$$P(m_0, \beta) = \frac{(\beta + m_0 - 1)!}{\beta! \, (m_0 - 1)!} \frac{E^{m_0}}{(1 + E)^{\beta + m_0}}, \quad (7)$$

$$P(m_0, n_0) = 0$$

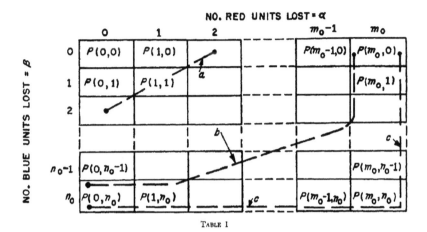

TABLE 1

All these probabilities can be expressed in a tabular form as shown in Table 1 The heavy dashed lines a, b, and c correspond to the situation at different "times" T For instance, for the line a, $T = 2$; for the line b, $T = n_0 + 1$ In case b, the cells crossed by the horizontal and vertical portions of the dashed line represent finished battles, those crossed by the diagonal portion of the line represent battles not yet finished Line c represents $T > m_0 + n_0$ after all possible battles have finished The sum of all the P's along any one of the dashed lines equals unity (as, of course, they must)

It will be apparent that for times corresponding to the lines b or c, the average number of combatants lost will not correspond to equations (1) for the Lanchester law In particular, a study of the case represented by line c shows that when the battle is continued to its finish, the result will be *either* a number of Blue units left *or* a number of Red units left For any particular values of m_0 or n_0 or E, the average number of survivors can be computed for these alternative possibilities

As an example, a table of the form shown in Table 1 can be computed for the case where there are initially five Red units and three Blue units, and where the exchange rate is unity From this tabular form one can compute the average number of combatants surviving on each side after T combats The results of these calculations are tabulated under "Prob" in the following

TABLE 2
$m_0 = 5$, $n_0 = 3$, $E = 1$

T	0	1	2	3	4	5	6	7+
Avg m, Prob	5 0	4 5	4 0	3 5	3 06	2 72	2 48	2 367
Avg m, Lan	5 0	4 5	4 0	3 5	3 0	2 5	2 0	2 0
Avg n, Prob	3 0	2 5	2 0	1 5	1 06	0 72	0 48	0 367
Avg n, Lan	3 0	2 5	2 0	1 5	1 0	0 5	0	0

Prob that the Red forces are annihilated $= (29/128) = 0$ 2266
If the Blues win, the expected no of Blue survivors $= 1$ 621
Prob that the Blue forces are annihilated $= (99/128) = 0$ 7734
If the Reds win, the expected no of Red survivors $= 3$ 061

The results of the probability calculation are compared with the solutions of Lanchester's equations (labeled "Lan ") We see that for this case there is approximately one chance in four that the battle will end with all the Red forces annihilated, and on the average, approximately 1 6 Blue units left. In the other three cases out of four (approximately) the Blue forces will be annihilated and an average of three Red units will be left The limitations of Lanchester's equations in the latter part of the battle are obvious Of course, it should be pointed out that for larger numbers the per cent deviations from Lanchester's laws would be smaller

4 3 2 The Square Law

In order to make a probability analysis of the Lanchester square law, we shall have to define an engagement as being an exchange of salvos, or a single attack of short enough duration so that the losses on each side cause no appreciable diminution in fire power during the engagement Suppose that at the beginning of the engagement there are m_0 Red units and n_0 Blue units Suppose also that during the engagement each Red unit shoots a certain fraction of the Blue units and vice versa To correspond with the notation of equation (5), we should have the fraction of the Blue units shot by a Red unit, on the average, as $(\tau \sqrt{E}/n)$, and the fraction of the Red units shot by the Blue unit, on the average, as $(\tau/m\sqrt{E})$, where τ is the duration of the engagement in the new units of time, defined by equation (4)

There will be a certain number of units which are hit more than once We are, however, interested in those units on each side which are *not* hit after the engagement The probability that a given Red unit is not hit is given by the expression $[1-(\tau/m\sqrt{E})]^n$ Again using the multinomial distribution, we find that the probability that α Red units are hit out of the total of m Red units, and the probability that a number β of the Blue units are hit during the engagement, is given by equation (8)

$$P_r(\alpha) = \frac{m!}{\alpha!(m-\alpha)!}\left(1 - \frac{\tau}{m\sqrt{E}}\right)^{n(m-\alpha)}\left[1 - \left(1 - \frac{\tau}{m\sqrt{E}}\right)^n\right]^\alpha,$$

$$P_b(\beta) = \frac{n!}{\beta!(n-\beta)!}\left(1 - \frac{\tau\sqrt{E}}{n}\right)^{m(n-\beta)}\left[1 - \left(1 - \frac{\tau\sqrt{E}}{n}\right)^m\right]^\beta. \quad (8)$$

From these expressions one can find the average number of Red and Blue units hit during the engagement These expressions are

$$\alpha_{avg} = m\left[1 - \left(1 - \frac{\tau}{m\sqrt{E}}\right)^n\right],$$

$$\beta_{avg} = n\left[1 - \left(1 - \frac{\tau\sqrt{E}}{n}\right)^m\right] \quad (9)$$

This expression does not correspond to the solution of Lanchester's equations except in the limit of small values of τ

If τ is not particularly small, but if the number of combatants on both sides is quite large, the equation may be reduced to somewhat more simple form

$$\alpha_{avg} = m[1 - e^{-(n\tau/m\sqrt{E})}],$$

$$\beta_{avg} = n[1 - e^{-(m\tau\sqrt{E}/n)}], \quad (10)$$

which still do not correspond with the solution of Lanchester's equations If, however, the quantities in the exponential are quite small, as they would be if the engagement is considered to last a very short duration $d\tau$, then the number of Red units lost (which equals $-dm$) is equal to $-(n/\sqrt{E})d\tau$, which checks completely with equation (5)

By going back to equation (8), however, we can extend the differential technique to the probabilities themselves For instance, if we define $P(m, n, t)$ as the chance that at the time t there are m Red units and n Blue units still unhit, then a detailed study of the elementary engagement lasting a time dt shows that the probability functions satisfy the following recursion relations

$$\frac{d}{dt}P(m, n, t) = (m\sqrt{E})[P(m, n+1, t) - P(m, n, t)]$$
$$+ \left(\frac{n}{\sqrt{E}}\right)[P(m+1, n, t) - P(m, n, t)],$$

$$\frac{d}{dt}P(m, 0, t) = (m\sqrt{E})P(m, 1, t), \quad (11)$$

$$\frac{d}{dt}P(0, n, t) = \left(\frac{n}{\sqrt{E}}\right)P(1, n, t)$$

These equations can be solved subject to the initial condition that $P(m_0, n_0, t)$ equals unity and all other P's equal zero at $t = 0$. The calculations are tedious for large numbers, but are straightforward

4.3 3   An Example

Detailed study of the solutions of equation (11) shows that the average values of m and n, as functions of time, are fairly accurately equal to those predicted by the solution of Lanchester's equations (5) for the early stages of the battle During the later stages, however, deviations occur from the Lanchester solution of a nature analogous to those displayed in

of the nonzero probabilities give the chances of the various outcomes In the example given in Table 3, the probabilities of the eventual results are expressed in Table 4 Therefore in the long run the chances are about 9 to 1 that the Reds will win. If they do win, they will have approximately four combatants surviving The Blues will have one chance in nine of winning, and, if they win, they will have approximately two combatants surviving

TABLE 3

$m_0 = 5$, $n_0 = 3$, $E = 1$, expressions for $P(m, n, t)$

No Blue units remaining $= n$

		3	2	1
No Red units remaining $= m$	5	e^{-8t}	$5e^{-7t}(1-e^{-t})$	$\dfrac{25}{2}e^{-6t}(1-e^{-t})^2$
	4	$3e^{-7t}(1-e^{-t})$	$11e^{-6t}(1-e^{-t})^2$	$\dfrac{113}{6}e^{-5t}(1-e^{-t})^3$
	3	$\dfrac{9}{2}e^{-6t}(1-e^{-t})^2$	$\dfrac{71}{6}e^{-5t}(1-e^{-t})^3$	$\dfrac{163}{12}e^{-4t}(1-e^{-t})^4$
	2	$\dfrac{9}{2}e^{-5t}(1-e^{-t})^3$	$\dfrac{49}{6}e^{-4t}(1-e^{-t})^4$	$\dfrac{159}{60}e^{-3t}(1-e^{-t})^5$
	1	$\dfrac{27}{8}e^{-4t}(1-e^{-t})^4$	$\dfrac{473}{120}e^{-3t}(1-e^{-t})^5$	$\dfrac{1191}{720}e^{-2t}(1-e^{-t})^6$

Table 2 An example will perhaps illustrate the nature of the phenomenon We choose the same initial number of combatants as that chosen for Table 2, in order to compare the probability calculations for the linear and the square law cases Table 3 gives values of the probability functions except for $m = 0$, or $n = 0$

The functions $P(m, 0, t)$ and $P(0, n, t)$ can be computed from the last two of equations (11) by simple integration

Table 3 differs from Table 1 in that the time enters into each expression in the present case; whereas the time is indicated by the dashed line in the former case Here the sum of all the P's is equal to unity at all times, whereas in the earlier case the sum of the quantities along each dashed line is equal to unity In the present case the eventual result is obtained by letting t go to infinity When this is done, only the lowest row (for $m = 0$) and the right-hand column (for $n = 0$) will differ from zero, indicating that the battle has come to an end with some of one side or some of the other side surviving The limiting values

The difference between these results and those given in Table 3 for the linear law are quite interesting For the linear case the chance of the Blues surviving was one in four, approximately, whereas for

TABLE 4

$m_0 = 5$, $n_0 = 3$, $E = 1$, limiting values of $P(m, 0, t)$ and $P(0, n, t)$

$m = 5$, $P(m, 0, \infty) =$	0 3721	$n = 3$, $P(0, n, \infty) =$	0 0362
4	0 2690		
3	0 1456	2	0 0469
2	0 0712		
1	0 0295	1	0 0295

Prob Reds win $= 0.8874$ with 3 994 survivors expected if Reds win

Prob Blues win $= 0.1126$ with 2 059 survivors expected if Blues win

the square law the chance of survival is one in nine, approximately This corresponds to the increased importance of outnumbering the opponent in the square law case The other striking difference is in the number of survivors In the linear case, if Red wins the expected number of surviving victors is three, whereas in the square case four are expected to remain The expected numbers, assuming a Blue victory, are 1 6 and 2, respectively. In general, therefore, one can expect a larger number of surviving victors for the square law case, a result which again illustrates the advantage in numbers which the square law case represents Even if the weaker side is lucky, and happens to win (it can happen in the case in question once in nine tries), this luck will most likely turn up early in the battle by a chance reversal of the numerical advantage Once this reversal *does* occur, the Blues can overwhelm the remaining Reds without much additional loss, and end up by having wiped out the Reds with an average loss to the Blues of only one unit

We have shown by these two examples that any differential equations representing war conditions (such as Lanchester's equations) have their limitations due to the fact that chance enters into the actual battle, and the exact outcome can never be predicted accurately As long as the equations are not pressed too hard (such as by going to the limit of annihilation of one force), however, the solutions of the equations will correspond quite closely to the "expected value" obtained from the probability analysis One must expect the actual results to deviate from the expected values, with the average deviation increasing as the solutions tend toward the ultimate annihilation of one force

4.4 THE GENERALIZED LANCHESTER EQUATIONS

The previous sections have dealt with the application of Lanchester's equations to more or less continuous engagements—to battles rather than wars Sometimes it is of interest to utilize the same sort of analysis in discussing the overall trend of a war, though any attempt to reduce the course of a war to the scope of a set of differential equations is such a sweeping simplification that we should not expect the results often to correspond closely to reality A discussion of the problems involved and the nature of the resulting solutions is, however, of considerable interest, if only as a basis of comparison with reality

In the first place, there is the question of the units of measure of the quantities m and n, the *fighting strengths* of the opposed forces Each side has, at any moment, a certain number of trained men, of battle-ships, planes, tanks, etc , which can be thrown into battle in a fairly short time, as fast as transport can get them to the scene of action The total strength of this force is determined by the effectiveness of each component part (as discussed in Section 3 3). At any stage of war we can say, very approximately, that a battleship is as valuable as so many armies, that a submarine is as valuable as so many squadrons of planes, etc To this crude approximation, each unit can be measured in terms of some arbitrary unit—so many equivalent army divisions, for instance Naturally, differences between submarines and tanks are qualitative as well as quantitative, and neglecting the qualitative side is part of the oversimplification of the present analysis When the forces involved are large, however, the quantitative aspect begins to overshadow the qualitative, and we can begin to think of a number which is the measure of the total fighting strength of a nation at some instant

This strength is continually changing with time In the first place, both sides are busy producing more strength training men, building planes, etc. The *rate of production* (in the same units as m or n are measured) for the Red side is P, and that for the Blue side is Q These will vary with time, but for our first analysis we will assume they are constant

4.4.1 Loss Rates

In addition, the strengths will be decreasing due to the fighting This rate of destruction must depend on the strengths of the two sides, and it is not certain what form of function most nearly represents the behavior of actual wars Certainly a Lanchester term of the form $(-an)$ for the rate of change of m is a reasonable one, since the rate of loss of Red units must increase as the Blue strength increases But there is also a term proportional to m needed in the rate of loss of m, to represent operational attrition The resulting expression for the Red operational loss rate, $(-an-cm)$, is the simplest expression which can represent the overall behavior of war When the Red strength is considerably larger than the Blue strength, then the Red side will determine the rate of fighting, and will work out replacement schedules for forces in action, so that it is not unreasonable to expect that the percentage losses for the Reds will be constant (i e , the Red loss rate will be proportional to m) and that the Blue loss rate will also be proportional to m. If the opposed strengths are about equal, we would expect that the loss rates of both sides would be proportional to the opposed strengths Consequently, only linear terms in m and n should be included These requirements are all met by the expression $(-an - cm)$.

The generalized Lanchester equations are therefore

$$\frac{dm}{dt} = P - an - cm,$$

$$\frac{dn}{dt} = Q - bm - dn,$$ (12)

where, in general, a and b are larger than c or d At first, we will consider the production rates, P and Q, to be constant Differential equations[b] of this sort have been discussed in relation to the struggle between animal species[11 12] and in chemical kinetics The unit of time can be the year The quantity P will then be the number of equivalent armies (or the equivalent number of battleships) which the Red nation can train and equip in a year, and so on

The solutions for equations (12) are

$$m = A + Ee^{(\mu-\lambda)t} + \frac{\mu+\kappa}{b} Fe^{-(\mu+\lambda)t};$$

$$n = B - \frac{\mu+\kappa}{a} Ee^{(\mu-\lambda)t} + Fe^{-(\mu+\lambda)t},$$

$$\lambda = \tfrac{1}{2}(c+d), \kappa = \tfrac{1}{2}(c-d), \mu = \sqrt{\kappa^2 + ab},$$

$$A = \frac{Qa - Pd}{ab - cd}, \quad B = \frac{Pb - Qc}{ab - cd}, \quad ab - cd = \mu^2 - \lambda^2,$$

$$E = \frac{ab}{2\mu(\mu+\kappa)} \left\{ \left[m_0 + \frac{d+\mu+\kappa}{ab-cd} P \right] \right. $$ (13)
$$\left. - \frac{\mu+\kappa}{b} \left[n_0 + \frac{c+\mu-\kappa}{ab-cd} Q \right] \right\},$$

$$F = \frac{ab}{2\mu(\mu+\kappa)} \left\{ \frac{\mu+\kappa}{a} \left[m_0 + \frac{d-\mu+\kappa}{ab-cd} P \right] \right.$$
$$\left. + \left[n_0 + \frac{c-\mu-\kappa}{ab-cd} Q \right] \right\}$$

Since ab is larger than cd, in general, we have μ greater than λ Therefore, the exponential in the second term of the equations for m and n continually

increases, whereas the exponential in the third term continually diminishes Consequently, if the constant E, as determined by the initial conditions, turns out to be positive, the Blue forces (n) are eventually annihilated, and, if E is negative, the Red forces (m) eventually go to zero

When the opposed units are equally effective, $a = b$ and $c = d$ In this case the equations take on a simpler form

$$a = b = \mu, \quad c = d = \lambda, \quad \kappa = 0,$$

$$m = A + Ee^{(a-c)t} + Fe^{-(a+c)t},$$

$$n = B - Ee^{(a-c)t} + Fe^{-(a+c)t},$$

$$A = \frac{Qa - Pc}{a^2 - c^2}, \quad B = \frac{Pa - Qc}{a^2 - c^2},$$ (14)

$$E = \frac{1}{2}\left[\left(m_0 + \frac{P}{a-c} \right) - \left(n_0 + \frac{Q}{a-c} \right) \right],$$

$$F = \frac{1}{2}\left[\left(m_0 - \frac{P}{a+c} \right) + \left(n_0 - \frac{Q}{a+c} \right) \right]$$

Here again the sign of the constant E, fixed by the initial conditions, determines which of the forces goes to zero Examining this factor, we see that the *total strength* of one side is equal to its initial fighting strength, plus the productive rate divided by the quantity $(a - c)$ The sign of E depends on which of these strengths is the largest

4 4 2   Typical Solutions

As an example of the behavior of the solutions of Lanchester's generalized equations, Figure 1 shows the results for eight different cases of initial strength The attrition rates have been chosen as follows $a = 2, c = 1$ The top set of four curves corresponds to the case when the initial fighting strengths of the opposed forces are equal, the lower four curves correspond to the case where the initial fighting strength of the Red forces is twice that of the Blue forces The first two curves on the top row present cases where initial forces and productive strengths are equally matched, so that the battle ends in a draw In the other cases, either the initial forces, the productive strengths, or both differ, so that one side or the other is eventually wiped out

The last curve on the bottom row is of particular interest. It represents a case where the eventual

---

[b] The biological equations contain a nonlinear term, proportional to the product (nm), which does not seem to be justified in the case considered in this volume

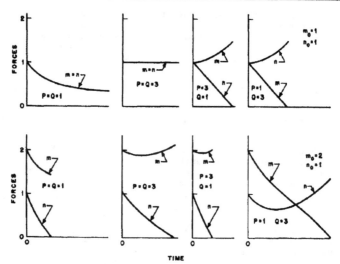

FIGURE 1   Solutions of the generalized Lanchester equations for $a = b = 2$, $c = d = 1$, for different productive capacities P and Q and different initial forces m_0 and n_0. $(dm/dt) = P - an - cm$, $(dn/dt) = Q - bm - dn$

winner started out with a two to one handicap in initial fighting strength This initial disadvantage was more than overcome by a three to one production advantage For the first third of the conflict, the Blue forces were still further depleted, and for more than half of the duration of the conflict the Blue forces were outnumbered by the Red forces Once the initial handicap had been overcome by the larger production, however, the advantage rapidly became decisive and the Red forces were wiped out in short order The increasing rapidity of the final debacle is a characteristic of Lanchester's equations and is met with, to a certain extent, in actual warfare

4.4 3   Destruction of Production

The generalized Lanchester's equations, discussed above, are capable of somewhat more sophisticated interpretation than has been given them in the first part of this section We there assumed that each combatant maintained his productive capacity constant This never has been exactly true, and since the advent of the strategic airforce it is far from being true. The productive capacity of a nation depends on the strength of the enemy's strategic forces, and also on the strength of its own defenses. Production diminishes as the enemy's strategic forces increase, and increases as its own defensive forces increase Each side must apportion its forces between defense and strategic offense, so as simultaneously to diminish the enemy's productive capacity and to wipe out the enemy's defensive forces in the most expeditious manner

It will be of interest to work out a crude approximation to this state of affairs We assume that both sides divide their total forces into two parts:

$$m = m_t + m_s, \qquad n = n_t + n_s ,$$
$$m_t, n_t \text{ tactical forces}, m_s, n_s, \text{ strategic forces}$$

The strategic forces are directed only against the enemy's productive capacity, whereas the tactical forces are directed against the enemy's strategic and tactical forces The tactical forces are the "fighting forces" and their attrition rates, therefore, correspond to the generalized Lanchester's equation discussed above (at least to the rough degree of approximation which concerns us here)

The effect of the strategic forces is shown in a modification of the enemy's productive rate It takes a certain amount of strategic force to keep a certain amount of the enemy's factories out of commission

Therefore, one might expect, to the first approximation, that the diminution in the enemy's production is proportional to the strength of one's strategic force. The effectiveness of this force, however, depends on the strength of the enemy's tactical force, which in part defends his productive capacity. To a very crude approximation, one might expect that this factor of effectiveness, for diminution of the enemy's productive capacity, would be proportional to the ratio between the strategic force and the opposing tactical force. In other words, the simplest possible formula representing the expected behavior is as follows

$$\text{Red production} = P\left(1 - \beta\,\frac{n_s}{m_t}\,n_s\right);$$

$$\text{Blue production} = Q\left(1 - \beta\,\frac{m_t}{n_t}\,m_s\right)$$

The formulas lead to absurdities if the ratio between strategic and tactical forces become too large. Nevertheless, it is not difficult to see that, within reasonable limits, these formulas are crude approximations to the behavior we have been discussing. We have made a further simplifying assumption in making the coefficients in the parentheses both equal to β. Our only excuse for thus limiting ourselves to cases where the opposing strategic forces are equally effective is that this assumption is not unreasonable, and any further complications introduced now will render the final solution too complicated for easy understanding. The more complicated case can be worked out by the reader, if this is desirable.

Our equations for the increase and decrease of the opposing forces, therefore, turn out to be

$$\frac{dm}{dt} = P - P\beta\frac{n_s^2}{m_t} - \alpha(n_t + m_t)\ ;$$

$$\frac{dn}{dt} = Q - Q\beta\frac{m_s^2}{n_t} - \alpha(m_t + n_t) \tag{15}$$

Here we have again simplified matters by letting the coefficients of the Lanchester terms all be equal to the same quantity, α. Our justification is again that this simplification does not invalidate the general behavior of the solutions, and it simplifies the formulas considerably. Once the behavior of the simplified equation is discussed, further complications can be added as desired.

4.4.4   Tactical and Strategic Forces

These equations cannot be solved immediately because we have not as yet laid down any rules as to the relative strengths of tactical and strategic forces. The commanding generals of the two sides must decide these distributions. Their decisions, of course, will be based on a great many things: politics, details of production, efficiency of intelligence service, etc. Presumably each side should distribute its forces between the tactical and strategic arms, in such a way as to make one's own loss rate as small as possible, and one's enemy's loss rate as large as possible. In terms of the crude model we are here considering, the commanding general of the Red side should strive to make the expressions

$$\frac{dm}{dt} - \frac{dn}{dt} = P - Q - \beta\left[P\frac{(n - n_t)^2}{m_t} - Q\frac{(m - m_t)^2}{n_t}\right]$$

$$= L(m_t, n_t)$$

as large as possible, and the commanding general of the Blue side should strive to make this same quantity as small as possible. At each instant, the values of (m, n) are fixed by the previous history of the situation. The Red general, at each instant must adjust m_t so that the quantity L is as large as possible.

This is an example of the "minimax principle" which is discussed in more detail in Chapter 5. In actual practice, each general must make his decision on inadequate knowledge of what the other general has decided. The "safest" decision for each general is to assume that the other general has made the best possible choice (for his side). This means that the Red general must assume that the Blue general is trying to *minimize* L, and the Blue general must assume that the Red general is trying to *maximize* L. These simultaneous adjustments can be made by requiring

$$\frac{\partial L}{\partial m_t} = 0\ ,\quad \frac{\partial^2 L}{\partial m_t^2} < 0\ ;\quad \frac{\partial L}{\partial n_t} = 0\ ;\quad \frac{\partial^2 L}{\partial n_t^2} > 0\ , \tag{16}$$

which is the minimax principle in one of its mathematical forms. If the Red general makes his choice according to these equations, then his situation will be as good as possible *if the Blue general makes the corresponding choice* for n_t. If the Blue general does *not* make this choice for the relative distribution of strength between tactical and strategic forces, then the Red general *can always improve his situation* by appropriate modification of his balance between tactical and strategic forces Consequently, the distribution above forms the safest solution of the problem with the forces at hand, and will be called the "basic solution " It is the best solution possible when the two opponents have equal intelligence, if one side departs from this solution, the other side can obtain still better results

4 4 5   The Minimax Principle

Applying the minimax principle to the approximate expression for L, we find that

$$P \quad n_i(n - n_i)^2 = 2Q \quad m_i^2(m - m_i) ,$$

$$2P \, n_i^2(n - n_i) = Q \, m_i(m - m_i)^2 ,$$

$$m_i = \frac{\rho}{2} \, (n - n_i) , \quad n_i = \frac{1}{2\rho} \, (m - m_i) ,$$

$$\tag{17}$$

where $\rho^3 = (P/Q)$ Therefore

$$m_i = \left(\frac{2}{3}\rho n - \frac{1}{3}m\right) , \quad n_i = \left(\frac{2}{3}\frac{1}{\rho}m - \frac{1}{3}n\right) ,$$

$$m_s = \frac{2}{3}(2m - \rho n) = 2\rho n_i, n_s = \frac{2}{3}\left(2n - \frac{m}{\rho}\right) = \left(\frac{2m_i}{\rho}\right),$$

is the *basic solution*, as long as $m < 2\rho n$ and $n < 2m/\rho$

These solutions are very interesting They show that, within certain limits, the size of the tactical force of one side should increase if the enemy's total forces increase (i e , the fraction of Red forces which should be assigned to the tactical arm depends linearly on the ratio between the Red and the Blue total forces) It also depends on the ratio between the initial productive forces of the two sides, through the quantity ρ, although the dependence on this ratio is only to the one-third power We notice that these formulas would require the value of m_i to be sometimes negative, when the ratios of the two forces become considerably unbalanced This is of course due to the crudity of our initial equations, and the solutions will have to be watched to prevent such absurdities from arising Aside from these crudities, the solution does correspond to what we might expect If the enemy strength increases, we put more of our forces in the tactical arm If our production is large, we need a somewhat greater defensive strength

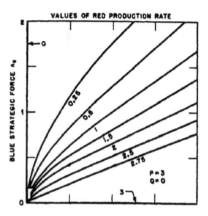

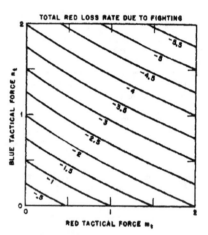

FIGURE 2   Contour plots of assumed production rates and total losses as function of own tactical force and enemy tactical and strategic force

(tactical force) On the other hand, if our own fighting forces are larger than the enemy's, we can afford to put more of our strength in the strategic arm, and so on

If we now assume that the generals on both sides continually adjust their forces, so as to correspond to the "basic solution," then it turns out that equations (17) inserted in equations (15) correspond

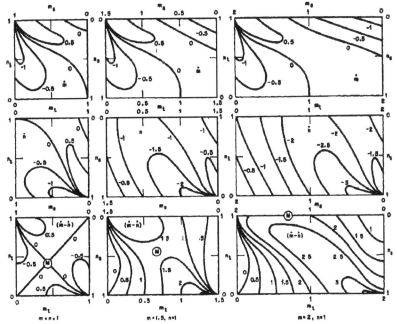

FIGURE 3   Contour plots of Red and Blue total loss rate, and of differential loss rate, for different values of total forces, for production and losses as given in Figure 2 Points marked M on the differential loss rate plots are the minimax points, corresponding to safe operation

to the generalized Lanchester's equations (12), with the following constants

$$a = \frac{\alpha}{3}\left[\frac{8P\beta}{\rho\alpha} + 2\rho - 1\right], \quad b = \frac{\alpha}{3}\left[\frac{8Q\rho\beta}{\alpha} + \frac{2}{\rho} - 1\right],$$

$$c = b - 4Q\rho\beta, \quad d = a - 4\left(\frac{P\beta}{\rho}\right), \quad \rho = \left(\frac{P}{Q}\right)^{1/3} \tag{18}$$

A graphical presentation of these arguments will perhaps make this more clear In so doing, we can use somewhat less crude expressions for production rate and for loss rate due to fighting Figure 2 shows possible contour plots for these quantities as functions of the strategic and tactical forces The upper contour is for the Red production rate If the Blue strategic force n_t is small and the Red tactical force m_t is large, the Red production rate has its full value If the relative strengths are reversed, the production rate falls nearly to zero The lower contour is the total

Red loss rate due to fighting This loss rate is zero if both tactical forces are zero, and it increases linearly with increase in either force, according to the general Lanchester term The Red loss rate depends more strongly on the size of the Blue tactical force, n_t than on m_t, as mentioned earlier

These curves can be combined in various ways to obtain the Red or Blue net gain as a function of (m_t, n_t) for various values of m and n This has been done for several different relative total strengths in Figure 3 The upper three sets of contours display values of the net rate of increase for Red forces, and the middle row shows values of the corresponding increase for the Blue forces Negative values mean net loss rate, and positive values mean net gain per unit of time The bottom row of contours shows values of the function L, the difference between Red and Blue gain According to equation (16) a minimax point is to be found on these surfaces

The minimax points are marked on the contours

by M Examining the center plot of the bottom row, for $m = 1\,5$, $n = 1\,0$, we see that the minimax point corresponds approximately to $m_t = 0\,65$ and $n_t = 0.55$ If the Red general changes his relative distribution of tactical and strategic forces, making n_t equal to $1\,0$, for instance, then the Blue general, by correspondingly increasing the Blue tactical forces, can reduce the Blue net loss and increase the Red net loss Consequently, it is safest for the Red general to distribute his forces corresponding to the minimax point, at least until he can determine whether the Blue general is doing likewise If the Blue general has not done so, then the Red general can adjust m_t to improve the situation, as can be seen from the contour

The differential equations corresponding to these loss rates can be solved numerically A contour plot for L has to be drawn for each instant of the war, the proper distribution of tactical and strategic forces can then be determined, and the corresponding loss rates for the two sides can be computed This is then inserted back into the equations for the rate of change of (m, n) to obtain a final solution

4 5   REACTION RATE PROBLEMS

Many problems concerned with the increase and attrition of forces can be analyzed by equations closely related to those used in chemistry to study reaction rates An example of this can be taken from a partial analysis of the antisubmarine war in the Atlantic The study concerns itself with the general problem of air offensive action against the German submarine It assumes that a certain amount of aircraft and number of crews are available for action against the submarine, over and above the number of aircraft and crews needed for protection of convoys It discusses the question as to how this offensive action should be distributed in order most effectively to reduce the total number of submarines in the Atlantic at any time

Three distinct types of offensive action against enemy submarines can be taken

1 Submarines can be hunted out in the Atlantic, and can be sunk or damaged there

2 The submarine repair bases along the coast of France can be bombed, so that fewer submarines per month can be reserviced and put to sea again.

3 The factories in Germany which produce submarines can be bombed, so as to reduce the production rate

Each of these offensive actions has its effect in re-

ducing the number of submarines in the Atlantic, either immediately or at some future date. An important strategic question, which must be decided from time to time, is how the available offensive air strength is to be distributed among these three activities in order to produce the greatest reduction in submarines in the Atlantic at the time when it is most needed Before deciding on the relative apportionment of strength, a great number of different factors must be taken into consideration Along with other factors, it is possible that a purely theoretical study of the effects on the submarine distribution of changes in production, sinking, or repair may be worth consideration It is certain that the analysis summarized in the following pages is entirely too simplified to represent the actual case in all its complications Nevertheless, it is felt that the results of this simple theoretical analysis should prove suggestive as to actual possibilities

4 5 1   Circulation of U-Boats

In order to study theoretically the relative effect of damaging the factories or the repair bases, or in attacking the submarine directly in the Atlantic, we must study the activities of the average submarine Submarines are produced at an average rate P per month, and are being sunk at an average rate S per month Therefore, the net increase in their number per month is $P - S$ which is called I We know that the average length of time the submarine stayed on patrol on the Atlantic was about two months. After this time the submarine went back to one of the bases along the French coast for repair, refueling, and resting the crew Therefore, on the average, about half the number of submarines in the Atlantic returned to their base each month

The length of time the submarine remained at the repair base depended on the amount of repair work which had to be carried out, and on the degree of efficiency of the base itself The average amount of repair work required depended on the average number of U-boats which were damaged each month, and the efficiency of the base depended on the amount of damage the base had received that month The details of this interrelation will be discussed more fully later on At this point it is only necessary to notice that the repair bases had a maximum capacity for refitting submarines, which capacity could be diminished either by bombing the bases or by increasing the average amount of damage to a submarine on patrol Thus the return flow of submarines from the repair bases to the Atlantic constituted a bottleneck, whose size had an important effect on the total number of submarines in the Atlantic at any one time

In fact, it is possible to see that a marked reduction in the flow rate L of submarines from bases to Atlantic would produce an effect on the number of submarines in the Atlantic in a relatively short time This is due to the fact that the U-boats remained in the Atlantic no longer than about two months, so that after a period of two months all the submarines which were originally in the Atlantic had been replaced by submarines which came from the repair bases within the two months time

In order to obtain results of a more quantitative nature, we must make certain reasonable assumptions about the interrelationships between the various rates and numbers

We define the following quantities

A = average number of U/B in Atlantic,

B = average number of U/B in bases,

P = production of U/B per month, constant,

S = number of U/B sunk per month,

$P-S = I$ = net increase in number of U/B per month,

t = time in months,

L = number U/B leaving bases per month, $L = M(1 - e^{-CB/M})$,

M = maximum rate of repairing U/B and returning them to Atlantic,

CB = rate of repairing U/B in very lightly filled base, C is usually 1,

$1/K$ = mean length of stay of U/B in Atlantic $\simeq 2$ months

The equation for L represents our assumption concerning the capabilities of the repair bases We assume that the average rate of sending submarines back from the bases to the Atlantic depends on the number in the bases at any one time, in the manner given by the equation This indicates that if there are a small number of submarines in the bases then the repair work can proceed efficiently enough so that the submarines can be sent out again about a month after they have come in from their previous cruise The equation shows this, for small values of B, the rate of leaving, L, is approximately equal to the number, B, in the bases When there are a large number of submarines present in the bases, however, the state of repair of the bases and the average damage to the submarines begins to make itself felt We

assume that there is a fixed maximum rate of repairing submarines at any given time, which number is indicated by M on the plot It is assumed that, at the time considered, no more than this number, M, can be put into operation each month, no matter how many submarines are present in the bases awaiting repair The curve for L therefore never rises higher than the value M

For the purposes of this study, it is the value of M which indicates the state of efficiency of the base Any increase in damage to the bases by bombing them, or any increase in average damage suffered by submarines in the Atlantic, will decrease the value of M temporarily The question of the relative effect of damaging the factories and damaging the bases, therefore, resolves itself to the question of the relative effect of a change in $I = P - S$ and a change in M

4 5 2 Equations of Flow

With these assumptions, the equations for the flow of submarines can be set up The fundamental equations for the change of A and B can be written in dimensionless form, if the variables are changed in the following manner

$$x = \frac{CA}{M}, \quad y = \frac{CB}{M}, \quad p = \frac{I}{M}, \quad k = \frac{K}{C}; \quad u = Ct$$

Then the operations become

$$\frac{dx}{du} = p - kx + (1 - e^{-y}), \quad \frac{dy}{du} = kx - (1 - e^{-y}) \quad (19)$$

Solutions of these equations, for the range $0 < u < 10$, and for the values $p = 0, \frac{1}{4}, \frac{1}{2}, 1, k = 0, \frac{1}{2}, 1$, were run off on the Differential Analyzer at MIT for the initial conditions $x_0 = 0, 1, 2, y_0 = 0, 1, 2$ Graphs have been obtained from these solutions

For small values of u, the following series expansions hold

$$x = x_0 + (p - kx_0 + 1 - e^{y_0})u + \cdot \quad \cdot$$

$$y = y_0 + (kx_0 - 1 + e^{y_0})u +$$

For large values of y (except for the cases $k = 0$ or $p = 0$)

$$x \to \frac{(p - 1)}{k}, \quad y \to x_0 + y_0 - \left[\frac{(p - 1)}{k}\right] + pu.$$

4.5.3   **Typical Solutions**

A few typical solutions are given in Figure 4 Curves are given for the average number of U-boats in port and in the North Atlantic, for different times after the start and for different net production of U-boats per month It will be noticed that at first

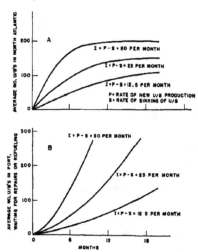

FIGURE 4 Typical solutions for the submarine "turn-around" problem Plots of submarines in port and on patrol as functions of time, for different values of net increase of submarines I Assuming average length of cruise 2 months, average stay in uncrowded port 1 month, maximum rate of servicing U/B in port = M = maximum rate of sending U/B out on cruise to be 50 per month

the number of U-boats in the bases is less than the number of U-boats in the North Atlantic However, after six months (for the value of M chosen in the example) the effect of the bottleneck in the repair bases begins to make itself felt The increase in the number of U-boats in the North Atlantic is not as great as at first, and the excess U-boats pile up in the bases, since they can not get repaired fast enough

However, such solutions, starting with the beginning, are not of the greatest amount of interest for our purposes here. We are more interested in finding out what happens to the curve when we suddenly change M, the maximum rate of returning U-boats to the Atlantic, or when we suddenly change I, the net rate of production of U-boats Such a sudden change would correspond to the serious attack on the

bases or on the factories, or on a sudden increase in the offensive against U-boats in the Atlantic A case in point is given by Figure 5, which shows A, the number of U-boats in the Atlantic before and after a single attack In this case we have taken one of the curves from Figure 4 for the initial increase. If there had been no attack, the number A would have continued along the dotted curve At the end of six and a half months, however, we assume an attack either on the factories or on the repair bases, In the curve

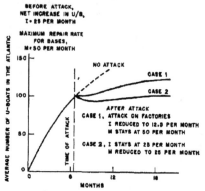

FIGURE 5 Solutions for submarine flow, or "turnaround," problem Effect of damage to submarine production and to repair facilities

marked "Case 1" we assume a reduction of the net production to one-half its original value In the curve "Case 2" we assume a net decrease of the maximum repair rate of the bases to one-half its initial value In the cases shown here it would seem that reducing the effectiveness of the repair bases is slightly more efficacious than reducing the effectiveness of the factories This is not always the case, however

The curves of Figure 5 are still not exactly the ones which we need to answer our questions Another set is given in Figure 6, this time plotted only for the months after the attack No assumption has been made as to the antecedent curve, except that at the time of the attack there are 100 U-boats in the Atlantic and 50 U-boats in bases (This was approximately the case at one time during World War II.) The curves plotted give the number of U-boats in the Atlantic against the number of months after the attack, for different assumed values of I, net increase in submarines per month, and M, the maximum rate of repair of submarines at all bases These curves show the effect of different reductions of effectiveness of the factories and of the repair bases

For some time during the war, the average value of I was between 12 5 and 25, and the average value of

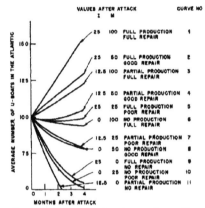

FIGURE 6   Solutions for the submarine flow problem Effect of damage to submarine production and repair facilities Fifty submarines left in repair base after attack I = net increase in submarines per month, M = maximum rate of repair of submarines per month

M was between 50 and 100 Consequently we would expect that the number of U-boats in the Atlantic would have followed a curve somewhere between curves 2 and 3 of Figure 6 (curve 3 is more likely) if no attacks had been made on bases or factories

Curve 6 indicates that if we attacked the U-boat factories strongly, so as to reduce the net production

to zero, this still would not have greatly decreased the number of U-boats in the Atlantic in a short time Curve 4 indicates that an attack on the bases which only reduced to one-half the maximum rate of repair would likewise not have diminished the number of U-boats in the Atlantic to an appreciable extent

Curve 7 indicates that although the factories are not touched, an attack on the bases which reduces the maximum rate of repair to a quarter of its initial value would appreciably reduce the number of U-boats in the Atlantic in a few months Curve 8 indicates that even though the factories are knocked out, it also requires a reduction of the bases to half their initial efficiency before there would be appreciable reduction in U-boats in the Atlantic within a reasonably short time

For the short-term effects, therefore, these curves seem to indicate that the damaging of the repair bases had a greater effect than the damaging of the factories These conclusions must be taken with some caution, however, since the solution here worked out is for a single attack at the beginning of the curves and for no change in rate of production or repair thereafter A balance of the probable effects of other factors, however, would indicate that the actual curves would fall above the curves considered here. Therefore, if the present curves do not show a certain type of attack to be satisfactory, it would not have been satisfactory in actual practice

Other curves can be drawn for other initial conditions They are not very dissimilar to the set in Figure 6, and lead to no different results

Chapter 5

TACTICAL ANALYSIS

SOME IMPORTANT CONTRIBUTIONS have been made by operations research methods in the analysis of tactics Many new situations arose in World War II, involving new equipment or new tactics on the part of the enemy, for which the correct tactical answer had to be found An immediate answer had, of course, to be worked out by the forces in the field, but it often turned out that such pragmatic solutions could be improved upon through further study The problem was usually approached by the operations research worker from two directions the observational, and the analytical At the onset of the new conditions the forces in the field would be forced to try a number of different tactics, if detailed data on the results of these trials could be obtained from the field, they could be studied statistically to see which tactic seemed most promising

These initial data, if they were complete enough, could be used to obtain approximate measures of effectiveness, and to obtain a general picture of the possible behavior of the forces involved As soon as this general picture could be obtained, together with the approximate measures of effectiveness involved in the operations, it was then possible to study the operations analytically Knowing the physical capabilities of the equipment involved, optimum tactics could be worked out theoretically For this theoretical work to be of much practical value, however, the magnitude of the constants involved must be determined, either from actual operational data, or from data obtained by carefully analyzed tactical tests

Section 5 1 will give illustrations where the correct tactics became reasonably obvious after a statistical study of the operational data As soon as the average results from the different actions were computed, it became clear which was the best action to take in a

particular circumstance. Later sections of the chapter will illustrate various methods of working out optimum tactics analytically, and will discuss some of the general principles which are often useful in such analysis Methods of studying tactical tests to obtain measures of effectiveness will be discussed in Chapter 7

5 1   STATISTICAL SOLUTIONS

An example of a case where operational data made clear the appropriate tactics comes from the problem of the ship maneuvering to dodge an incoming suicide plane In spite of our combat air patrol and our antiaircraft [AA] fire, a number of Japanese suicide planes survived long enough to make final dives on some of our naval units As soon as it was clear that the plane was in a dive heading for a particular ship, this ship could attempt to avoid being hit by violent maneuvers, or could continue on a steady course and trust to its antiaircraft fire alone to destroy the enemy's aim It was important therefore, to find out whether radical ship maneuvers would spoil the aim of the incoming Kamikaze more than they would spoil the aim of the defensive antiaircraft fire

5 1 1   Damage Due to Suicide Planes

In order to answer this question, accounts were collected of 477 cases where the enemy plane was obviously a suicide plane heading toward a particular ship Thirty-six per cent of these planes, 172 of them, hit the ship they were aiming for, the others missed. As a result of the 172 hits, 27 ships were sunk. This is shown in the following table

	Larger fleet units			Smaller fleet units				All ships
	BB CA, CL	CV	CVE CVL	DD, APD DM, DMS	AP, APA AKA, AKN	LSM LST, LSV	Small craft	
Number of attacks	48	44	37	241	21	40	37	477
Per cent hits	44	41	48	36	43	22	22	36

Of the 477 attacks studied, only 365 reported in enough detail to be able to ascertain the behavior of the ship and the ultimate state of the plane (i e , whether it was severely damaged or destroyed by antiaircraft fire, or not) These attacks were analyzed to determine the percentage of hits, for large and small ships, according to whether they were maneuvering or not

	Large units	Small units	Total
Maneuvering			
Number of attacks	36	144	180
Per cent hits on ship	22	36	33
Nonmaneuvering			
Number of attacks	61	124	185
Per cent hits on ship	49	26	34

5.1.2 The Effects of Maneuvering

The results indicate that battleships, cruisers, and carriers should employ radical maneuvers when attacked by a suicide plane The percentage of suicide hits on these ships is considerably smaller when they maneuver than when they do not The table, of course, tells nothing about what sort of maneuvers should be employed, but it clearly demonstrates that these larger ships benefit from maneuvering radically in the face of a suicide attack

Destroyers and smaller fleet units, as well as auxiliaries, should not maneuver with radical turns, according to this table, because they receive a higher percentage of hits when they do than when they do not maneuver The table does not indicate whether the smaller ships would profit from the use of slow turns, but it does show that they should not use a combination of high speed and full rudder

Part of the reason why large fleet units should maneuver and smaller ones should not apparently lies in the effect of radical maneuvers on AA effec-

	Large units	Small units	Total
Maneuvering			
Number of attacks	36	144	180
Per cent AA hits on plane	77	59	63
Nonmaneuvering			
Number of attacks	61	124	185
Per cent A A hits on plane	74	66	69

tiveness This is shown in the preceding table, giving percentages of suicide attackers which are seriously damaged by AA fire during their dive attacks

The data reported in the table are not particularly accurate, since it depends on the judgment of the officer writing the action report as to whether the incoming plane was seriously damaged or not by the AA fire Such judgments are not always accurate, nor are they always clearly stated in the reports Nevertheless, the results seemed to show that for large units the AA fire is about as effective when the unit is maneuvering as it is when not maneuvering, whereas the fire from the smaller units seems to be less effective when the ship is maneuvering The difference between 66 and 59 per cent is probably significant, considering the number of cases reporting The rolling and pitching of smaller craft, when performing radical maneuvers, probably upsets the stability of the gun platform sufficiently to cause serious AA errors, whereas this does not seem to be true in the case of larger ships

Dividing these data still further, into cases where the suicide plane came in on high dives, and other cases where it came in on low dives, does not seem to alter the conclusions concerning maneuvering It is apparent from the details that, no matter what the dive angle, destroyers and smaller fleet units should not employ radical maneuvers in order to escape suicide bombers

5 1 3 The Effect of Angle of Approach

The first three tables showed that radical maneuvers were good or bad depending on the type of ship being considered Nothing was said, however, about what maneuvers were particularly good or bad By considering the effect of the suicide plane's angle of approach, some notion may be had as to what, if any, maneuvers should be employed by the vessel under attack A breakdown of the data to show this effect is given in the table on page 83

Because of the difficulties of determining angle of approach on maneuvering ships and because of the effect of maneuvers on AA effectiveness, only nonmaneuvering ships have been considered here Furthermore, because of the small number of attacks in which the required data are known, no attempt has been made to break the data down by ship types Grouping all ships together for this study is not unreasonable because all ships are of the same general shape and the relative distribution of fire power around all ship types is very similar In other words, there does not appear to be any reason to suppose that the effect of angle of approach would be markedly different among ship types

	Per cent hits on ships	Number of cases
High dives		
Ahead	100	1
Bow	50	6
Beam	20	10
Quarter	38	13
Astern	80	5
Low dives		
Ahead	36	11
Bow	41	17
Beam	57	23
Quarter	23	13
Astern	39	23

Two facts are apparent from the table High divers achieve a greater measure of success if they approach from an angle other than the beam, but low divers do best if they approach on the ship's beam. Put conversely, a ship is safer if it presents its beam to a high diver and turns its beam away from a low diver The latter fact is contrary to much opinion on the subject, and certainly calls for some explanation

5 1 4   Reasons for the Results

A discussion of the relative safety of ships against various angles of approach must be based on two independent arguments, that which considers the amount of AA fire power which can be brought to bear at a given angle, and that which considers the relative target dimensions presented to a plane approaching from that same angle It is the relative weight of these two arguments, rather than the conclusion of either by itself, which must decide the issue

The argument concerning AA fire power is clearcut More AA fire power can be brought to bear on the beam than on the bow or stern And this is true no matter what dive angle is being considered Thus, on the basis of this argument alone, it would appear as though the ship were always safest if the plane approached from the beam, regardless of the dive angle

The argument concerning target dimensions is somewhat more involved. First we must consider the relative size of range and deflection errors made by suicide divers In the case of high dives, when all suicide misses of 500 yards or more are eliminated, the average errors in the point of crash are about 50 yards in range and 15 yards in deflection. The range error is measured along the plane's track and the deflection error normal to the plane's track, assuming the bridge structure of the ship to be the point of aim. These figures are necessarily rough because of the lack of precision in the action reports They are sufficiently accurate, however, to indicate that range errors are about three times as large as deflection errors In order to take advantage of this error distribution, it is apparent that the small dimension of the ship should be placed parallel to the track of a high diver in order to increase the safety of the ship; in other words, a high-diving plane should be placed on the beam Thus both this argument and that concerning AA fire power indicate that the ship is safest if a high-diving plane approaches from the beam

In the case of a low-diving plane, the problem is somewhat different If the deflection error is small enough, and if the plane is flying only a few feet above the water, it is apparent that range errors are of little importance The plane simply continues flying until it hits the ship Put differently, a very large *effective* target in range is presented to the low-flying plane no matter from what angle it approaches Since range errors cannot very well be taken advantage of in this case, it will be better to take advantage of deflection errors by placing the small dimension of the ship normal to the plane's course, or, in other words, by turning the beam away from the plane For low divers, then, the AA fire power consideration argues that the beam is a safe aspect to present to the attacker, but the consideration of target dimensions argues that the beam is a dangerous aspect to present The figures of the preceding table indicate that the second argument is the more important Apparently the distribution of fire power around the ship does not vary sufficiently to overcome the differences in target dimensions presented to a low diver

Further confirmation of these results is given by an independent analysis of data concerning maneuvering destroyers The table on page 84 presents the results broken down according to dive angle and whether the destroyer was turning its beam toward or away from the plane.

The figures clearly indicate that a maneuvering destroyer should present its beam to a high diver They also indicate, but less conclusively, that the destroyer should not attempt to present its beam to a low

	Suicide success, per cent	Number of cases
High dives		
Maneuvering to present beam	17	6
Maneuvering to turn beam away	73	11
Low dives		
Maneuvering to present beam	67	9
Maneuvering to turn beam away	45	11

diver Although the number of cases here is small, the figures do confirm the results of the analysis of angle of approach on nonmaneuvering ships, and hence are given added significance

5 15   Suggested Tactics

On the basis of data included in this study, the following conclusions are justified

1 All ships should attempt to present their beams to high-diving planes and to turn their beams away from low-diving planes This recommendation, it should be noted, is based on the assumption that no great difference exists in the damage done by planes crashing from different angles of approach. If there is considerable difference, it might be necessary to change this recommendation

2 Battleships, cruisers, and carriers should employ radical changes of course in order to evade suicide planes

3 Destroyers and smaller fleet units and all auxiliaries should turn slowly to present the proper aspect to the diving plane, but should not turn rapidly enough to affect the accuracy of their AA

The importance of ships employing these optimum tactics is illustrated by the fact that only 29 per cent of the dives on ships using the proper tactics, as defined above, were successful, whereas 47 per cent of the dives were successful on ships using other than these tactics

5 16   Submarine Casualties

An extremely interesting attack on a very difficult problem by the use of statistical analysis was the investigation of the causes of the losses of our own submarines in the Pacific during World War II Except for intelligence sources, the calculations here have to be made by indirect methods One hears the stories of those submarines which have been damaged, but have managed to return. One does not hear what has happened to those submarines which do not

return On the other hand, it is extremely important for the submarine forces to know what tactic of the enemy is causing the greatest number of these casualties

One might expect that the answer could be obtained by collecting information on the causes of damage for those submarines getting home, and extrapolating the results to the case of those which did not Such an extrapolation was made for U S submarines in the Pacific, the results did not reasonably explain the known losses An extrapolation, using reasonable ratios of casualties to damage for surface and air attacks resulted in figures for expected casualties which were only about one-third of the actual casualties

This discrepancy might, of course, have indicated that our expected ratio of casualties to damage was too small by a factor of 3, nevertheless, there was a fair possibility that another cause of casualty was entering, which did not enter into the cause of damage If some type of enemy tactic resulted either in a complete miss or a total casualty, then the submarines which came back damaged could tell us nothing concerning this type of tactic It was suggested that the effects of enemy submarines would answer this description, any torpedo hit would presumably so damage our submarine as to prevent it from returning to base, whereas a torpedo miss might be noticed but would not cause damage, and so might not be stressed in the action report The following analysis was made in an attempt to estimate how many of our submarines could have been sunk by enemy submarines, by counting how many of our submarines sank Japanese submarines

In general, available information concerning encounters of our submarines with the enemy does not provide answers concerning our losses As a trite example, it would be illogical to attempt to estimate our submarine casualties caused by destroyers on the basis of the destroyers our submarines have sunk Similarly the ability of submarines to shoot down enemy planes bears no relation to the ability of enemy planes to sink submarines This is simply because for these cases there exist no common bases for comparison

5 17   Comparison with Japanese Submarine Casualties

However, in the special case where our submarines encounter enemy *submarines*, a basis for comparison does exist Although it is not true that U S and

Japanese submarines are identical either in design or tactical use, certainly no U S submarine will ever encounter any Japanese craft more like itself than a Jap submarine, although opposing submersibles, when compared, show detailed differences, they still are fundamentally alike in that they operate in the same medium, with the same weapons, and enjoy or suffer the same general advantages or disadvantages. It is this feature of submarines vs submarines which permits comparative results to be deduced

Since direct evidence from sunk U S submarines was unobtainable, indirect evidence was substituted The next best information to that directly concerning submarines lost is information concerning those which were attacked but missed. Presumably the number of U S submarines claiming to have been fired at and missed by enemy submarines bears a direct ratio to the number fired at and not missed, and consequently unable to report the action Thus, for cases where our submarines were unsuccessfully attacked by submarine torpedoes, there must exist a proportionate number of attacks on our submarines with less fortunate results

While there are several independent methods for estimating our submarine losses, preference must be attached to those depending on the fewest assumptions The most direct approach is simply to assume that Japanese attacks on submarines suffer about the same percentage of misses that ours do, and apply this figure to the number of times we have been attacked and missed There was no reason to suppose that the percentage success of attacks Japanese submarines made against U S submarines was greatly different from the percentage success of our attacks on Japanese submarines

5 1 8   **The Operational Data**

From the beginning of the war to 15 June 1944 there were 27 submarine attacks on our submarines and 43 attacks by our submarines on Japanese submarines In 17 of these 43 attacks by U S submarines the Japanese submarine was sunk or damaged, and in the other 26 cases it was missed The breakdown by years is shown in Table 1

From these data the best overall figure for our per cent misses is 26/43, or 60 per cent, for all types of attacks on Japanese submarines, whether by day or night, and whether surfaced or submerged, hence, we hit about two-thirds as many Japanese submarines

as we missed Applying this factor to the numbers of cases in which a U. S. submarine was attacked and missed gives the probable losses from Japanese submarine action shown in Table 2 The second column gives the calculated figures; the first, the rounded-off estimates

TABLE 1 Torpedo attacks, submarine versus submarine

	Sunk or damaged	Submarine missed
Attacks on Japanese submarines		
1942	8	8
1943	4	11
1944	5	7
Total	17	26
Attacks on U S submarines		
1942	?	9
1943	?	11
1944	?	7
Total	?	27

It turned out that at the time of the analysis, reasonable estimates of the effectiveness of Japanese antisubmarine planes and ships explained our submarine casualties only in part, and left approximately 15 casualties unexplained The surprising correlation between this number 15 and the number 18, estimated by the above argument to have been sunk by

TABLE 2 Estimated losses of U S submarines by Japanese submarine action

1942	6	(6 0)
1943	7	(7 3)
1944	5	(4 7)
Total	18	(18 0)

Japanese submarines, made it appear likely that at least some of these casualties had been caused by Japanese submarines. It was probable that not all the 15 casualties were due to Japanese submarines, for it was likely that the enemy submarines were not as effective as ours, which was the assumption made in obtaining Table 2 In addition, there must have been a certain number of casualties caused by enemy mines and by ordinary operational accidents, which would account for some of the 15 Nevertheless, the above analysis indicated that Japanese submarines were likely causes of some of the casualties Such a possibility had not been seriously considered before.

5 1.9   Suggested Measures

When this analysis was brought to the attention of the higher command, the results suggested the addition of certain equipment on our submarines to detect incoming torpedoes, and certain tactical measures (which will be discussed in the next section) to protect against this unexpected danger

It has since been learned that Japanese submarines actually sank far fewer than 18 of ours, and that many of the unexplained 15 casualties were due to enemy mines and operational accidents Nevertheless, the analysis had indicated a source of danger which had been previously minimized, and suggested new equipment and tactics to safeguard our submarines against this danger After these safeguards had been put into use, reports from submarine commanders indicated that the new equipment and tactics probably saved 3 or 4 additional submarines from being sunk

5.2   ANALYTICAL SOLUTIONS INVOLVING SEARCH THEORY

A great deal of tactical analysis involves the principles of the theory of search The details of this theory are presented in another volume of this series, but one theorem is so important for our present discussion that it will be worth while discussing it here also This theorem might be called the "mean free path theorem," by its analogy with certain concepts in statistical mechanics.

5 2 1   Covered Area

The theorem concerns the probability of locating, or of damaging, or of colliding with some object, called the target, which is placed at random somewhere within an area A The search object, which is to collide with, or damage, or find the target, can be a patrol plane, a torpedo, a bomb, a 16-inch shell, etc Each object has an effective range of action against the target: effective range of sighting, lethal radius, target width for torpedoes, etc After a certain length of time, some portion of the area A will have been covered by one or more of the search objects, so that, if the target is within this covered area, it will have been discovered or damaged at least once For instance, if the search object is a patrol plane, the *covered area* is equal to twice the effective lateral range of vision of the plane, times the speed of

the plane, times the length of time spent in searching the area A If the test object is a 16-inch shell, the covered area is equal to the number of shells fired inside A, times the lethal area of the 16-inch shell for the target considered If the search object is a torpedo, the covered area is equal to the effective width of the target ship, times the length of track of the torpedo; and so on

We assumed that this covered area is distributed *at random inside* the area A There may be some overlap, in that the area is covered more than once, but we assume that this is done in a random manner. The "mean free path theorem" gives the probability of success as a function of the ratio between the covered area and the total area A

5 2 2   Probability of Hit

To find the value of this probability, we consider the situation at some given instant when the covered area is equal to α We can call $P(0, \alpha)$ the value of the probability that the target is not yet discovered or damaged before this instant We then increase the covered area by an amount $d\alpha$ If this new covered area is placed at random inside the area A, then the chance that the target *will* be found or damaged in this new area is equal to the ratio between $d\alpha$ and total area A, multiplied by the probability that the target has not yet been found or damaged before this In other words,

$$dP(0, \alpha) = -(d\alpha/A)P(0, \alpha)$$

The solution of this differential equation, which satisfies the initial condition that the probability of no hits when α is zero is equal to unity, is the following

$$P(0, \alpha) = e^{-\phi}, \quad \phi = \left(\frac{\alpha}{A}\right) = \text{Coverage factor}$$

A = Total area, α = Covered area   (1)

Probability of hit = $P(>0) = 1 - e^{-\phi}$

Referring back to equation (28) of Chapter 2, we see that the probability of no hits, $P(0, \alpha)$ is just the Poisson distribution probability of obtaining zero points when the expected number is ϕ A little study of the relation between the present case and the case discussed for the Poisson distribution shows the complete analogy, and indicates why the coverage factor ϕ is equal to the expected value of the number of hits To carry the analogy farther, we can say that the probability that the target will have been discovered, or damaged, or hit m times when the covered area is α is $P(m, \phi)$, where

$$P(m, \phi) = \left(\frac{\phi^m}{m!}\right) e^{-\phi}, \quad \phi = \left(\frac{\alpha}{A}\right),$$

(2)

$$P(> 0) = \sum_{m=1}^{\infty} P(m, \phi) = 1 - P(0, \phi) = 1 - e^{-\phi}.$$

5 2 3   Merchant Vessel Sinkings

A few simple examples will illustrate the usefulness of this theorem For instance, suppose a merchant vessel can make $2\frac{1}{2}$ trips, on the average, across the ocean before it is sighted by an enemy submarine, and suppose that on the average 1 out of every 4 ships sighted by the submarine is torpedoed Then the "mean free path" of a ship before it gets hit would be 10 trips across the ocean, and the expected number of hits in n trips would be $(n/10)$ Here, instead of an area, a line is covered (namely the distance covered by the ship) and the coverage factor ϕ is equal to the ratio between the number of trips and the "mean free path" (in this case, 10 trips) The probability of coming through n trips unscathed is $P(0, \phi)$, obtained from equation (2), with $\phi = (n/10)$

5.2 4   Area Bombardment

Another example can be taken from the study of area bombardment. A mortar emplacement, for instance, is somewhere within an area A The lethal area of the average 5-inch shell for damaging a mortar is a Then if n 5-inch shells are fired at random into the area A, the chance that the mortar will be undamaged is $e^{-\phi}$, where the coverage factor ϕ equals (na/A) The probability of the mortar getting hit m times is given in equation (2)

Now suppose that the probability that a single hit on the mortar will damage it beyond repair turns out to be p_0, so that the probability of being able to repair the mortar after m hits is $(1 - p)^m$ Combination of probabilities shows that the overall probability of completely disabling the mortar by n shells fired into the area A is

Probability damage beyond repair

= 1 − probability reparability.

Probability reparability

$$= \sum_{m=0}^{\infty} (1 - p)^m P(m, \phi) = e^{-\phi} \sum_{m=0}^{\infty} \frac{(1-p)^m \phi^m}{m!}$$

$$= e^{-\phi} e^{(1-p)\phi} = e^{-p\phi}, \quad \phi = \left(\frac{na}{A}\right)$$

(3)

Therefore, the probability of escaping complete destruction can be expressed in terms of a new coverage factor $\phi' = (pna/A)$ This shows that in many cases the coverage factor for complete destruction can be obtained from the coverage factor for a hit, by multiplying by the probability of complete destruction when hit This simple property of ϕ is typical of the Poisson distribution

Another example of the "mean free path theorem" can be taken from the study of the effectiveness of mine fields An influence mine has a range of action R for a given ship If there are n mines in a given area A, then the probability that the ship will hit a mine is given by

Probability of hitting at least one mine

$$= 1 - e^{-\phi}, \quad \phi = \left(\frac{2nRL}{A}\right),$$

where L is the length of the ship's track through the mine field The mean free path of the ship in the field is thus $(A/2nR)$.

5 2.5   Antiaircraft Splash Power

Another example of considerable use in the study of antiaircraft defense involves the definition of the splash rate for a given battery of antiaircraft guns From the accuracy and rate of fire of these guns, it is possible to compute the probability that a given plane will be shot down between range r and range $r + dr$. This can be written as $s(r)dr$, where $s(r)$ is called the "splash rate " Ordinarily this rate is small for large values of r and increases as r diminishes In this case the coverage factor ϕ is called the *splash power*, which is obtained by integration

$$\text{Splash power, } \phi(r) = \int_r^\infty s(r)dr;$$

$$s(r) = \text{splash rate.} \tag{4}$$

The probability that the plane is splashed before it reaches range r is $1 - e^{-\Phi}$ By drawing contours of constant splash power about the antiaircraft battery, one can determine the effectiveness of this battery in various directions, and, if necessary, can work out its weak points Since the splash power is additive, the powers of different batteries can be added together to give an overall contour plot Contour plots of this sort have been useful in determining the correct tactics for our own planes against enemy antiaircraft fire, as well as evaluating the effectiveness of our own antiaircraft batteries

5.2.6   Ships Sighted and Sunk by Submarines

A more complicated example comes from the comparison of the effectiveness of submarines used on independent patrol against those used in coordinated attack groups Suppose N submarines are assigned to patrol a given shipping lane Suppose the shipping lane has a width W and that each submarine has an effective range of vision r Then by an analysis similar to that carried through above, we see that the average number S of ships sighted (by one or more submarines) per month is

$$S = F(1 - e^{-2Nr/W})$$

Initial sightings per month per submarine

$$= \frac{F}{N}(1 - e^{-2Nr/W}) , \quad (5)$$

where F is the total traffic in ships per month We see that there is a definite saturation effect as we increase the number of submarines, due to the fact that the additional submarines often sight ships which have already been sighted

When the submarine is on independent patrol, it will carry through its attacks separately and will not call in the other submarines to help If P is the probability of sinking a merchant vessel once it has been sighted, then, by arguments similar to those employed in obtaining equation (3), we can compute the average number of ships sunk per month by the N submarines on independent patrol

$$H_i = F(1 - e^{-2NPr/W})$$
$$= \text{No ships sunk by } N \text{ submarines on} \quad (6)$$
$$\text{independent operation}$$

5 2.7   Independent Patrol

This property of the Poisson distribution, which enables us to multiply the coverage factor for sighting by the probability of sinking once the sighting is made, to obtain the coverage factor for sinking, has an interesting effect on the saturation of forces As an example of this, suppose we consider the case where the shipping lane is twice as wide as the range of vision of a submarine Then, on the average, a single submarine would see a fraction 0 63 of all of the shipping traveling along the lane Two submarines would, on the average, sight 0 86 of all the ships. Consequently, the addition of the second submarine on independent patrol would add to the total number of new sightings by only about one-third of the number of sightings the first submarine had obtained, an example of the saturation effect This does not mean that the second submarine does not see as many ships as the first one, it only means that most of the ships sighted by the second submarine have already been sighted by the first, and that only one-third of the second submarine's sightings are *new* ones

If now, on the average, only one-quarter of the ships sighted by the submarine are sunk, we can use equation (6) to determine the number of ships sunk by a number N of submarines on independent patrol The results are given in the following table

On the average
($2r/W = 1$, Prob sinking if sighted $= P = 0$ 25)

1 submarine sinks 0 22 of shipping flow,

2 submarines sink 0 39 of shipping flow, the second sub giving a gain of 0 77 of the first sub's catch,

3 submarines sink 0 53 of shipping flow, the third sub giving an added gain of 0 64 of the first sub's catch,

4 submarines sink 0 63 of shipping flow, the fourth sub giving an added gain of 0 45 of the first sub's catch, and so on

Here we see that although the second submarine does not make many *new sightings*, it does account for nearly as many *additional sinkings* as does the first submarine This is due to the fact that the first submarine does not sink three-quarters of the ships it sights Therefore, although the second submarine usually sights the same ships sighted by the first one, it has an additional chance to sink them, which is nearly as good as the first submarine However, as we keep on adding submarines the saturation effect comes in again, though not as quickly The fourth submarine accounts for less than half the additional number one might expect, due to the saturation effect.

5 2 8   Group Operation

Now suppose these N submarines act together as a group, instead of attacking ships independently In this case they will patrol station independently, but whenever any submarine sights a ship it will signal all the others, who will rendezvous on the submarine making the initial sighting and will also attempt to sink the ship We will assume first that all of the submarines in the group of N manage to home on the first one and get their chance at sinking the ship In this case, the probability that the ship is sunk is $1 - (1 - P)^N$ instead of the value P which it had if only one submarine carried out the attack By the same arguments as before, we see that the number of ships sunk by a group of N submarines is

$$H_g = F\{1 - e^{-(2Nr/W)[1-(1-P)^N]}\}$$
$$= \text{No ships sunk by } N \text{ submarines in} \qquad (7)$$
$$\text{group operation}$$

The relative advantage of group action over independent action is given by the ratio

$$R = \frac{H_g}{H_1} = \frac{1 - e^{-(2Nr\,W)[1-(1-P)^N]}}{1 - e^{-(2NrP/W)}} \qquad (8)$$

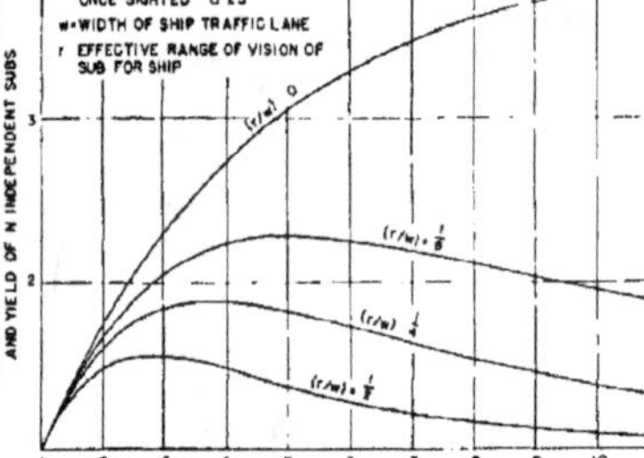

FIGURE 1   Relative advantage of group action over independent action for submarines against merchant vessels

Values of this ratio are plotted in Figure 1 We see that, when the shipping lane is narrow, saturation soon sets in, and there is a certain optimum size for the group. When the shipping lane is very wide, how-

ever, the advantage continually increases as we add more and more submarines to the group, to the degree of approximation considered here.

Actually, of course, other inefficiencies, besides saturation, enter as the group gets quite large Not all of the submarines are able to home on the one which has made the sighting The Germans seldom managed to home more than one-half their pack for simultaneous attack, and U S submarines in the Pacific seldom homed more than one additional submarine In addition, when the pack size is large, interference would discourage the less aggressive Consequently, due to all of these effects, the gain would be less than that shown in Figure 1, although it would be greater than unity

If the shipping travels in convoys, the advantage to group action is again increased, for there are a number of advantages in combined attack on a convoy, some of them mentioned in Section 3 2

Although the German "wolf packs" sometimes reached a dozen or more, analysis of the sort outlined above, using data on Japanese shipping, indicated that groups of U S submarines of about three per group would give optimum results in the Pacific Following this analysis, group tactics were tried. After the operational tactics had been perfected by practice, it turned out that the yield per submarine in a group of three was about 50 per cent greater than the yield per independent submarine Thus the analysis was borne out in practice

5 2.9   Disposition of CAP Protection About Task Forces

Many analyses of tactical problems involve the geometrical combination of velocities and tracks which also enter into the theory of search One interesting example of this comes from the study of the proper distribution of combat air patrol [CAP] units about a task force, to protect the force from enemy bomber planes During World War II, the task force itself had the search radar which made the first detection of the enemy planes This detection was not always made at the same range, there was a certain probability distribution F of detection, which depended on the type of search radar used To be specific, the probability that the enemy unit is detected between a range R and a range $R + dR$ is equal to $F(R)dR$ The integral of F over all values of R must be unity or less, for this integral equals the fraction of enemy planes detected at some range In actual practice, during World War II, this integral was nearly equal to unity, for nearly all enemy planes were detected before they reached the task force An average curve for this probability of detection F is shown in Figure 2. It was obtained from operational

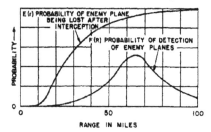

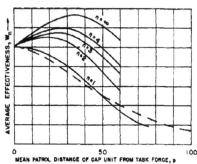

FIGURE 2   Lower curves give average effectiveness, in keeping off enemy bombers, of n combat air patrol units, each patrolling along a circle of radius about the task force When enemy planes are detected, only the nearest unit is vectored to intercept   Curves at top give F, the probability of detection of the enemy planes between R and $R + dR$, and E the average per cent loss of enemy planes when the interception is made at range r (obtained from operational data)

data taken, during the last year of World War II, from actions in the Pacific

Detection is not enough, of course, the combat air patrol must be vectored to intercept the enemy planes and shoot them down Since the speed of the combat air patrol is approximately equal to that of the enemy bombers, both enemy and friendly planes will have traveled an equal distance between the time that the enemy planes are detected and the time the patrol planes intercept the enemy. This situation is shown in Figure 3, where we have assumed that the enemy planes are coming in on a straight course di-

rected at the task force, and that the nearest combat air patrol unit is vectored correctly. Consequently, the farther away the CAP unit is from the enemy at the instant of detection, the nearer to the task force will be the interception We should place the units so they can make interception as soon as possible

It is rather obvious that it is desirable to intercept the enemy bombers as far away from the task force as possible This gives the CAP unit a longer time to

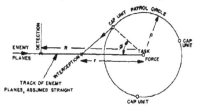

FIGURE 3   Defense of task force from enemy planes by combat air patrol units At instant of detection, nearest unit is vectored to intercept Angle ϕ is random, since bearing of enemy planes is random

"work over" the enemy unit and to scatter it or shoot it down. Even though the planes are not all shot down, a scattered enemy unit seems to find it more difficult to get into the task force, perhaps because the leader is a better navigator than the other planes in the enemy unit and, if the planes scatter, they lose their leader It is of advantage, therefore, to place the CAP units in such a way that the interception will take place, on the average, as far from the task force as possible The operational data on the fraction of enemy planes lost after interception, as a function of range of interception, shown in Figure 2, emphasizes this point

5.2.10   Analysis of Tactical Situation

The tactical situation, which is to be analyzed, can now be stated The CAP units are made large enough to be able to handle the enemy unit without undue loss Suppose that only a number n of such units can be kept aloft at the same time If we do not know the direction of the enemy attack, the CAP protection should be symmetrically placed, so we assume that the units are uniformly spaced around a patrol circle of radius ρ about the task force At the instant of detection the nearest unit is vectored to interception as shown in Figure 3 We assume that the speed of the CAP unit is the same as that of the enemy planes

The range of interception r depends on the angle ϕ as well as on ρ and R, according to the equation

$$r = \frac{R^2 - \rho^2}{2(R - \rho \cos \phi)} \quad R > \rho \quad (9)$$

We also assume that the fraction of enemy planes lost, when an interception takes place at a range r from the task force, is $E(r)$ An approximate curve for E, obtained from operational data, is shown in Figure 2

At the instant of detection the CAP unit, which is vectored to the interception, happens to be at the position corresponding to the angle ϕ, where ϕ is less in magnitude than (π/n) (or else this unit would not be the nearest one to the enemy planes) If the enemy planes are equally likely to come in from any direction, any value of ϕ is possible between the limits (π/n) and $-(\pi/n)$ Consequently, the average value of E, the fraction of enemy planes *not* getting through after the interception is given by

$$\bar{E}_n(R, \rho) = \begin{cases} \dfrac{n}{2\pi} \displaystyle\int_{-\pi/n}^{+\pi/n} E(r)d\phi & R > \rho \\[2mm] 0 & R < \rho \end{cases} \quad (10)$$

However, ranges of first detection are not always the same, but vary according to the distribution function $F(R)$ The average value of the fraction of enemy planes lost by CAP interception for all values of detection range is given by

$$W_n(\rho) = \int_\rho^\infty F(R)\bar{E}_n(R, \rho)dR , \quad (11)$$

which might be called the *effectiveness of the CAP patrol disposition.*

5 2.11   A Simple Example

These calculations cannot be carried through analytically unless the functions E and F are extremely simple If we rate the effectiveness of an interception as a linearly increasing function of the range of interception r, then the first step in the calculation can be carried through analytically

Assume $E(r) = (r/R_m)$, then

$$\bar{E}_n = \frac{n}{2R_m} \sqrt{R^2 - \rho^2} \left\{ \frac{1}{2} - \frac{1}{\pi} \sin^{-1}\left[\frac{\rho - R \cos(\pi/n)}{R - \rho \cos(\pi/n)}\right] \right\} ,$$

$$\bar{E}_1 = \frac{1}{2R_m} \sqrt{R^2 - \rho^2}, \quad R > \rho$$

Even this simplification does not allow the second integration, shown in equation (11), to be accomplished analytically, except for $n = 1$. For this special case and for a simple assumption concerning the distribution function F we obtain,

assuming $F = \left(\dfrac{R}{R_0^2}\right)e^{-R/R_0}$,

$$W_1 = -\left(\frac{R_0}{R_m}\right)\left(\frac{z^2}{2}\right)K_2(z) ; \quad z = \left(\frac{\rho}{R_0}\right)$$

The probability function F starts at zero for $R = 0$, rises to a maximum at $R = R_0$, and then approaches zero again for very large values of R

The average effectiveness of a single CAP unit is given by W_1, where the function K_2 is the Bessel function of the second kind, of imaginary argument, and of second order, as defined by Watson [18] This function is plotted as a dashed curve in the lower set of curves in Figure 2, for $R_0 = 25$ miles We note that its maximum value is at $\rho = 0$, indicating that, if there is only one CAP unit which can be kept aloft at a time, it is most effective to keep this unit directly above the task force, as long as one does not know the direction from which the enemy planes are likely to come, for if the single unit were patrolling at a distance from the task force it might get caught "off base" by an enemy unit coming in to the task force from the opposite side This result turns out to be true for other reasonable assumptions as to E and F: if only a single CAP unit is aloft at a given time, its most effective position is directly over the task force (unless the direction of enemy attack is known).

5.2 12   Several CAP Units

The integration for the more general case, with several CAP units aloft, must be carried through numerically Consequently we might as well use the curves for E and F obtained from the operational data, shown in Figure 2 The results of this calculation are shown in the lower set of solid curves in Figure 2 The maximum values of these curves indicate the optimum radius of the patrol circle for the n units of combat air patrol We notice that, for the curves of E and F used if only one CAP unit can be kept aloft at a time, it should patrol over the task force, if two units can be kept aloft, they should patrol on opposite sides of the task force and about 20 miles away from the task force; if three units are aloft, they should patrol on a circle of radius 25 miles, spaced 120 degrees apart along this circle, etc Even for an extremely large number of CAP units, if these are distributed on a single circle, the diameter of the circle should only be 35 miles in radius, equal to about one-half the mean range of detection

The discussion presented here is only the beginning of the complete tactical study One must investigate the possibilities of vectoring out a second unit to "back up" the first unit, for it sometimes happens that the first unit does not make an interception effectively This can be taken into account to some extent by successive use of the function E, but, strictly speaking, the mean free path theorem should be used to obtain a more detailed answer In many cases, also, it is more likely that the enemy units will approach from one side rather than another In this case, the integration over the angle ϕ must include the probability of the enemy units coming in from a given direction The results would indicate how the disposition of CAP units would have to be modified The present calculations also do not include the effect of the altitude of the enemy units on the interception problem Many of these aspects have been dealt with in various ORG studies, space cannot be given to them here

5 2 13   Tactics to Evade Torpedoes

The last example given in this section will continue the analysis of the submarine versus submarine problem discussed in Section 5 1 There it was shown that there was a possibility that our own submarines in the Pacific were being torpedoed by Japanese submarines, and that there was a good chance that several of our casualties were due to this cause Presumably the danger was greatest when our submarine was traveling on the surface and the enemy submarine was submerged It was important, therefore, to consider possible measures to minimize this danger One possibility was to install a simple underwater listening device beneath the hull of the submarine, to indicate the presence of a torpedo headed toward the submarine Torpedoes driven by compressed air can be spotted by a lookout, since they leave a characteristic wake, electric torpedoes, on the other hand, cannot be spotted by their wake All types of torpedoes, however, have to run at a speed considerably greater than that of the target, and therefore their propellers generate a great deal of underwater sound This sound, a characteristic high whine, can be detected by very simple underwater

microphones, and the general direction from which the sound comes can be determined by fairly simple means

Microphone equipment to perform this function had already been developed by NDRC; it remained to determine the value of installing it In other words, even if the torpedo could be heard and warning given, could it be evaded? The chief possibility, of course, lay in radical maneuvers A submarine (or a ship) presents a much smaller target to the torpedo end on than it does broadside Consequently, as soon as a torpedo is heard, and its direction is determined, it is advisable for the submarine to turn toward or away from the torpedo, depending on which is the easier maneuver

5 2 14   Geometrical Details

The situation is shown in Figure 4 Here the submarine is shown traveling with speed u along the

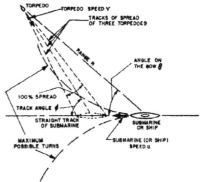

FIGURE 4   Quantities connected with analysis of torpedo attack on submarine or ship

dash-dot line It discovers a torpedo at range R and at angle on the bow θ headed toward it For correct firing, the torpedo is not aimed at where the submarine is, but at where the submarine will be when the torpedo gets there The relation between the track angle ϕ, the angle on the bow θ, the speed of torpedo and submarine, and the range R can be worked out from the geometry of triangles The aim, of course, is never perfect, and operational data indicate that the standard deviation for torpedoes fired from U S submarines is about 6 degrees of angle

In most cases, more than one torpedo is fired For

instance, if three torpedoes are fired in a salvo, the center torpedo is usually aimed at the center of the target If the other two are aimed to hit the bow and stern of the target, the salvo of three is said to have a 100 per cent spread Due to the probable error in aim, it turns out to be somewhat better to increase the spread to 150 per cent, so that, if the aim were perfect, the center torpedo would hit amidships, and the other two would miss ahead and astern Analysis of the type to be given in Chapter 6 shows that a salvo of three with 150 per cent spread gives a somewhat greater probability of hit than does a salvo with 100 per cent spread

A glance at Figure 4 shows that if the *track angle* ϕ is less than 90° the submarine should turn as sharply as possible toward the torpedoes in order to present as small a target as possible, if the track angle is greater than 90° the turn should be away from the torpedoes Assuming a three torpedo salvo, with 150 per cent spread and 7° standard deviation in aim, and knowing the maximum rate of turn of the submarine and the speed of the submarine and torpedo, it is then possible to compute the probability of hit of the salvo, as a function of the angle-on-the-bow θ and the range R at which the submarine starts its turn If the range is large enough, the submarine can turn completely toward or away from the torpedoes (this is called "combing the tracks") and may even move completely outside of the track of the salvo If the torpedoes are not discovered until at short range, however, very little improvement can be obtained by turning

One can therefore compute the probability of hitting the submarine if it starts to turn when it hears a torpedo at some range and angle-on-the-bow This can be plotted on a diagram showing contours of equal probability of sinking, and these can be compared with contours for probability of sinking if the submarine takes no evasive action, but continues on a straight course A typical set of contours is shown in Figure 5

The solid contours show the probabilities of a hit when the submarine takes correct evasive action The dotted contours give the corresponding chances when a submarine continues on a steady course One sees that the dotted contour for 30 per cent chance of hit covers a much greater area than a solid contour for the same chance In other words, at these longer ranges the evasive action of the submarine has a greater effect The contours for 60 per cent chance of hit do not show the corresponding improvement,

since, by the time the torpedo is so close to the submarine, maneuver has little chance of helping the situation One sees that, if one can hear the torpedo as far away as 2,000 yards, a very large reduction in the chance of being hit can be produced by the correct evasive maneuvers

Since these contours represent, in effect, vulnerability diagrams for torpedo attack, they suggest the directions in which lookout activity should be em-

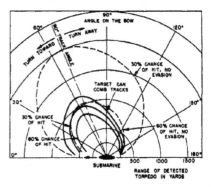

U S FLEET TYPE SUBMARINE AT 16 KNOTS
3 TORPEDO SALVO (150% SPREAD) AT 45 KNOTS

FIGURE 5　Chance of surviving torpedo salvo by sharp turns as soon as torpedo is detected, as function of torpedo range and bearing when detected, compared to chance of survival when no evasive action is taken

phasized. The greatest danger exists at a relative bearing corresponding to a 90 degree track angle, and the sector from about 30 degrees to 105 degrees on the bow should receive by far the most attention. The narrow separation of the contours corresponding to evasive action emphasizes the extreme importance of the range of torpedo detection In many instances a reduction of 500 yards in detection range may cut in half the target probability of escaping

Another factor vital to the efficacy of evasive turning is the promptness with which it is initiated For 45-knot torpedoes, every 10 seconds delay in execution of the turn corresponds approximately to a reduction of 250 yards in the distance from the torpedo to the target. Thus it is apparent that a 20 seconds delay in beginning the evasive turning will probably halve the chances of successful evasion

These same calculations, with different speeds and different dimensions for the target vessel, may be used to indicate to the submarine where it is best to launch its torpedoes in order to minimize the effect of evasive turning of the target ship One sees that it is best to launch torpedoes, if possible, with a track angle of approximately 90 degrees One sees also the importance of coming close to the target before firing the salvo, since evasive action is much less effective when begun with the torpedo less than 2,000 yards away

This study showed the value of good torpedo-detection microphones, with ranges of at least 2,000 yards, and supported the case for their being installed on fleet submarines Publication of the study to the fleet indicating the danger from Japanese submarines and of the usefulness of evasive turns, produced an alertness which saved at least four U S submarines from being torpedoed, according to the records

5 3   MEASURE AND COUNTER-MEASURE

Some of the most urgent tasks and the most exciting opportunities for operations research lie in the field of the devising of countermeasures to new enemy tactics or weapons Nearly every aspect of World War II showed an interplay of measure and counter-measure the side which could get a new measure into operational use before the enemy realized what it was, or which could get a countermeasure into use before the enemy had perfected his methods of using some measure, was the side which gained tremendously in this interplay Operations research workers helped considerably in speeding up these reactions, by following technical developments closely and by relating them to the most recent operational data In a narrow sense, of course, this is not operations research, but operations research workers proved most useful, since they were familiar with the tactical situation

Most of the operational decisions and planning on countermeasures require a great deal of technical background Information from espionage and other intelligence sources often comes through in fragmentary form, and unless the persons analyzing the information know the technical possibilities, only a fraction of the important information may ever be discerned Knowledge of new enemy measures must then be carried to those laboratories which are capable of turning out countermeasures quickly and accurately. Since it often happens that the weak points of an enemy measure are things which could easily be remedied by the enemy if he thought it

necessary, it is usually quite important to keep our knowledge of such information at a high security level The problem of introducing enough technical men to the intelligence information in order to solve a problem rapidly, while maintaining proper security, is one of the reasons these problems are difficult ones

5 3 1   Countermeasures to Acoustic Torpedoes

The first information on the German T-5 Acoustic Torpedo came from espionage The first information which was of technical value came from fragmentary descriptions of the torpedo by prisoners By piecing together these descriptions, a fairly sensible picture of the design was obtained, and, by using the two available guesses as to size, the dimensions of important units could be estimated roughly The problem was serious enough to warrant requesting a laboratory to build an acoustic control head according to the estimated specifications In the meantime, calculations involving the properties of diffraction and of acoustic resonance were utilized in order to obtain a preliminary estimate of the acoustical behavior of this torpedo Combining measurements on the sample built by the laboratory, theoretical calculations, and further detailed intelligence information made it possible to obtain a rough estimate of its characteristics

The important characteristics were the speed of the torpedo, its turning radius, the extent of the region around the torpedo within which the hydrophones were sensitive to sound, the frequency for optimum response of hydrophones, and the sensitivity of response in the steering mechanism to changes of direction of the sound source The torpedo was to be fired from a considerable distance and to travel as an ordinary torpedo for the majority of its run. The hydrophones were then turned on, the speed of the torpedo was reduced to reduce self-noise, and the torpedo steered toward whatever noise source was in front of it.

Since the sensitive element was a pair of hydrophones, which could only tell whether the torpedo was steering to the right or left of the source, the torpedo probably would follow a pursuit course, not a collision course On a pursuit course the torpedo constantly points toward the source of sound, which the launcher hopes will be the ship's propellers If the torpedo is initially forward of the ship, the torpedo path will exhibit a greater and greater curvature until the torpedo turns around the stern of the ship and begins a stern chase (unless the torpedo track is so nearly a collision track that it hits the hull of the ship as it goes by) If the track angle is large, the greatest curvature of this pursuit path may be less than the maximum curvature possible for the torpedo In many cases, however, the torpedo will not be able to turn sharply enough to follow the pursuit course At this point, whether the torpedo eventually swings back on the ship's track to complete its stern chase, or whether it loses the target completely, depends on how concentrated, around the bow direction, is the directional listening pattern of the torpedo's hydrophones

The obvious countermeasure to such a torpedo is to tow after the ship an underwater noisemaker, which is enough louder in the proper frequency range than the propellers, so that the torpedo will steer for the noisemaker rather than for the propellers Noisemakers could be tossed overboard to drift astern, but this would require too large an expenditure of material, so it was preferable to tow the noisemaker, if this would provide sufficient protection Pursuit curves, for various intensities of the noisemaker and for various distances astern of the ship, had to be computed, using different reasonable assumptions concerning the spread of the directional listening pattern of the torpedo and its range of acuity On the basis of these calculations, it was decided that a single noisemaker, towed some distance astern, would provide reasonable protection against a torpedo with the acoustic and control properties which seemed most probable The specifications also required a certain minimum intensity of the noisemaker in the important frequency range, which by that time had been determined to be within 10 and 15 thousand cycles per second

The experimental tactical unit of the Antisubmarine Development Detachment, Atlantic Fleet, was then utilized to make full-scale measurements on various types of noisemakers The parallel-pipe vibrators called FXR turned out to be as loud as most and to be somewhat easier to handle than most. By this time a working model, estimated to correspond to the German torpedo, was built and could be used to verify the calculations The results were satisfactory and the countermeasure gear, the FXR, was supplied to the antisubmarine craft for their protection, together with the necessary doctrine for its use

Most of these calculations and tests had already been finished by the time the Germans came out with the T-5 torpedo in operation A few destroyers were sunk by the torpedo before the countermeasure gear could be supplied; but no destroyers were hit by T-5 torpedoes when they were towing the noisemaker according to doctrine, although many acoustic torpedoes were fired at such destroyers (and several noisemakers were blown up by direct torpedo hits!) The German U-boat Command was greatly disappointed at the rapidity with which this countermeasure was gotten into use and the consequent failure of their new torpedo

5.3.2 Radar Countermeasures

The radar field was the greatest arena of countermeasures in World War II, and the struggle reached its greatest complexity in the aspects connected with strategic bombing The activities in this field are sufficiently complex to require several volumes to explain them, and space forbids their discussion here The radar countermeasure struggle in the anti-U-boat campaign was a comparatively simple one, but it demonstrates most of the elements of the problem, and will be discussed here for its simplicity. A preliminary discussion of this phase has already been given at the end of Section 3 1

Radar has been only one of the many weapons applied to counter the enemy use of U-boats, but it played an important role at certain critical times and caused grave concern to the U-boat Command The moves and countermoves of the radar war offer an interesting example of the importance of quick and accurate evaluation of enemy measures, and of the operational effectiveness of enemy countermeasures Only rarely is a countermeasure widely enough applied or sufficiently effective to justify the extreme tactic of abandoning the weapon, usually the prompt application of counter-countermeasures will restore effectiveness This is particularly true of the radar vs search-receiver competition, which was a continuing problem throughout the U-boat war

From the start of the war the Germans were fully aware of the possibilities of meter ASV radar and had developed their own airborne search equipment When, in the summer of 1942, they concluded correctly that the Allies were using radar for U-boat search, they initiated a "crash" program for the development of search receivers [GSR] to detect the radiations. The first equipment to be installed on U-boats was the R600 or "Metox," with a low-wavelength limit of 130 cm It was of the heterodyne type, thought to be the only type capable of sufficient sensitivity, and it radiated energy in fact, if it had been designed as a transmitter it could hardly have radiated more power Its operational success against the British Mark II radar was undeniable, and it was accepted as a satisfactory warning receiver by U-boat captains

Meanwhile, Allied development of S-band radar was proceeding, based upon the magnetron transmitter tube, and was put into operational service in early 1943 as the U S ASG and the British Mark III types From the start this met with operational success and U-boat sinkings increased The Germans became convinced that Allied aircraft were using some new detection device, and started a frantic activity to identify and counter it For a time they occupied themselves with the idea that it was an infrared detector, and experimented with their own infrared detectors and with special paints intended to give no infrared reflections They also considered the possibility of a frequency-scanning radar and developed a scanning receiver with a cathode-ray tube presentation This was of definite advantage to the operator, but it still covered the same meter-wave band

The sinkings of U-boats continued In desperation, they jumped to the conclusion that their GSR radiations were being homed on The Metox receiver was outlawed, and the "Wanz" G1 introduced This was of an improved design and radiated much less power However, the almost pathological fear of radiations which had been bred in the minds of U-boat captains prevented them from trusting it Continued sinkings and skepticism of the technical advantages kept it from being used Next, the German scientists turned to the much less sensitive crystal detector receiver, which was entirely free from radiation, and produced the "Borkum " This was a broad-band intercept receiver which covered the 75–300 cm band

Finally, in September 1943, the U-boat Command recognized that 10 cm band radar was being used for U-boat search One of these sets had been captured intact at Rotterdam by the German Air Force in March 1943, and German scientists had soon determined its characteristics but the news reached the German Navy in September How this six months' delay occurred is one of the mysteries of the war and a significant factor in the U-boat war (it can perhaps be explained only by a criminal lack of liaison between the German air and naval technical staffs) A further delay of six months intervened before the first effective S-band receivers became operational, in April, 1944 During this interval the frantic ex-

perimentings of the German Technical Service became evident in such incidents as the patrol of the U-406 carrying one of their best GSR experts, Dr Greven, and his staff, with a full complement of experimental search receivers The U-406 was sunk, and Dr Greven was captured Other experimental patrols had even shorter careers

5.3 3   Naxos Search Receiver

Out of this confusion finally came the "Naxos" intercept receiver covering the 8–12 cm band The first models were crude, portable units mounted on a stick and carried up through the conning tower on surfacing The range was short, due to the crystal detector principle, the broad-band coverage and the small, nondirectional antenna, estimates of range from P/W reports are 8 to 10 miles The equipment was subject to rough handling on crash dives and was often out of order Continued development improved the reliability, and it eventually proved its value in giving warning of Allied S-band radar, usually at ranges about equal to radar contact ranges This resulted in an increase in the number of "disappearing contacts" on the radars and an even greater number of successful evasions which can only be estimated

Allied reaction to intelligence reports about Naxos as early as December 1943 brought the fear that S-band radar was compromised A serious morale problem developed among Allied ASV flyers with this news and with the related drop in U-boat contacts Radar was turned off completely in several squadrons Tactics were improvised to salvage some usefulness for the radars, on the assumption that the GSR could outrange the radar On the approach "searchlighting" the target, sector scan, or change of scan rate were not allowed, since such changes would indicate to the GSR operator that radar contact had been made, and the U-boat could take evasive action Attenuators, such as "Vixen," were initiated to cause a slow and steady decrease in transmitted power as range closed, so as to confuse the GSR operator. In order to use this successfully, the contact must be made at a range of 15 miles or greater Since this was greater than average radar contact range under many conditions, it could only be used for about half the contacts Production was slow and installations slower, Vixen never did have an operational opportunity of justifying the effort spent in its development An interim tactic of a "tilt-beam" approach to reduce signal intensity as range closed was proposed.

This required unusual skill and cooperation between pilot and radar operator to be effective, and its value was never adequately proven Almost in desperation the tactic of turning the spinner aft (for the 360-degree scanning radars) and approaching by dead reckoning was suggested The chances of a successful navigational approach were small, however, as compared to radar homing on the target

5 3.4 Allied Reaction

The chief error made by the Allies at this phase was in *overestimating* the capabilities and efficiency of the Naxos GSR Analyses of sighting data, mentioned in Section 3 1, soon showed that the GSR was far from being certain protection for the U-boat Efforts were made to revive the confidence in radar and keep it in operation The validity of this view was indicated by the continued high rate of U-boat sinkings up through August 1944, when the withdrawal from French coastal ports caused a large drop in U-boat activity

The use of radar of an even higher frequency was an obvious next step Development and allocations of X-band equipments even preceded the advent of Naxos, and were further stimulated by the problem it presented However, the Germans were not caught napping this time An H2X blind-bombing A/C was lost over Berlin in January 1944, and from the damaged remains the Germans learned of the frequency band It was assumed that this frequency would also be applied to ASV radar, and the development of X-band intercept receivers was started even before use of X-band radar by the Allies in U-boat search became operationally effective A well-designed receiver, known as "Tunis," which consisted of two antennas, the "Muecke" horn for X-band and the "Cuba Ia (Fliege)" dipole and parabolic reflector for S-band, was developed and installations started in the late Spring of 1944 Installations seem to have been completed during the period of inactivity following the withdrawal to Norwegian and German bases Two amplifiers with a common output to the operator's earphones made it possible to search both bands simultaneously The chief feature was the directional antennas, which gave increased sensitivity and range; the range probably exceeded radar contact range for all X and S radars of that time To obtain full coverage the antennas were mounted in the D F loop on the bridge and rotated manually at about two revolutions per minute The unit still was to be dismounted and taken below on submerging,

and so could be used only in the surfaced condition. It seems to have been a reliable and effective warning receiver

5.3 5 Intermittent Operation

Intermittent operation of ASV radar might have become a valuable counter to such directional receivers A schedule of two or three radar scans at intervals of one to two minutes for a narrow-beam radar will point the beam "on target" for only short time intervals The probability of detection is determined by the chance of coincidence of these time intervals with the intervals when the receiver antenna is directed toward the radar Knowledge of the radar and GSR beam widths and scan frequencies make it possible to compute the probability of detection per minute, P_1, for each intermittency schedule The cumulative probability of detection in the time required for the radar aircraft to approach from GSR range to average radar contact range is given by $P_t = 1 - (1 - P_1)^t$ The probability of undetected approach to a radar contact ($Q_t = 1 - P_t$) can be made as high as 70 per cent by proper choice of the intermittency schedule A small reduction in radar contact efficiency or sweep width is to be expected, but is, in general, much less than the loss in search receiver-detection probability, and the result is net gain.

The above tactic of intermittent use of radar is of most value against highly directional search receivers such as Tunis All-round-looking receiver antennas will not be countered to the same extent. However, the psychological confusion of the receiver operator in interpreting the short and infrequent signals will result in a definite but incalculable reduction in efficiency Furthermore, the shorter range and reduced sensitivity of the nondirectional antennas will mean that a shorter time interval is involved So there may be advantages of intermittent radar operation even for such nondirectional search receivers

One of the most important results of the intensive Allied use of search radar was in driving U-boats under the surface and so, in blinding and partially immobilizing them, reducing their effectiveness Hold-down, or flooding, tactics to achieve this end are of recognized value for convoy coverage and in congested areas Radar will no doubt continue in use even though a future GSR of greater sensitivity and more perfect coverage is produced, in order to prevent U-boats from again adopting surfacing tactics Furthermore, no device is ever 100 per cent efficient operationally and will occasionally fail Continued use of radar will capitalize on this inefficiency and will result in some successful contacts.

5 3.6   Estimate of Effectiveness of Enemy's Measures

The preceding discussion of radar countermeasures illustrates one of the most important problems for operations research in the field of countermeasures namely, the proper estimation of the time to introduce the countermeasure It was pointed out above that there was a tendency among the Allied antisubmarine forces to turn off their microwave radar before the German microwave search receiver had become effective Thus the Allied antisubmarine aircraft were reduced by a factor of 2 or 3 in effectiveness before it was really necessary to make the reduction A detailed comparison between visual and radar contacts in the Western Atlantic showed that there was little actual reduction in the ratio of visual to radar sweep rate until the end of the war Therefore, even if the Germans were using their search receiver, it was not doing them much good at that time, and there was no reason to hamper our own radar search aircraft by introducing countermeasures until effectiveness had improved

This situation is typical of a great number of cases There are indications that the enemy has begun, or is likely to begin, the use of a countermeasure which may destroy the effectiveness of one of our measures We have in turn developed a counter to this which may or may not reduce the effectiveness of the enemy's countermeasure, but which is detrimental to our measure unless the enemy is using its countermeasure. In a few cases, the effects of the enemy's countermeasure are so apparent that we can nearly always tell when he uses it We can then follow the situation, and can introduce our own counter when the enemy uses his countermeasure a great enough percentage of times to make our counter worth while

In a great number of cases, however, we cannot be sure in each encounter whether the enemy was using his countermeasure or whether he was just lucky in that particular case A certain percentage of the time the enemy's countermeasure is not used and our measure is effective, in another per cent of the time our measure fails even though the countermeasure is not used, in a part of the time the enemy's countermeasure is used but is not effective, and the remainder of the time the enemy's countermeasure is used and is effective In such cases, we are not as interested in knowing what percentage of the time the enemy uses his countermeasure as we are in knowing whether our countermeasure would be able to help the situation

Such a question can only be answered by trial in operation Each month we try a certain number of times using the countermeasure, and the remainder of the times we do not use it If the results show that the counter to the enemy's countermeasure gives better results, we then use it, if it does not, we try again later to see whether the enemy has improved his countermeasures Since all such trials are random affairs, we must be sure that our results have meaning statistically Consequently, it is well to provide criteria for determining when our tests have meaning

5 3 7   Discrete Operational Trials

There are two cases which must be considered separately The first is where the operation consists of a discrete try, such as a firing of a torpedo or guided missile The other case is where the operation involves continuous effort, such as the aircraft searching for a submarine, or the submarine waiting for a ship The first case can be exemplified by the following example we have been using air-launched, antiship guided missiles against the enemy with fair success This success has recently been reduced, which leads us to suspect that the enemy is using certain jamming methods which disturb the homing mechanism in the guided missile We have developed an antijamming device which can be inserted in the homing mechanism of our missiles This device is complex enough so that in a certain number of cases the homing mechanism will break down and fail

On the other hand, when it does not fail, it will counteract the enemy's jamming equipment in a certain percentage of the cases We are sure that if the enemy is *not* using jamming equipment, the antijamming equipment would be a detriment to install If the enemy *is* using jamming equipment enough of the time, however, it probably would be best to install the antijamming mechanisms We must make a series of tries with and without the antijamming equipment in order to see which is the best result, on the average Since the enemy is probably changing his tactics from time to time, we must continue to make these tests, at the same time, however, we must arrange our actions so that the majority of the time we use that operation which we believe will give best results

5 3 8 Mathematical Details

To see what should be done we first consider the general case where we have made n trials without the antijamming equipment (Tactic 1) and N trials using the antijamming equipment (Tactic 2) Suppose in s of the n trials without antijamming equipment, we are successful (i e , the guided missile sinks a ship), and in S cases, out of the N tries with Tactic 2, we have success Then, if (s/n) is larger than (S/N), our information would lead us to think that the enemy's countermeasure was not effective enough to make it worth while to install antijamming equipment yet. However, the results we have actually obtained might be due to fluctuation and might not represent the average case We should like to determine, by our series of tests, the values of the *probability of success p* and P of the two tactics If p is larger than P, then we should definitely use Tactic 1, if (p/P) is smaller than unity, we should use Tactic 2 (antijamming device)

If we actually knew the values p and P, we could compute the probability of obtaining the result we did From Chapter 2, equation (14), we see that this probability is

$$\frac{n!N!}{s!(n-s)!S!(N-S)!}p^s(1-p)^{n-s}P^S(1-P)^{N-S}$$
$$= f_d(p, P)$$

Unless n and N are both small, this expression is a rather difficult one to handle In general, however, we will have to make enough trials to be sure of our answer, so that n and N will *not* be small If these quantities are not small, however, we can use the approximation methods discussed in obtaining equation (24) of Chapter 2. These same methods give the approximate result

$$f_d(p, P) \simeq \frac{n^2N^2}{4\pi^2sS(n-s)(N-S)}$$
$$\exp\left[-\frac{n^2}{2s(n-s)}\left(p-\frac{s}{n}\right)^2 - \frac{N^2}{2S(N-S)}\left(P-\frac{S}{N}\right)^2\right]$$

This probability has a maximum at $p = (s/n)$ and $P = (S/N)$, as shown in Figure 6 In terms of this

figure, we see that our question is as follows: We have obtained results s and S, what is the probability that p is larger than P? From the figure we see that this must equal the integral $f(p, P)$ over all the space to the right of the diagonal dashed line A great deal of algebra is needed to show that this probability is

Prob. $p > P$

$$= F_n\left\{\left[\frac{s(n-s)}{n^3} + \frac{S(N-S)}{N^3}\right]^{-1/2}\left[\frac{s}{n} - \frac{S}{N}\right]\right\}, \quad (12)$$

where F_n is the function given in equation (24) of Chapter 2 According to Figure 11 of Chapter 2 this probability is 50 per cent if the quantity in the

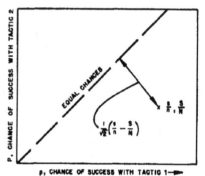

FIGURE 6 Calculation of probability that Tactic 1 or Tactic 2 is more successful.

braces is zero, it is approximately 10 per cent if this quantity is $-1\,4$, and it is 90 per cent, approximately, if the quantity is $+1.4$.

We can say that, if s, S, n, N have such values that this probability (that Tactic 1 is better than Tactic 2) is less than 1 chance in 10, we would naturally prefer to use Tactic 2 (antijamming device) Since the enemy is likely to change his countertactics, however, it is well to keep a certain percentage of Tactic 1 going in order to keep a continuous check. If the probabilities of Tactic 1 being better than Tactic 2 are less than 1 chance in 10, however, we should not use Tactic 1 very often, it should be used less than one-tenth of the time, as a matter of fact Similarly, if the probability P_n is larger than 90 per cent, we should not use Tactic 2 any more than 1 in 10 times, etc.

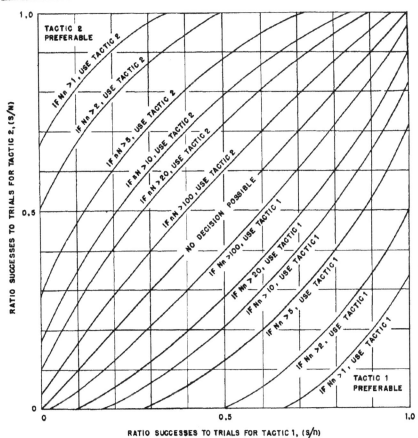

FIGURE 7.   For s successes out of n discrete trials of Tactic 1, S successes out of V trials of Tactic 2, a point is determined on the plot   Rules in text tell how future action should depend on position of point with respect to contours

539   **Rules for Trials**

With this sort of reasoning in mind, we proceed to make rules of procedure, which of necessity must be more clear-cut than the probabilities ever can be These rules, which nevertheless give a fairly good approximation to the discussion of the last paragraph, are as follows

1. If the quantity in the braces in equation (12) is less than $-1\,4$, use Tactic 1 one-tenth as often as Tactic 2

2 If the quantity in the braces is between $-1\,4$ and 0, use Tactic 1 one-half as often as Tactic 2.

3 If the quantity is between 0 and $+1\,4$, use Tactic 1 twice as often as Tactic 2

4 If this quantity is larger than $+1\,4$, use Tactic 1 10 times as often as Tactic 2

5 If situation (1) or (4) continues for several months, and if other intelligence indicates that it is likely to continue, discontinue Tactic 1 or Tactic 2 entirely

These requirements can be presented graphically,

in Figure 7 From the results of the week's (or month's) trials, we plot on this chart the point (s/n), (S/N). If this point falls to the right of the diagonal line marked "No Decision Possible," then it is more likely that Tactic 1 is preferable How sure we are of this result, however, depends on the size of the quantity (Nn) The rule as given above can therefore be translated into the following

1 If the point (s/n), (S/N) is to the right of the lower contour line corresponding to the product of the number of times Tactic 1 was tried and the number of times Tactic 2 was tried, then use Tactic 1 10 times as often as Tactic 2

2 If the point is between the lower contour for (Nn) and the diagonal line, use Tactic 1 twice as often as Tactic 2

3 If the point is to the left of the diagonal line, but is to the right of the upper contour for (nN), use Tactic 1 half as often as Tactic 2

4 If the point is to the left of the upper contour for (nN), use Tactic 1 one-tenth as often as Tactic 2

5 If situation (1) or (4) continues for several months, and if other intelligence indicates that it is likely to continue, discontinue Tactic 1 or Tactic 2 entirely

Thus we have derived a set of rules which tell us what to do about introducing any particular countermeasure when the operation consists of discrete tries

One notices that the greater the product (nN) is, the sharper can be the distinction between courses of action. This corresponds to the general principle of probability, that a large number of trials reduces the chance of a misleading result due to fluctuations This condition is sometimes difficult to achieve in practice, for the enemy is changing his tactics, and it would not do to lump together data taken before and after a change in enemy tactics From this point of view, it is preferable to use data taken over as short a period of time as possible, which means a small value for n and N General rules cannot be made up for handling such situations, each case must be dealt with on its own merits, utilizing all available information, and exercising common sense

5 3 10   Continuous Operations

The second situation, where a continual effort must be made, is dealt with in an analogous manner As an example, we can consider the search for U-boats by antisubmarine aircraft Tactic 1 will be the search by radar planes, and Tactic 2 can be the search by

visual means with the radar set shut off As long as the enemy does not use radar warning receivers effectively, the radar planes will discover more U-boats per thousand hours of flying than will visual planes. This situation, however, will change when the warning receivers begin to get effective

Let us suppose that during the last month radar planes have flown e hours, searching for U-boats During the same time and over the same portion of ocean, we suppose that nonradar planes have flown E hours During this time, the radar planes have made m contacts with U-boats and the visual planes have made M contacts If the effectiveness of radar planes, in contacts per hour, is p, and if the effectiveness of the visual planes is P, then the probability that the number of contacts mentioned is actually obtained turns out to be

$$\frac{(pe)^m (PE)^M}{m! \, M!} \; \exp\left(-pe - PE\right) = f_c(p, P)$$

from equation (28) of Chapter 2

If m and M are large enough, this expression may be approximated by one which is similar to the discrete case discussed above

$$f_c(p, P) \simeq \frac{e^2 E^2}{4\pi^2 mM}$$

$$\exp\left[-\frac{e^2}{2m}\left(p - \frac{m}{e}\right)^2 - \frac{E^2}{2M}\left(P - \frac{M}{E}\right)^2 \right]$$

Returning now to Figure 6, we see that this function has its maxima at $p = (m/e)$, $P = (M/E)$ An argument entirely analogous to that given for equation (12) shows that the probability that the effectiveness of Tactic 1 is greater than the effectiveness of Tactic 2 is given by the following expression

$$\text{Prob } p > P = F_n\left[\left(\frac{m}{e^2} + \frac{M}{E^2}\right)^{-1/2}\left(\frac{m}{e} - \frac{M}{E}\right)\right], \quad (13)$$

where F_n is the function defined in Chapter 2, equation (24)

By arguments analogous to the discrete case discussed above we can devise a new contour chart which will guide us in our decisions in the continuous case This chart is given in Figure 8 The results of our test operations are expressed in terms of the position of the point (e/E), (n/N) Rules similar to those discussed above for the discrete case with

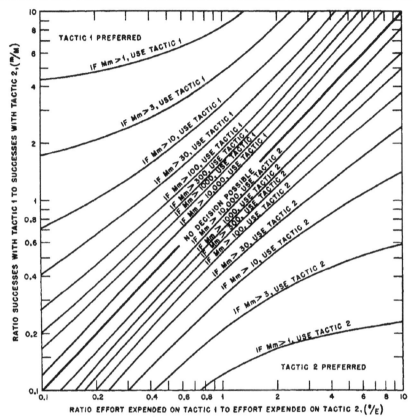

FIGURE 8 Continuous effort e and E expended on Tactics 1 and 2, resulting in m and M successes Rules for future action, based on graph, are given in text

Tactic 1 and 2 reversed, apply here We notice again that it is important to get as many contacts per month as possible, for the enemy is likely to change his tactics

5 4   THEORETICAL ANALYSIS OF COUNTERMEASURE ACTION

The previous subsection considered the case where we were not sure how effective the enemy countermeasure was, nor how often he was using it It also assumed that the enemy's action was slow, so that data taken over a month would represent a particu-lar situation, which could be relied on to hold for another month or so In other cases, however, intelli-gence is more complete and both sides know reason-ably well what the other side can do, and what value the choices have Suppose both sides are keeping watch over the results of each action, and can change from one tactic to another as rapidly as they see what tactic the opponent chooses, if they can gain by change

In this case it pays to analyze the play in advance The enemy has the choice of using a measure or not using it Correspondingly, our own forces have the choice of using a countermeasure or not using it This makes four possible combinations, each of which have a certain value to our side and a corresponding damaging effect to the opposite side This can be illustrated in the following diagram

W_{ij}, Value to our side, or damage to enemy

		Enemy action	
		No use of measure	Use of measure
Our action	No use of counter-measure	W_{11}	W_{12}
	Use of counter-measure	W_{21}	W_{22}

Sometimes W_{21} is smaller than W_{11}, indicating that our use of the countermeasure is a detriment to us if the enemy is not using the measure On the other hand, W_{12} is usually much smaller than W_{22} if the countermeasure is at all effective, and W_{12} is smaller than W_{11} if the measure is to profit the enemy (a small W is best for the enemy) As soon as we know the tactics of the enemy, we must adjust our own tactics so that the value W_{ij} is as large as possible Correspondingly, the enemy will try to adjust his tactics so as to make W as small as possible This is an example of a situation which also occurs in many games Its enunciation is usually called the minimax principle [4] One side wishes to maximize W, and the other wishes to minimize it This has been discussed in connection with equation (1b) of Chapter 4

5 4 1 Definite Case

There are a number of possibilities, which may be analyzed separately The first, which we can call the definite case, occurs when W_{21} is larger than W_{11} (we have already assumed that $W_{22} > W_{12}$ and $W_{11} > W_{12}$) In this case we should always use the countermeasure, for, no matter what the enemy does, we would profit by its use ($W_{21} > W_{11}$ and $W_{22} > W_{12}$) The enemy, if his intelligence is good, would know this, and would choose always to use the measure if $W_{22} < W_{21}$, or not to use it if $W_{21} < W_{22}$ The point here is that, if both sides know the values of all the combinations, they will always prefer the one tactic which will give them the most gain (or the least loss) no matter what the other does A similar case occurs when $W_{11} > W_{21}$, but $W_{21} > W_{22}$, for here it is always to the advantage for the enemy to use his measure

5.4.2 Indefinite Case

The other case, which will be called the indefinite case, for reasons which will shortly become clear, is where $W_{11} > W_{21}$ and $W_{22} > W_{21}$ (we lose by using the countermeasure if the enemy is not using the measure, and the enemy loses by using the measure if we are using the countermeasure) We can see the difficulty if we try to figure out what we should do if the enemy's espionage were perfect, and compare it with what the enemy should do if our espionage were perfect (To make the analysis specific, let us take $W_{22} > W_{11} > W_{12} > W_{11}$) In the first case, if we should decide to use the countermeasure, the enemy, knowing our decision in advance, would use no measure and we would get W_{21}, if we should decide not to use the countermeasure, the enemy would use his measure, and we would get W_{12} Since $W_{21} > W_{12}$, we would prefer to use countermeasures in this case, since W_{21} is the maximin of the array (i e , in each row there is a minimum value; W_{21} is the largest of these) On the other hand, if we knew beforehand that the enemy was going to use his measure, we certainly would use our countermeasure, getting W_{22}, or, if we knew the enemy were not going to use his measure, we would not use our countermeasure, and the result would be W_{11} In such a case, it would behoove the enemy not to use his measure, for $W_{11} < W_{22}$, W_{11} being the minimax of the array (i e , in each column there is a maximum value, W_{11} is the least of these)

The property of the definite case, which makes it definite, is that the minimax is the same as the maximin, so that there is no question as to which each side should do In the indefinite case, however, the minimax is not the same as the maximin, so that it is not obvious what either side should do The correct solution[4] is that neither side should stick to one tactic, but should alternate them at random, with some predetermined relative emphasis between the two choices The difficult part of the problem is the determination of this emphasis.

5.4.3 Solution for the Indefinite Case

To make the problem specific, let us choose values for the W's

		They		
		No measure	Measure	
We	No CM	2	0	(Value
	CM	1	3	to us)

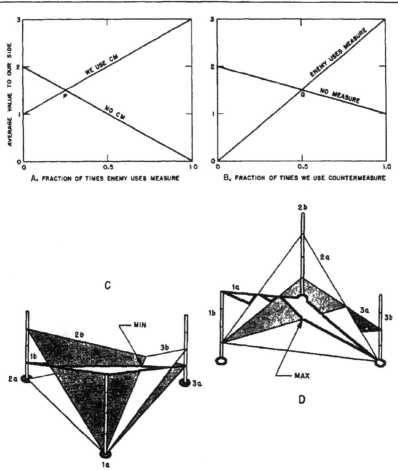

FIGURE 9   Choice of mixed tactics.

Now suppose the enemy varied his tactics, sometimes using the measure and other times not using it We could plot the average return to our side as a function of the percentage of times the enemy used his measure, one curve for when we used the countermeasure, and another for when we did not. These are shown in Figure 9A. We see that the safest mixture for the enemy is to use the measure one-quarter of the time (point P). For if he tries any other mixture we can get better results, for instance, if he uses his measure 50 per cent of the time, we can get best results by using our countermeasure all of the time, and, if he uses his measure only 10 per cent of the time, we can win by not using our countermeasure His mixture of tactics, moreover, must be made completely at random, otherwise we might be able to gain by following his pattern of choice The average value to us is 1 5, if he uses the safest mixture.

We also must protect ourselves by using a random pattern of tactics, as is shown in Figure 9B Unless we use equal amounts of countermeasure and no countermeasure (point Q), the enemy may be able to gain an additional advantage This mixture must also be distributed at random We must, of course, keep track of the enemy's frequency of using his measure, so that if he drifts off point P (or if any of the W's change value) we can adjust our tactics to gain by it

5 4 4　　Case of Three Choices

The problem above was concerned with two choices on the part of each adversary, but similar problems can occur with more choices We can consider the possibility of two different measures (or none) on the part of the enemy, and two possible countermeasures (or none) on our part. This is indicated in the following table where Tactic 3a might be no measure and Tactic 3b might be no countermeasure, with 1a and 2a two different counters

		Side a		
		Tactic 1a	Tactic 2a	Tactic 3a
	Tactic 1b	4	1	1	(Value
Side b	Tactic 2b	0	3	1	
	Tactic 3b	0	0	2	to side b)

Here we must plot the results of mixed tactics on a triangular chart, where the distance in from each edge represents the percentage of use of one of the tactics, and the distance perpendicular to the plane of the triangle is the value to side b Such plots are shown in Figure 9C and D At the edge of each side is a side view giving the traces of the planes representing pure tactics for the other side The shaded parts of the triangle give the best choice of tactic for any mixture of opponent's tactics We see that, if side a uses any mixture other than $\frac{1}{3}$ of 1a, $\frac{2}{3}$ of 2a, and $\frac{4}{3}$ of 3a, side b will be able to gain, if side b uses any other mixture than $\frac{1}{3}$ of 1b, $\frac{1}{3}$ of 2b, and $\frac{1}{3}$ of 3b, side a will be able to make more The net value to side b, if both sides play "correctly," is $\frac{4}{3}$. If side b tried to make more than this, an alert enemy could arrange it so side b would make less Therefore, this mixed solution is the safest solution, presumably it should be used whenever we do not know what the enemy is liable to do, and should only be modified when we are reasonably sure the enemy has departed from his "safe" mixture

5 4.5　　Barrier Patrol for Submarines

There are cases with an infinite variety of choices of tactics and countertactics, where a mixture of tactics is necessary for safety An example is in the (much simplified) problem of the barrier patrol of a plane guarding a channel from passage by a submarine We suppose that the submarine cannot be caught by the plane when it is submerged, but that it can only run a distance a submerged. Each day the plane can fly back and forth across the channel in one part, though the next day it can patrol another part of the channel If it patrols a wide part of the channel it cannot do it as efficiently, but, if it always patrols across the narrowest part, the submarines can dive and elude it The position of patrol along the channel must be varied from day to day so as to keep the submarine from being certain.

The situation is illustrated in Figure 10 A channel of length larger than a is to be patrolled by the planes. If the barrier patrol is at point x and if the submarine attempts to go by on the surface, the probability that the plane will contact the submarine is given by $P(x)$ as shown in the lower half of Figure 10.

As we have said above, the barrier cannot be placed always at the same point x, it must be placed here and there along the channel so that the submarine can never be sure exactly where it is placed. The extent of the range of values of x over which the barrier is placed must, of course, be longer than a; otherwise the submarine could dive under the whole distribution The relative frequency of times the barrier is placed at a point x is proportional to the probability density $\phi(x)$ Since the barrier is to be placed somewhere each day, the integral of ϕ over x must be unity. Side A must then adjust the shape of the curve ϕ so that it gets good results no matter what the submarine does. The submarine can also have a choice of its point of submergence It will always run submerged its maximum distance a It can, of course, come to the surface before a distance a, and resubmerge for the rest of a at some other region in the channel, if this seems best There will be, therefore, a certain probability $\psi(x)$ that the submarine is submerged at the point x The integral of ψ over x must equal a, if the submarine is to have a maximum submerged range of a The submarine (Side B) must, therefore, adjust probability ψ so that it gets as good a result as possible no matter where the barrier is placed

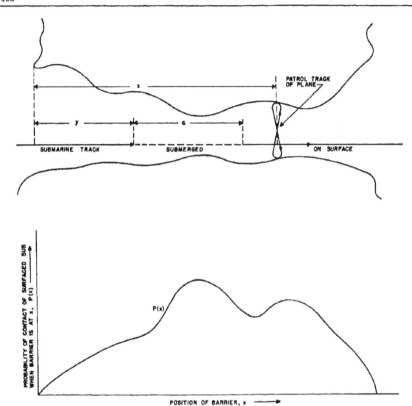

FIGURE 10   Barrier patrol versus diving submarine

This is indicated in the following equations

$P(x)$ = Probability of contact if barrier is at
 x and submarine is surfaced

$\phi(x)$ = Probability density for barrier at x

$$\int \phi(x) dx = 1$$

$\psi(x)$ = Probability that submarine is sub-   (14)
 merged at x $\int \psi(x) dx = a$.

G = Probability of contact

$$= \int P(x)\phi(x)[1 - \psi(x)]dx$$

Side A adjusts the probability density ϕ so that
the probability of contact G is as large as possible and
is independent of the tactics of the submarine, within
reason Conversely, Side B, the submarine, adjusts
the probability of submergence ϕ so that G is as small
as possible and is independent of the placing of the
barrier, within reason The problem is to determine
the function ϕ and ψ for safe tactics for both sides
when the probability P is known

We will first determine the tactics of the submarine, determined by the function ψ Suppose the submarine has chosen a function ψ, and suppose by
chance side A has found out what this function is A
glance at the equation for G shows that, if the quantity, $P(x)[1 - \psi(x)]$, has a maximum value, then

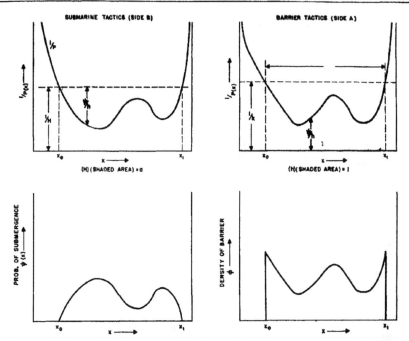

FIGURE 11   Solutions of problem shown in Figure 10 for safe tactics for both sides It turns out that $H = K$, and that the probability for contact G is equal to H, which equals $K = h(L - a)$ Function $\phi(x)$ controls the frequency of placing barrier at point x, and $\psi(x)$ is optimum probability that submarine is submerged at x

Side A will get the best results by placing its barrier always at the x corresponding to this maximum value The submarine would like to make this quantity zero, but this is not possible, since the channel is longer than the maximum range of submergence, a In any case, however, the submarines can choose ψ so that the quantity $P(1 - \psi)$ has *no single maximum*, i e , is flat along the top This is done as follows

Safe tactics for Side B (submarine)

Over as great a range of x as possible, choose ψ so that

$$P(x)[1 - \psi(x)] = H, \text{a constant, i e ,}$$

$$\psi(x) = \begin{cases} 1 - \dfrac{H}{P(x)}, \text{ when } P(x) > H , \\ 0, \text{ when } P(x) < H \end{cases} \quad (15)$$

H is determined by the condition

$$\int \left(1 - \frac{H}{P}\right) dx = a$$

Probability of contact $G \leqq H$

The integral determining H ensures that H is as small as possible If now the barrier is placed anywhere in the range of x where the submarine submerges, the probability of catching the submarine will be H, if the barrier is placed in a position where ψ is zero (where the submarine does not submerge) then we have adjusted things so that the probability of contact G is smaller than H Consequently, this distribution of diving is the best the submarine can manage

The details of the solution are indicated in the two drawings of Figure 11 representing the submarine tactics We plot the reciprocal of the probability P and draw a horizontal dashed line of height $(1/H)$ so adjusted that the area between this dashed line and the $(1/P)$ curve is equal to (a/H) When this is done, the probability of submergence will be proportional to the difference between the horizontal dashed line and the $(1/P)$ curve, as shown in the second drawing The probability of contact is therefore equal to H if the barrier is anywhere in the region between x_0 and x_1, and is less than H if the barrier patrol is placed outside of this range If a is small, it may turn out that the horizontal dashed line must be so low as to break the shaded area into two parts (for the type of P shown) In such a case, it is best for the submarine to submerge in two separated regions, since it must conserve its short range of submergence for those regions where the probability of detection is highest

We must now see what the side controlling the barrier (Side A) is to do about its choice of the density function ϕ Suppose it chooses a particular function ϕ, and suppose the submarine learns what its values are The submarine will then always submerge in those regions where $P(x)\phi(x)$ is largest As with the submarine, therefore, the barrier patrol plans must be made so as *not to have any maxima* for the function $P\phi$ Consequently, no barrier will be flown at positions where the probability P is less than some limiting value K, and, where P is larger than K, the barrier density will be inversely proportional to P, in order that the product $P\phi$ will be constant in these regions The equations corresponding to this requirement are

Safe tactics for Side A (barrier).

Choose $\phi(x)$ so that $P\phi$ is constant over a range of x, i e,

$$\phi(x) = \begin{cases} \dfrac{h}{P(x)}, & \text{when } P(x) > K, \\ 0, & \text{when } P(x) < K, \end{cases} \quad (16)$$

where the range over which $P > K$ is between x_0 and $x_1(x_1 - x_0 = L)$

The value of h is determined by the condition

$$\int_{x_0}^{x_1} \frac{dx}{P(x)} = \left(\frac{1}{h}\right)$$

Probability of contact $G \geqq h(L - a)$, which is maximum when $K = H$.

The problem for the distribution of the barrier is not yet completely solved, since we can vary the value of L and readjust the value of h It certainly would not be advisable to make L smaller than a, for then the submarine could dive completely under the system of barriers On the other hand, it would not do to make L too large, for then h would become too small In fact, we must adjust h and L so that the quantity $h(L - a)$ is a maximum

A certain amount of algebraic juggling must be gone through to show that the requirements that $h(L - a)$ is a maximum correspond to the requirements that $K = H$ In other words, the range of x which is covered by the barrier turns out to be the same range which is covered by the submerging submarine This is, of course, reasonable, for any overlap on the part of either side would represent waste motion and reduced effectiveness The technique for obtaining the distribution for barrier patrol ϕ is shown in the right-hand curves in Figure 11 One again plots the reciprocal of $P(x)$, chooses K equal to H and the end point x_0 and x_1 to be the same as in the analysis for the submarine We choose the normalizing factor h to be such that h times the area shaded in the right-hand figure equals unity Therefore, the best the submarine can do, if the barrier patrol is fully alert, and the best the barrier patrol can do, if the submarine commander is clever, is the set of tactics defined by equations (15) and (16), with the resulting probability of contact given below

Safe tactics for both sides

Integration is carried out over that region of x where $P(x) > H$ The constant H is related to the maximum submerged range a by

$$H = h(L - a), \quad \text{where } \frac{1}{h} = \int \frac{dx}{P(x)},$$

and $L = \int dx$ is the total range of x over which P is greater than H. The probability of submergence for the submarine is then given in equation (15), the barrier density is

$$\phi(x) = \begin{cases} \dfrac{H}{(L - a)P(x)}, & P(x) > H, \\ 0, & P(x) < H, \end{cases} \quad (17)$$

and the probability of contact of plane and submarine is

$$G = H = h(L - a) = \frac{L - a}{\displaystyle\int \frac{dx}{P(x)}}.$$

A number of other examples might be considered, where this method of analysis of tactic and counter-tactic would be useful. The difficulties at present are in finding a general technique for the solution of such problems The studies of Von Neumann and Morgenstern[4] show that there *are* solutions to each problem and show the general nature of these solutions They do not show, however, the technique for obtaining a solution. We have seen examples of the problems and how their solutions can be obtained in three cases A great deal more work needs to be done in finding solutions to various examples before we can say that we know the subject thoroughly.

It is to be hoped that further mathematical research can be undertaken on this interesting and fruitful subject

Chapter 6

GUNNERY AND BOMBARDMENT PROBLEMS

IN THIS CHAPTER we shall consider a class of problems which arise in the evaluation of such weapons as guns, bombs, and torpedoes, and in analyzing the best methods for their use All these weapons are used for the destruction of targets, such as ships, gun emplacements, factories, and the like The effectiveness of any such weapon against a given kind of target can be measured, at least in part, by the ratio of the number of targets destroyed to the number of shells, bombs, or torpedoes used

The majority of this sort of analysis should, of course, be carried out by scientists in the service laboratories, where the weapons are designed or produced However, the operations research worker should be familiar with the techniques of evaluating weapon performance, and should know enough about the behavior of the weapon to be able to analyze its action if necessary The operations research worker often is useful as a technical adviser to the *users* of equipment giving unbiased advice on technical details of use, although his primary task is the broader one of helping fit equipment, personnel, training, intelligence, etc , into an effective *operation* This chapter is included, as was Chapter 2, because it is believed that ability in the broader problems is improved by mastery of the narrower technical details

The number of shells, bombs, or torpedoes required, on the average, to destroy a target depends on two primary factors, the destructiveness of the weapon, i e , the probability that the target is destroyed if the weapon hits it, and the accuracy of the weapon, i e , the probability that the weapon will hit the target In addition, if weapons are used in groups rather than singly (for example, spreads of torpedoes, sticks of bombs) the result depends on the firing pattern used In this chapter we shall describe methods of calculating the probabilities of destroying targets, and of determining the patterns which create the maximum destruction

6 1   THE DESTRUCTIVENESS OF WEAPONS—LETHAL AREA

The simplest case of measurement of destructiveness occurs when the weapon must hit the target in order to destroy it, but always does destroy the target if it hits Such a case is found, for example, in use of medium-caliber (e g , 5-inch) shells against open gun emplacements. The walls of such emplacements are, in general, strong enough to protect the guns and men within them against the blast and fragments from shells which strike outside the emplacement, whereas, if such a shell hits inside the emplacement, both guns and men are destroyed The probability that a shell destroy the emplacement is therefore just the probability that the shell hits a certain area, called the *lethal area* The magnitude of the lethal area is a measure of the destructiveness of the shell against these targets

As a slightly more complicated example, let us consider some cases of antisubmarine ordnance The simplest case is that of a small contact charge (hedgehog or mousetrap) This situation is very similar to the last the charge must hit the submarine to destroy it, and it is usually assumed that a single hit is sufficient to cripple the submarine In this case the lethal area is the area of the horizontal cross section of the submarine or, better, of its pressure hull

If we consider the case of a depth charge with a proximity (or influence) fuze, it is no longer necessary actually to hit the submarine to destroy it, for the proximity fuze will convert a near miss into a destructive explosion We let R be the radius of action of the proximity fuze If the charge is sufficient so that an explosion within this radius from the submarine will sink the submarine, then the lethal area is increased to the area included within a curve surrounding the horizontal cross section of the submarine, at a distance R from its boundary Finally, if we consider the case of the depth charge set to explode at a preset depth, we no longer have a lethal area at all, but a lethal volume, for, to sink the submarine, the depth charge must explode within the volume enclosed by a surface surrounding the submarine at a distance equal to the lethal radius of the depth charges

6 1 1   Multiple Hits

In many cases a single hit is not enough to destroy a target A typical case is that of a torpedo hitting a ship Even for merchant ships a single torpedo hit is not usually enough to sink it, and heavy combatant ships are designed to withstand many torpedo hits To treat such cases exactly, we should determine the probabilities D_1, D_2, D_3, etc , of sinking the ship if the ship is hit 1, 2, 3, etc , times Then, if, for a given method of firing torpedoes, the probabilities of 1, 2, 3, etc , hits are P_1, P_2, P_3, etc , the probability of sinking the ship would be

$$P_s = D_1 P_1 + D_2 P_2 + D_3 P_3 + \cdots \qquad (1)$$

The probabilities D_1, D_2, D_3, etc , are sometimes called the *damage coefficients*

As a matter of operational experience it has been found that the damage coefficients in many cases are related, to a very good approximation, by the law

$$D_n = 1 - (1 - D_1)^n , \qquad (2)$$

which is just the law of composition of independent probabilities (see Chapter 2) In other words, the chance of sinking a ship with any torpedo hit is always the same, regardless of how many previous hits there have been This may be interpreted as meaning that a torpedo will only sink a ship if it hits a "vital spot," and that hits on other than vital spots will damage, but not sink, the ship This "vital spot" hypothesis, while not to be taken too seriously as an actual description of what happens when ships are hit by torpedoes, does serve to reduce the number of unknown quantities D_n to one, and has been found to give fairly satisfactory results in many cases, not only for sinking cargo ships by torpedoes, but also in many other cases, such as AA hits on aircraft However, it is not a very good approximation for battleships, with many compartments

When the "vital spot" theory can be applied, the *lethal area* of a target is defined as the product of the effective area of the target and the probability D (the same as our previous D_1) that a hit on this area will destroy the target For example, a torpedo hit on a merchant vessel has a probability of about 1/3 sinking the ship Hence $D = 1/3$, and the lethal area is 1/3 of the length of the ship

In some problems it is necessary to take into account the variation of the probability of destroying the target as a function of the point at which the hit is made If we consider, for example, the effect of proximity-fuzed AA shells on aircraft, the probability of destruction is high if a shell hits or passes very close to the aircraft As the trajectory moves further

away from the aircraft the probability of destruction decreases until finally a distance is reached at which the fuze is no longer activated, and the chance of destruction falls to zero In such cases we must express this probability as a function $D(x,y)$, the *damage function*, where x and y are coordinates centered on the target in a plane perpendicular to the trajectories When this has been done, the lethal area may be defined as

$$L = \iint D(x, y) dx dy , \qquad (3)$$

where the integration is over all the area for which $D(x, y)$ is greater than zero It is easy to see that the simpler definitions of lethal area are included in (3) as special cases in which $D(x, y)$ has a constant value over the target area The modification of (3) to cases of one- or three-dimensional targets is obvious

6 1 2   Random or Area Bombardment

In cases where bombs or shells are dropped at random over an area, the lethal area is sufficient to determine the destruction which will be caused For any given target in the area, the chance that a given bomb or shell will hit the element of area $dx dy$ is just $(dx dy / A)$, where A is the total area bombarded The probability that this bomb or shell will destroy the target is therefore

$$P_1 = \int D(x, y) \frac{dx dy}{A} , \qquad (4)$$

or

$$P_1 = \frac{L}{A} \qquad (5)$$

If n bombs or shells are dropped, the probability that a given target is destroyed is

$$P_n = 1 - e^{-nL/A} . \qquad (6)$$

This is not only the probability that one particular target is destroyed, but also represents the expected fraction of all the targets in the area which are destroyed The result is a generalization of that given in Section 5 2

As a numerical example, let us suppose that an area of 1 square (nautical) mile is to be bombed with 1,000-pound GP bombs The area contains 100 gun emplacements (each of lethal area 400 square feet) and personnel in trenches [total lethal area per man, determined by equation (3) of 900 square feet] Since 1 square mile is 36,000,000 square feet, the ratio L/A is 1/90,000 for the gun emplacements, and 1/40,000 for the personnel A plot of the fraction of the gun emplacements and personnel destroyed, as a function of n, is shown in Figure 1 It will be noted that

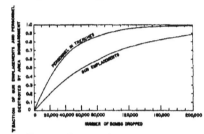

FIGURE 1   Destruction by area bombardment

an enormous expenditure of ammunition is required to accomplish much destruction by area bombardment

8.1 3   Aimed Fire—Small Targets

We now consider the case in which the bombs or shells are not distributed at random over an area, but are each individually aimed at a target For the present, however, we shall suppose that the target dimensions are small compared to the aiming errors When this is the case, we may neglect the variation over the target area in the probability of hitting an area element $dxdy$, and again the lethal area is sufficient to determine the destructiveness

If the bombing errors follow the normal distribution law (usually a safe assumption), with a standard deviation in range σ_r, and a standard deviation in deflection σ_d, then the probability of hitting the area element $dxdy$ at x, y, where x is the range error and y the deflection error, is

$$P(x,y)dxdy = \frac{1}{2\pi\sigma_r\sigma_d}\, e^{-(x^2/2\sigma_r^2)-(y^2/2\sigma_d^2)}\, dxdy\, . \quad (7)$$

Near the target this has the value

$$P(0,0)dxdy = \frac{dxdy}{2\pi\sigma_r\sigma_d}\, .$$

The probability of destroying the target with a single bomb or shell is

$$P_1 = \iint \frac{D(x,y)dxdy}{2\pi\sigma_r\sigma_d} \cong \frac{L}{2\pi\sigma_r\sigma_d}\, . \quad (8)$$

If n bombs or shells are dropped *independently*, the probability of destruction is

$$P_n = 1 - \left(1 - \frac{L}{2\pi\sigma_r\sigma_d}\right)^n .$$

Since by hypothesis L is small compared to $\sigma_r\sigma_d$, this is approximately

$$P_n = 1 - e^{-nL/2\pi\sigma_r\sigma_d} \quad (9)$$

To compare this result with the case of area bombardment, let us consider that the square mile of our last example contained 100 gun emplacements (each of lethal area 400 square feet), and that the standard deviations of the bombing errors, σ_r and σ_d, are each 200 feet Then the ratio $L/2\pi\sigma_r\sigma_d = 400/(2\pi)(200)^2 = 1/600$ approximately The number of bombs which we must expect to drop to destroy all 100 emplacements would be 60,000 bombs It should be noted that this is the number which would be required if each target was bombed until it was destroyed If it were arbitrarily decided to drop 600 bombs on each gun emplacement, then by equation (9) the fraction destroyed would be $(1 - e^{-1})$ or 0 63, a much poorer showing

6 1.4   Aimed Fire—Large Targets

When the assumption can no longer be made that the target area is small compared to the aiming errors, it becomes necessary to consider the variation of the probability of hitting an area element $dxdy$ over the target area, and the idea of lethal area loses most of its usefulness If $f(x, y)dxdy$ is the probability of hitting an area element, the chance that the target is destroyed by a single shot becomes

$$P_1 = \iint D(x,y)f(x,y)dxdy\, , \quad (10)$$

and further progress depends on our ability to evaluate this integral Once evaluated, however, we have, as before, the result that the expected number of shots to destroy the target is $1/P_1$, and the probability of destroying the target in n shots is

$$P_n = 1 - (1 - P_1)^n, \qquad (11)$$

which, if P_1 is small, can be written

$$P_n = 1 - e^{-nP_1} \qquad (12)$$

If $D(x,y)$ has a constant value D over the target area, then equation (10) represents just the chance of hitting the target, multiplied by D If the target is of simple shape, and the probability density $f(x, y)$ is not too complicated, then the evaluation can be carried out As an example of this type of calculation, consider the following problem

A submarine fires torpedoes at a merchant ship 200 feet long, and at a track angle of 90 degrees The errors in firing are normally distributed with a standard error of 100 mils (somewhat larger than the errors experienced in World War II, but taken here as an example), its shots are fired from 2,000 yards, and the probability of sinking due to a torpedo hit is $1/3$ We wish to know the chance of sinking the ship with n shots, each fired independently

The standard deviation of the torpedoes in distance along the target's track is $100/1,000 \times 2,000 = 200$ yards or 600 feet Hence the probability of an error of between x and $x + dx$ feet measured from the center of the target is

$$\frac{1}{\sqrt{2\pi}\ 600} \exp\left(-\frac{x^2}{2(600)^2}\right) dx$$

The probability of hitting the ship is therefore

$$\int_{-100}^{100} \frac{1}{\sqrt{2\pi}\ 600} e^{-(x^2/2\ 600^2)} dx$$

$$= \frac{1}{\sqrt{2\pi}} \int_{-1/6}^{1/6} e^{-(y^2/2)}\ dy = 0\ 132$$

The chance of sinking the ship is $1/3$ of this or $0\ 044$ The probability of sinking the ship with $1, 2, \quad \cdot\ 6$ torpedoes is given in the following table

No torpedoes	Prob. of sinking
1	0 044
2	0 086
3	0 126
4	0 165
5	0 202
6	0 237

The expected number of torpedoes required to sink the ship is 23

As a second example, let us consider the gun emplacements we have considered before Let us consider them to be circular, with a radius of 11 feet, and let $D(x, y) = 1$ inside this radius, and 0 outside. We shall suppose that the standard deviations of the errors in range and deflection are now 50 feet, instead of the previous values Then

$$\phi(x, y)dxdy = \frac{1}{2\pi(50)^2} e^{-(x^2+y^2)/2(50)^2} dxdy$$

$$= \frac{1}{2\pi(50)^2} e^{-r^2/2(50)^2}\ r\ drd\theta$$

where r and θ are the usual plane polar coordinates. Then

$$P_1 = \int_0^{2\pi}\int_0^{11} \frac{1}{2\pi(50)^2} e^{-r^2/2(50)^2} rdrd\theta$$

$$= \int_0^{11/50} e^{-(\rho^2/2)} \rho d\rho = \left[-e^{-(\rho^2/2)}\right]_0^{11/50}$$

$$= 0\ 0239$$

If this is compared with the small-target result

$$P_1 = \frac{\pi(11)^2}{2\pi(50)^2} = 0\ 0242\ ,$$

we see that the agreement is very good If, on the other hand, the radius had been 50 feet, then

$$P_1 = \int_0^1 e^{-(\rho^2/2)} \rho d\rho = \left[-e^{-(\rho^2/2)}\right]_0^1 = 0\ 39\ ,$$

while the small-target approximation would have given

$$P_1 = \frac{\pi(50)^2}{2\pi(50)^2} = 0\ 50\ .$$

In this case the small-target approximation is not satisfactory

6 2   PATTERN FIRING—NO BALLISTIC DISPERSION

There are many tactical situations where it is advantageous to fire several shots (or torpedoes, or bombs) more or less simultaneously, instead of aiming each shot individually and firing consecutively

They can all be fired in the same direction (*salvo firing*), or each shot can be displaced a predetermined amount with respect to the others (*pattern firing*), the relative advantages of the two methods are determined by the errors involved There is, first, the error in the aiming of the salvo or the center of the pattern, this is called the *aiming error* Secondly, there is the spread of the individual shots as they travel toward the target, converting the salvo into an irregular pattern, and changing a regular pattern into an irregular one, this is called the *ballistic error*

If the dispersion of the ballistic errors is larger than the dispersion of the aiming errors and also larger than the lethal area of the target, the best one can do is to fire a salvo (zero pattern spread) On the other hand, if the aiming dispersion is larger than the ballistic dispersion and also larger than the lethal dimensions of the target, it is usually better to use pattern firing When salvos are fired, if the ballistic errors are very small, the shots will either all hit or none will hit, whereas, if the shots are spread into a pattern, it will be more likely that at least one shot hits This is the shotgun method, as opposed to the rifle Since this case often occurs in practice, it is important to study methods for determining optimum pattern shape and size

To bring out the fundamental principles involved, we shall first consider that the ballistic dispersion is negligible compared to the aiming dispersion If a regular pattern is fired, a regular pattern will arrive near the target We shall soon see that, if the pattern is too small, either several shots will hit or they will all miss, as the pattern size is increased, the chance of at least one hit increases to a maximum, representing the optimum pattern For still larger patterns the probability of at least one hit decreases again This is the basic philosophy of dropping bombs in sticks or firing torpedoes in spreads

6 2 1   Example from Train Bombing

The fundamental problem to be solved in pattern firing is that of finding the best pattern to use To illustrate, let us consider the following simple case A plane carries two bombs to attack a single-track railroad A single bomb hit within 25 feet of the center of the track is sufficient to destroy the track The plane therefore flies along a course perpendicular to the track, and drops a pattern of two bombs, spaced a distance 2a apart, aiming the midpoint of the pattern at the center of the track We wish to determine the best stick spacing

If the error of aiming the pattern is x, i e, if the midpoint of the pattern falls a distance x beyond the track, then the track is destroyed if $-25 < (-a + x) < 25$, or if $-25 < (a + x) < 25$ We may therefore introduce the *pattern damage function*, $D_p(x)$, the probability that the target is destroyed if the center of the pattern falls at the point x, which is given, in this case, by

$$D_p(x) = \begin{cases} 1, \text{ if } -25 < (-a + x) < 25 \text{, or} \\ \quad -25 < (a + x) < 25 \\ 0, \text{ otherwise} \end{cases}$$

If $f_p(x)(dx)$ is the probability that the center of the pattern falls in the element dx, then the probability of destroying the target is

$$P(a) = \int D_p(x) f_p(x)(dx) . \tag{13}$$

This equation is completely analogous to equation (10) It will be noted, however, that the pattern spacing enters this as a parameter The best pattern is that which makes $P(a)$ a maximum

In the present case, equation (13) reduces to the form

$$P(a) = \begin{cases} \int_{-a-25}^{a+25} f_p(x)(dx) & (a < 25) \\ \int_{-a-25}^{-a+25} f_p(x)dx + \int_{a-25}^{a+25} \phi_p(x)dx & (a > 25) \end{cases} \tag{14}$$

In every practical case the aiming error has a normal distribution, so that, if σ is the standard deviation of the aiming error,

$$f_p(x) = \frac{1}{\sqrt{2\pi}\,\sigma} e^{-x^2/2\sigma^2}$$

Then

$$P(a) = \begin{cases} \dfrac{1}{\sqrt{2\pi}\,\sigma} \displaystyle\int_{-a-25}^{a+25} e^{-x^2/2\sigma^2}\,dx \\ \quad = \dfrac{2}{\sqrt{2\pi}} \displaystyle\int_{0}^{(a+25)/\sigma} e^{-\xi^2/2}\,d\xi, \quad (a < 25) \\[4pt] \dfrac{1}{\sqrt{2\pi}\,\sigma} \displaystyle\int_{-a-25}^{-a+25} e^{-x^2/2\sigma^2}\,dx \\ \quad + \dfrac{1}{\sqrt{2\pi}\,\sigma} \displaystyle\int_{a-25}^{a+25} e^{-x^2/2\sigma^2}\,dx \\ \quad = \dfrac{2}{\sqrt{2\pi}} \displaystyle\int_{(a-25)/\sigma}^{(a+25)/\sigma} e^{-\xi^2/2}\,d\xi \quad (a > 25). \end{cases} \tag{15}$$

In the range $0 < a < 25$, $P(a)$ is obviously increasing, while in the range $25 < a < \infty$, $P(a)$ is decreasing $P(a)$ is therefore maximum for $a = 25$ Hence the

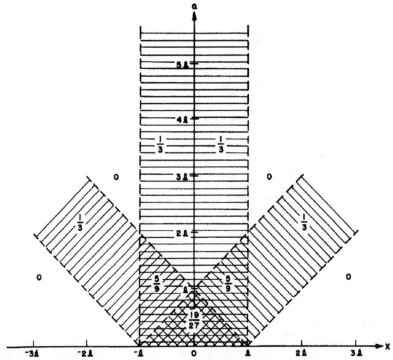

FIGURE. 2   Damage function for spread of three torpedoes No ballistic dispersion $D_p = 19/27$ in triple-shaded region, 5/9 in double-shaded region, 1/3 in single-shaded region, 0 in unshaded region

best stick spacing is $2a = 50$ feet This is obvious without calculation for the present simple case, but in many cases the analysis is necessary to obtain the correct answer

It is of some interest to compare the chance of destruction in the three cases (1) two bombs dropped together in salvo, (2) two bombs spaced 50 feet, (3) two bombs dropped on separate runs over the target The chances of destruction in the three cases are

Case (1) $P_a = \dfrac{2}{\sqrt{2\pi}} \displaystyle\int_0^{2a/\sigma} e^{-\frac{1}{2}\xi^2}\, d\xi\,,$

Case (2) $P_b = \dfrac{2}{\sqrt{2\pi}} \displaystyle\int_0^{50/\sigma} e^{-\frac{1}{2}\xi^2}\, d\xi\,,$

Case (3) $P_c = 1 - (1 - P_a)^2 = 2P_a - P_a^2$

The values of these probabilities, for a number of values of σ, are shown in the following table

Table of probability of destroying railroad track
(at least one hit)

P_a = probability with 2 bombs in salvo,
P_b = probability with 2 bombs, 50 feet spacing,
P_c = probability with 2 independent bombs

Standard deviation of bombing error (σ)	P_a	P_b	P_c
10 ft	0 9876	1 0000	0 9998
20	0 7888	0 9876	0 9554
30	0 5934	0 9050	0 8347
40	0 4680	0 7888	0 7170
50	0 3830	0 6828	0 6193
60	0 3256	0 5934	0 5452
70	0 3812	0 5222	0 4833
80	0 2434	0 4680	0 4276
90	0 2206	0 4246	0 3925
100	0 1974	0 3830	0 3558

One sees that as long as ballistic errors are negligible, and as long as only one hit is needed for destruction, the salvo is never as effective as the pattern or as independent bombs

As a second simple example, suppose that a submarine, knowing it can fire only one spread of three torpedoes at a ship, wishes to obtain the greatest probability of sinking the ship We shall suppose that the torpedoes run perfectly true, that the center torpedo is aimed at the center of the target, and the other two are equally spaced on either side We shall assume the vital spot hypothesis with $D_1 = 1/3$, so that with one hit the chance of sinking the ship is $1/3$, with two hits, $5/9$, and with three hits, $19/27$. Let $2l$ be the length of the ship, and a the distance apart, at the ship, of adjacent torpedoes in the spread Let x be the aiming error of the spread. The damage function for any value of x and a will be that shown in Figure 2 (the three bands in the figure are the regions in which each of the torpedoes hit) Applying this to equation (13), and assuming normal aiming errors, we find

$$P(a) = \begin{cases} \dfrac{19}{27} \dfrac{2}{\sqrt{2\pi}} \displaystyle\int_0^{(l-a)/\sigma} e^{-u^2/2}du \\[2mm] + \dfrac{5}{9} \dfrac{2}{\sqrt{2\pi}} \displaystyle\int_{(l-a)/\sigma}^{l/\sigma} e^{-u^2/2}du \\[2mm] + \dfrac{1}{3} \dfrac{2}{\sqrt{2\pi}} \displaystyle\int_{l/\sigma}^{(l+a)/\sigma} e^{-u^2/2}du, \quad (a \le l) \\[3mm] \dfrac{1}{3} \dfrac{2}{\sqrt{2\pi}} \displaystyle\int_0^{(a-l)/\sigma} e^{-u^2/2}du \\[2mm] + \dfrac{5}{9} \dfrac{2}{\sqrt{2\pi}} \displaystyle\int_{a(-l)/\sigma}^{l/\sigma} e^{-u^2/2}du \\[2mm] + \dfrac{1}{3} \dfrac{2}{\sqrt{2\pi}} \displaystyle\int_{l/\sigma}^{(a+l)/\sigma} e^{-u^2/2}du, \quad (l \le a \le 2l) \\[3mm] \dfrac{1}{3} \dfrac{2}{\sqrt{2\pi}} \displaystyle\int_0^{l/\sigma} e^{-u^2/2}du \\[2mm] + \dfrac{1}{3} \dfrac{2}{\sqrt{2\pi}} \displaystyle\int_{(a-l)/\sigma}^{(a+l)/\sigma} e^{-u^2/2}du, \quad (2l \le a) \end{cases}$$

The curves of $P(a)$ against a for a number of values of σ are shown in Figure 3 The curve of the optimum value of a as a function of σ is shown in Figure 4

6 2 2　　　The Squid Problem

As a somewhat more complicated example, we shall now consider the problem of determining the

effectiveness of the antisubmarine device known as *Squid* This is a device which throws three proximity-fuzed depth charges ahead of the launching ship in a triangular pattern In order to simplify the problem we shall make the assumption that the heading of the submarine is known, and also the assumption

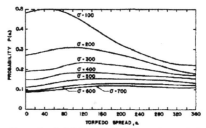

FIGURE 3　Probability of sinking ship with spread of three torpedoes

that the aiming errors are distributed in a circular normal fashion, with the same standard deviation for all depths We shall also assume that, if a single depth charge passes within a lethal radius R of the submarine, the submarine will be sunk We wish to determine the best pattern for the depth charges

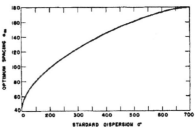

FIGURE 4　Optimum spread as a function of dispersion of aiming errors

For any given pattern, the pattern damage function depends on two variables, x and y, the aiming errors along and perpendicular to the course of the submarine For any pair of values of x and y, $D_p(x, y)$ is 1 if the submarine is sunk, and 0 otherwise A typical case is shown in Figure 5 The origin is the point of aim, and the positions of the depth charges in the pattern are indicated by crosses Each possible position of the center of the submarine is represented by a point in this plane (Note that x and y are actually the *negatives* of the aiming errors) The three shaded regions represent the positions at which the submarine is destroyed by each of the three depth charges. The pattern damage function is 1 inside the shaded regions, and 0 in the unshaded regions.

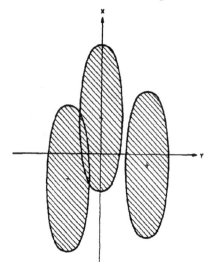

FIGURE 5   Damage function for *Squid* pattern

Let $f(x, y) dxdy$ be the probability that the center of the submarine be in the area element $dxdy$ Then the probability of destroying the submarine is

$$P = \int D(x,y)f(x,y)dxdy$$

$$= \int_D f(x,y)dxdy \qquad (16)$$

In the last equation the region D of integration is just the shaded area in Figure 5 Because of the irregular shape of this region, analytical evaluation of this integral is impractical, and graphical methods must be used In problems of this type a very convenient aid is a form of graph paper known as "circular probability paper." This paper is divided into cells in such a way that, if a point is chosen from a circular normal distribution, the point is equally likely to fall in any of the cells. If an area is drawn on the paper, the chance of a point falling inside the area is proportional to the number of cells in the area It

follows that the integral of equation (16) can be easily evaluated by drawing the damage function to the proper scale on circular probability paper, and counting the cells in the shaded area

This method gives a rapid means of finding the probability of destroying the submarine with any given pattern To find the best pattern, we note that changing the position of any one of the depth charges amounts to shifting the corresponding shaded area in Figure 5 parallel to itself to the new position If three templates are made by cutting the outline of the shaded area for a single depth charge out of a sheet of transparent material, to the correct scale to go with the circular probability paper, then the best pattern can be found by moving the templates around on a sheet of circular probability paper until the number of cells within the lethal area is a maximum

6 3   PATTERN FIRING—BALLISTIC DISPERSION PRESENT

Up to this point we have neglected the fact that bombs, shells, and torpedoes do not hit the exact point they are aimed at, even if the aim is perfect. The dispersion of the errors arising from this source is called the *ballistic dispersion* of the projectiles We shall always assume that these errors are independent of each other, and of the aiming error of the pattern as a whole

As a result of the ballistic dispersion we cannot tell the exact number of hits which will be obtained with a given pattern, even if we know the exact aiming error made We can, however, calculate the probabilities of 0, 1, 2, hits for each possible aiming error, and combining these with the damage coefficients we can find the probability of destroying the target as a function of the aiming error We thus calculate a *pattern damage function* which can be used exactly like the one we have treated previously for the case of no ballistic dispersion

To illustrate the effect of ballistic dispersion, let us reconsider the problem of the airplane dropping bombs on a railroad Let us suppose again that two bombs are dropped, and that a hit by either within 25 feet of the track will destroy the track Let us suppose that the standard deviation of the error of the aiming of the stick is 100 feet and that there is a ballistic dispersion of 25 feet for the bombs

Before calculating the damage function for a stick of bombs, let us first find the probability of destroying the railroad with a bomb aimed so that if there were no ballistic dispersion it would hit at a distance y from the center of the track This is easily seen to be

$$F(y) = \frac{1}{\sqrt{2\pi}(25)} \int_{-y-25}^{-y+25} e^{-x^2/2(25)^2} dx$$

$$= \frac{1}{\sqrt{2\pi}} \int_{-(y/25)-1}^{-(y/25)+1} e^{-u^2/2} du \qquad (17)$$

The form of this function is shown as the solid curve in Figure 6 [If there had been no ballistic error, $F(y)$

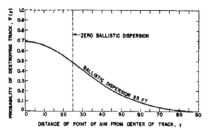

FIGURE 6   Probability of destroying railroad with one bomb as function of aiming error (ballistic dispersion included)

would have been unity for $|y| < 25$ and zero for $|y| > 25$, as shown by the dotted curve in the figure]

Now if the bombs are dropped with stick spacing $2a$ the values of y for the two bombs are $x - a$ and $x + a$, where x is the bombing error Since the ballistic dispersion of each bomb is independent of the other, the damage function is therefore

$$D_p(x) = 1 - \{[1 - F(x-a)][1 - F(x+a)]\},$$
$$D_p(x) = F(x-a) + F(x+a) - F(x-a)F(x+a) \qquad (18)$$

The damage function for $a = 25$ feet is plotted in Figure 7 to illustrate its form (If there had been no ballistic error, D_p would have been unity for $|x| < 50$ feet and zero for $|x| > 50$ feet as shown in the figure) When the damage function has been found, we take into account the distribution of the aiming errors, so that the probability of destruction is, by equation (10),

$$P(a) = \frac{1}{\sqrt{2\pi}(100)} \int D_p(x) e^{-x^2/2(100)^2} dx \qquad (19)$$

The evaluation of this integral is best made graphically A plot of $P(a)$ as a function of a then shows

the best value of a, and the probability of success. Such a plot is shown in Figure 8, with the corresponding curve for no ballistic dispersion It will be seen that the ballistic dispersion requires an increase in

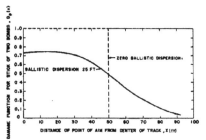

FIGURE 7   Damage function for stick of two bombs (ballistic dispersion included)

stick spacing from 50 feet to 85 feet, and has the effect of lowering the chances of success from 0 38 to 0 34

6 3 1 Approximate Solution for Large Patterns

The method of solution given in the previous section becomes very laborious for large patterns, particularly if one has no previous idea as to the correct

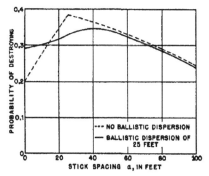

FIGURE 8   Probability of destroying railroad with stick of two bombs as a function of stick spacing

pattern to use In this section we shall describe an approximate treatment of the problem which can be used to obtain solutions more quickly for large patterns If more accurate results are required, this solution may serve as a starting point for a solution by exact methods

Consider a coordinate system fixed at the center of the pattern Because of ballistic dispersion there is probability $f(x,y)dxdy$ that a projectile will hit the area element $dxdy$ The integral

$$N = \iint f(x, y) \, dxdy \qquad (20)$$

is equal to the number of projectiles in the pattern By changing the pattern we can cause extensive changes in the function $f(x, y)$. Our approximation will consist of the assumption that $f(x, y)$ can be changed *arbitrarily* by shifting the pattern, subject only to the condition that equation (20) remains satisfied We can call f the *pattern density function*

If the lethal area of the target is L, then the expected number of lethal hits on the target, if the center of the target is at x, y, is $Lf(x, y)$ Assuming that the number of lethal hits is given by the Poisson law, the probability of at least one lethal hit, and hence the probability of destroying the target, is

$$D(x, y) = 1 - e^{-Lf(x\,y)} \qquad (21)$$

We shall therefore take this as our approximation to the pattern damage function

The total probability of destroying the target is then by equation (10)

$$P = \iint [1 - e^{-Lf(x\,y)}]f_p(x, y)dxdy \qquad (22)$$

where f_p is the probability density for aiming the pattern, usually the normal density We wish to find the function $f(x, y)$ which maximizes P, subject to the condition (20) To determine the maximum let us consider the effect of increasing $f(x, y)$ by a small amount δ in an element at x_1, y_1, and decreasing (x, y) by an equal amount δ at the point x_2, y_2. This obviously does not change the value of N in (20), and changes P by an amount (to the first order).

$$[e^{-Lf(x_1\,y_1)}f_p(x_1, y_1) - e^{-Lf(x_2\,y_2)}f_p(x_2, y_2)]\,\delta dxdy$$

When neither $f(x_1, y_1)$ nor $f(x_2, y_2)$ is 0, $[f(x, y)$ cannot be negative, but may vanish] then, if

$$e^{-Lf(x_1,y_1)}f_p(x_1, y_1) > e^{-Lf(x_2,y_2)}f_p(x_2, y_2),$$

P can be increased by a positive choice of δ If

$$e^{-Lf(x_1,y_1)}f_p(x_1, y_1) < e^{-Lf(x_2,y_2)}f_p(x_2, y_2),$$

then P can be increased by a negative choice of δ Hence for the function $f(x, y)$ which makes P a maximum, we must have

$$e^{-Lf(x_1\,y_1)}f_p(x_1, y_1) = e^{-Lf(x_2,y_2)}f_p(x_2, y_2)$$

for all pairs of points at which $f(x, y) > 0$ Hence for all such points

$$e^{-Lf(x\,y)}f_p(x, y) = \phi_0, \qquad (23)$$

where ϕ_0 is some positive constant

Now let x_1, y_1 be a point, as before, where $f(x, y) > 0$, and let x_2, y_2 be a point at which $f(x, y) = 0$ Then if we *decrease* $p(x_1, y_1)$ by a small amount δ (which must now be positive) and *increase* $f(x_2, y_2)$ by this amount, then P is increased by the amount

$$[f_p(x_2, y_2) - e^{-Lf(x_1,y_1)}f_p(x_1, y_1)]\,\delta dxdy$$
$$= [f_p(x_2, y_2) - \phi_0]\delta dxdy .$$

This is positive if $f_p(x_2, y_1) > \phi_0$ Hence $p(x, y)$ cannot vanish unless

$$f_p(x, y) \le \phi_0 \qquad (24)$$

From (23) and (24) we find our solution

$$f(x, y) = \begin{cases} \dfrac{1}{L} \ln \left[\dfrac{f_p(x, y)}{\phi_0} \right], & f_p(x, y) > \phi_0 \\[3mm] 0, & f_p(x, y) \le \phi_0 \end{cases} \qquad (25)$$

The unknown constant ϕ_0 remains to be determined. It must be chosen so that (20) is satisfied, i e , so that

$$N = \frac{1}{L} \iint_{f > \phi_0} \ln \left[\frac{f(x, y)}{\phi_0} \right] dxdy . \qquad (26)$$

In some cases ϕ_0 can be found analytically, in others it must be found graphically by plotting the integral on the right of (26) as a function of ϕ_0 Compare this detailed analysis with the preliminary discussion in Section 5 2.

The most important special case of this treatment

is that in which the probability density for aiming the pattern, $f_p(x, y)$, is the normal distribution

$$f_p(x, y) = \frac{1}{2\pi\sigma_x\sigma_y} \exp\left[-\frac{1}{2}\left(\frac{x^2}{\sigma_x^2} + \frac{y^2}{\sigma_y^2}\right)\right].$$

For this case (25) becomes

$$f(x, y) = \frac{1}{L}\left[-\ln(2\pi\sigma_x\sigma_y) - \frac{1}{2}\left(\frac{x^2}{\sigma_x^2} + \frac{y^2}{\sigma_y^2}\right) - \ln\phi_0\right],$$

over the region where this is positive, and $f(x, y) = 0$ everywhere else Using (26) to evaluate ϕ_0 gives the final result

$$f(x, y) = \frac{1}{L}\left[\sqrt{\frac{LN}{\pi\sigma_x\sigma_y}} - \frac{1}{2}\left(\frac{x^2}{\sigma_x^2} + \frac{y^2}{\sigma_y^2}\right)\right] \quad (27)$$

over the region where this expression is positive, and $f(x, y) = 0$ elsewhere The mean density of the pattern, therefore, should be concentrated near the maximum of the aiming probability density, and should decrease parabolically as one goes out from the point of aim in any direction

In the one-dimensional case the corresponding solution is

$$f(x) = \frac{1}{L}\left[\left(\frac{3LN}{4\sqrt{2}\sigma}\right)^{2/3} - \frac{1}{2}\frac{x^2}{\sigma^2}\right] \quad (28)$$

6 3 2   Example of the Approximate Method

As an illustration of the method of the previous section, let us consider the design of a depth charge pattern Let us suppose that the errors of the attack are circularly normal, with $\sigma_x = \sigma_y = 300$ feet, and that proximity-fuzed depth charges are dropped or thrown The lethal area of the submarine is 10,000 square feet, and 13 depth charges are to be used

Putting the given constants into equation (27) gives

$$10^4 f = 0\,678 - \frac{r^2}{18 \times 10^4},$$

where $r^2 = x^2 + y^2$ The value of f falls to 0 at $r = 350$ feet, so the entire pattern should be enclosed within a circle of 350 feet radius The number of charges which should be dropped within a radius r of center is

$$N_r = \int_0^r 2\pi r f\,dr$$

$$= 2\,13\frac{r^2}{10^4} - 0\,0873\frac{r^4}{10^8}$$

This function is plotted in Figure 9 To approximate this curve we may use the function indicated by the dotted line, which arises if we take a pattern consisting of one depth charge at the center, a ring of 6

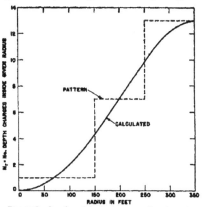

FIGURE 9   Number of depth charges inside radius r for 13-depth charge pattern

depth charges at a radius of 150 feet, and a second ring of 6 depth charges at a radius of 250 feet If these rings are staggered in a reasonable way we arrive at the pattern shown in Figure 10 (It should

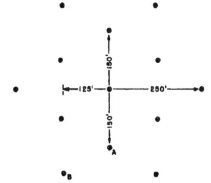

FIGURE 10   Possible depth charge pattern for maximum lethality Standard error 300 feet

be noted that practical requirements on the number of throwers on destroyers may force a modification of this pattern If the course of the destroyer is up the center of Figure 10, the two charges thrown 250 feet to the side would be replaced in actual practice by two more stern-dropped charges)

6.3.3 Probability Estimates by the Approximate Method

If equation (25) is substituted into equation (22) we find, for the probability of destruction,

$$P = \iint [f(x, y) - \phi_0] dx dy , \qquad (29)$$

where the integration is over the region in which $f > \phi_0$ If we put equation (25) into equation (20), we may write.

$$NL = \iint [\ln f(x, y) - \ln \phi_0] dx dy , \qquad (30)$$

(where the same region of integration is used), we have two equations between which ϕ_0 can be eliminated to produce an equation connecting the probability of destruction, P, with the number of projectiles, N This relationship is of great importance for making rapid estimates of P, or of the number of projectiles needed to obtain a desired value of P

The special case in which the aiming error has a normal probability density is so common that we will consider it in detail

In the one-dimensional case, with

$$f(x) = \frac{1}{\sqrt{2\pi}\sigma} e^{-x^2/2\sigma^2} ,$$

it is easily shown that for a pattern extending from $-x_0$ to x_0, equation (29) becomes

$$P = \frac{1}{\sqrt{2\pi}} \int_{-x_0/\sigma}^{x_0/\sigma} e^{-u^2/2} du - \sqrt{\frac{2}{\pi}} \left(\frac{x_0}{\sigma}\right) e^{-x_0^2/2\sigma^2} , \quad (31)$$

while (30) becomes

$$\frac{NL}{\sigma} = \left(\frac{2}{3}\right)\left(\frac{x_0}{\sigma}\right)^2 \qquad (32)$$

If (x_0/σ) is small, P is given approximately by

$$P \simeq \frac{1}{3}\sqrt{\frac{2}{\pi}}\left(\frac{x_0}{\sigma}\right)^3 = \frac{1}{\sqrt{2\pi}}\frac{NL}{\sigma} , \qquad (33)$$

so that the probability of destruction is proportional to the number of projectiles. Figure 11 shows the exact relationship between P, (x_0/σ), and (NL/σ).

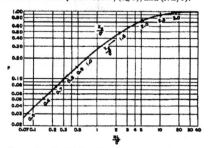

FIGURE 11. Probability of destruction and size of pattern as function of number of projectiles — one dimension

In the two-dimensional case, with

$$f = \frac{1}{2\pi\sigma_x\sigma_y} \exp\left[-\frac{1}{2}\left(\frac{x^2}{\sigma_x^2} + \frac{y^2}{\sigma_y^2}\right)\right] ,$$

the pattern extends over the region in which

$$\left(\frac{x^2}{\sigma_x^2} + \frac{y^2}{\sigma_y^2}\right) < r_0^2 ,$$

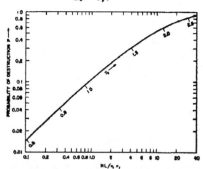

FIGURE 12 Probability of destruction and size of pattern as function of number of projectiles — two dimensions

and the equations for P and N are

$$P = 1 - \left(1 + \frac{1}{2}r_0^2\right) e^{-(r_0^2/2)} , \qquad (34)$$

$$\frac{NL}{\sigma_x\sigma_y} = \frac{\pi}{4}r_0^4 \qquad (35)$$

When r_0 is small, P is given approximately by

$$P \simeq \frac{1}{8} r_0^4 = \frac{NL}{2\pi\sigma_x\sigma_y}, \qquad (36)$$

so that the probability of destruction is again proportional to the number of projectiles The exact relationship between P, r_0, and $(NL/\sigma_x\sigma_y)$ is shown in Figure 12.

As an example of the use of these curves, let us obtain an approximate probability of destruction for the depth charge pattern shown in Figure 10 Here $N = 13$, $L = 10,000$ square feet and $\sigma_x = \sigma_y = 300$ feet Hence $(NL/\sigma_x\sigma_y) = 1\,44$ For this value, Figure 12 gives $r_0 = 1\,2$ and $P = 0\,14$ The value $r_0 = 1\,2$, of course, corresponds to the 350-feet pattern radius found in Figure 9

6 4   THE SAMPLING METHOD

While the method discussed in the latter part of the foregoing section gives a rapid approximate solution to pattern problems, its approximate nature makes it unsuitable for work in which precision is required Since exact analytical solutions are usually impractical or very tedious to carry out, we present here a method which can, in principle, give any desired degree of accuracy, and which at the same time is of such a character that rough approximations can be found with little more effort than the approximate method just given

The method operates by a simple process of sampling A pattern is selected for trial, and its probability of destruction is obtained by repeated trials (on paper) of the pattern, observing on each trial whether the target is or is not destroyed Each trial is conducted by selecting at random an aiming error from a suitably constructed artificial population of aiming errors In addition, a ballistic error for each projectile is selected in a similar way from a population of ballistic errors The position at which each projectile lands is thus found From these positions the damage to the target is found By taking a sufficiently large number of trials and averaging the results, the expected damage for the pattern is found By repeating this process for various patterns, the best pattern can be calculated In the following sections we consider the technique of carrying out these processes

6 4 1   Construction of Sampling Populations

As a basis for the construction of our sampling populations of aiming errors, ballistic errors, and the like, we shall use a *table of random digits*. Such a table may be constructed by any process which selects one of the digits 0, 1, 2, 3, 4, 5, 6, 7, 8, 9 in such a way that each of the ten digits is equally likely to be selected, and the selection is in no way affected by the result of previous selections One way of selection might be, for example, to mark ten identical balls with the ten digits, and form the table by drawing the balls from an urn, replacing the ball after each drawing and mixing well between drawings Another method would be to roll a die twice for each digit, translating the rolls into digits according to the following table

		Second Roll				
	1	2	3	4	5	6
1	1	2	3	4	5	6
2	7	8	9	0	1	2
First Roll 3	3	4	5	6	7	8
4	9	0	1	2	3	4
5	5	6	7	8	9	0
6	X	X	X	X	X	X

If the first roll is a 6, the die is rolled again It should be obvious that if the die is true, the ten digits are equally likely to be chosen (The reader is warned that if two dice are thrown together, it must be possible to distinguish the two, marking one No 1 and the other No 2)

It is most convenient to use one of the published tables, such as Tippett's,[14] which have been very carefully examined for randomness A short table of random digits is given at the back of the book as Table I

If we now wish to sample a stochastic variable x (for example a ballistic error), we may take a sequence of random digits, preceded by a decimal point, as a value of the distribution function F (as defined in Chapter 2) for the variable The functional relationship between x and F is therefore a method of converting from a table of random digits to a sample population of the stochastic variable x

To illustrate, let us sample a normal distribution The distribution function is

$$F_n = \int_{-\infty}^{x} \frac{1}{\sqrt{2\pi}} e^{-u^2/2\sigma^2} du$$

If we take the first five groups of five digits in Table I

as values of F, we obtain the following results, by using Table V to convert from F_n to x

F	(x/σ)
0 57705	0 19
0 13094	−1 13
0 60835	0 36
0 36014	−0 36
0 35950	−0 36

Continuing in this way a table of random values of (x/σ) can be constructed. Two such tables are given at the back of the book Table II is a table of random angles (in degrees), while Table III is a table of random normal deviates

6 4 2   A Rocket Problem

As a first illustration of the sampling method, let us consider the following problem A plane fires two rockets at a circular gun emplacement from a 30-degree glide at a range of 1,500 yards The gun emplacement is R feet in radius, and is destroyed if either rocket hits it The rockets are fired from parallel rails, 10 feet on either side of the center line of the plane The aiming error is normal, with $\sigma_x = \sigma_y = 10$ mils, and the ballistic error of the rockets is also normal, with $\sigma_x = \sigma_y = 5$ mils We wish to compute the probability of destroying the target

First translating the mil errors into lengths at 1,500 yards a 10 mil error is 15 yards or 45 feet, while a 5 mil error is 22 5 feet These are the standard errors in a plane perpendicular to the line of flight of the rockets On the ground, the range errors are increased by a factor of cosec 30 degrees = 2 This increases the aiming range error to 90 feet, and the ballistic range error to 45 feet We thus have the following standard deviations

Aiming	Range	$\sigma_{xa} = 90$ feet
	Deflection	$\sigma_{ya} = 45$ feet
Ballistic	Range	$\sigma_{xb} = 45$ feet
	Deflection	$\sigma_{yb} = 22\ 5$ feet

If x_1, y_1 are the coordinates of the landing point of the starboard rocket, then

$$x_1 = x_a + x_{b1},$$
$$y_1 = y_a + y_{b1} + 10, \quad (37)$$

where x_a, y_a are the aiming errors of the salvo, x_{b1}, y_{b1} are the ballistic errors of the rocket, and the 10 is the

displacement of the rails from the center line The coordinates of the landing point of the port rocket are

$$x_2 = x_a + x_{b2},$$
$$y_2 = y_a + y_{b2} - 10. \quad (38)$$

Each salvo therefore requires the sampling of six numbers. $x_a, y_a, x_{b1}, y_{b1}, x_{b2}, y_{b2}$ from normal populations with the standard deviations given above

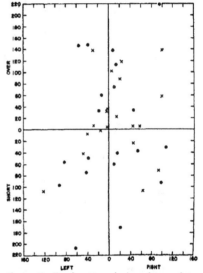

FIGURE 13   Sample pattern of salvos of two rockets Nearer rocket of each pair is marked with cross, farther with circle

The work of sampling is shown in the computation sheet in Table 1 A sample of 20 salvos is illustrated (rather smaller than should be used in practice) The first column (x_a) is obtained by taking the first 20 normal deviates in Table III, and multiplying each by the standard deviation, 90 feet The next five columns are obtained from the following sets of 20 normal deviates, multiplying them by the appropriate σ's. The next four columns are obtained by using equations (37) and (38).

In Figure 13 the positions of the rocket hits are plotted In each salvo, the rocket hitting closer to the center point is marked with a cross, the farther being marked with a circle. The distance of the closer rocket from the center is entered in the eleventh

TABLE 1. Calculation of probability of hit by sampling

x_a	y_a	x_{b1}	y_{b1}	x_{b2}	y_{b2}	x_1	y_1	x_2	y_2	R	Rank
72	7	−67	−20	−40	−15	5	−3	32	−18	6	1
−62	−27	21	−30	6	−45	−41	−47	−56	−82	62	11
34	33	−58	3	40	−12	−24	46	74	11	52	9
12	52	−61	−25	−6	15	−49	37	6	57	58	10
156	17	−37	−3	−18	1	119	24	138	8	122	16
−49	88	−22	−5	−48	14	−71	93	−97	92	117	15
−19	71	−12	26	24	−16	−31	107	5	45	45	8
−54	−54	47	5	−21	23	−7	−39	−75	−41	40	7
−143	−66	−64	−5	36	−45	−207	−61	−107	−121	162	19
−54	16	17	28	52	−21	−37	54	−2	−15	15	2
38	84	−131	5	21	26	−93	99	59	100	116	14
150	63	69	4	−11	47	219	77	139	100	172	20
60	−17	−23	6	0	14	37	−1	60	−13	37	6
5	−11	−46	17	27	18	−41	16	32	−3	32	5
123	−11	−35	22	25	−17	88	21	148	−38	90	12
−43	28	77	8	66	−4	34	46	23	14	27	3
−102	53	−4	1	−69	−21	−106	64	−171	22	124	17
45	11	58	−16	68	13	103	5	113	14	103	13
−17	−11	−43	10	24	−7	−60	9	7	−28	29	4
106	−14	41	−51	32	−5	147	−55	138	−29	141	18

column of the computation sheet (headed R) Finally the salvos are ranked in order, the salvo with the closest hit being numbered 1, the next 2, and so on It is now a simple matter to plot the number of salvos with at least one hit inside a target of radius R, as a function of R The result is the step curve shown in Figure 14 Finally the step curve is smoothed as shown in the same figure

To estimate the precision of this curve, we may calculate the standard deviation of the value of P, the probability of at least one hit If the true value for any value of R is P_0, the standard deviation of the value for a sample of n is

$$\sqrt{\frac{P_0(1 - P_0)}{n}}$$

Since $P_0(1 - P_0) \leq 1/4$, the standard deviation is everywhere less than $1/2\sqrt{n}$ For our sample of 20 this has the value 0 11 The step curve may therefore be expected to depart from the true curve by amounts of the order of 0 11, measured along the P axis It will be noticed that the smooth curve departs from the step curve in Figure 14 by amounts of this order

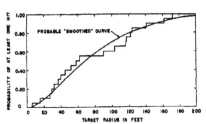

FIGURE 14   Probability of at least one hit as function of target size, from sample shots of Figure 13

The smoothing undoubtedly reduces the sampling error, but it is not possible to estimate how much. Obviously the precision can be increased to any desired extent by taking a large enough sample, although the precision increases only slowly with n.

6 4 3   Short Cuts in the Sampling Method

There are many short cuts and tricks which may be used to lighten the work of the sampling method These usually depend on special features of the problem to be solved, so that no general rules can be given. It may, for example, be possible to determine the damage function of a pattern analytically, but not to carry out the final integration In such a case the final integration can be made by a sampling process. In other cases there may be independent intermediate probabilities which can be found by sampling methods, and the results combined by analytical methods The recognition and use of such devices depends on the skill and ingenuity of the worker, rather than on previous knowledge

A very common device is illustrated by the following example Suppose that an exact evaluation of the depth charge pattern of Figure 10 is needed To carry out the calculation by direct sampling requires the selection of 29 sample numbers for each trial two for each depth charge to determine its ballistic error, two for the aiming error, and one to determine the orientation of the submarine The work, however, may be shortened in the following way A master chart of the depth charge pattern is prepared Ten sample ballistic errors for each depth charge are then found, and the resulting actual positions of the depth charges are marked on the chart, using different colors or symbols to designate the position the depth charge was supposed to have For instance, around the point A in Figure 10 (the point where the charge would fall if there were no ballistic error) will be a scatter of ten points, which can be labeled $A1$, $A2$, , $A10$, and around point B is another scatter, labeled $B1$, $B2$, , $B10$

When this drawing is completed, samples of positions and orientations of the submarine are drawn This may be rather complicated if one wishes to take into account the maneuverability of the submarine when computing its distribution function (for instance in some cases of interest one knows the position and velocity of the submarine a certain time before the pattern is dropped, but does not know its maneuvers thereafter) in any case a *random* sample of possible positions and orientations is drawn By means of a template showing the outline of the lethal area of the submarine (or, if one is finicking, the contours of equal probability of destruction D) each sample submarine position is examined for hits, and the probability of destruction can be found for that position

For example, if the template in one of the sample positions shows that 2 of the 10 points around point A ($A3$ and $A6$, for instance) and 1 of the 10 points around B ($B1$, for instance) are inside the lethal area,

and no others, then the probability of destruction in that position is recorded as

$$1 - \left(1 - \frac{2}{10}\right)\ \left(1 - \frac{1}{10}\right) = 0\ 28$$

If 100 sample positions are taken, a good approximation to the desired probability will be found by averaging the probabilities in the various positions The whole process involves 560 sampling numbers, whereas 100 direct trials would take 2,900 sampling numbers Needless to say, auxiliary tables for the combination of probabilities should be constructed and used

§ 4.4   Train Bombing

Another example of the use of the sampling method is in the calculation of the probability that a stick of bombs will damage a target As an example, let us take the case where the ballistic deviation (in range and deflection) equals the aiming deviation in deflection, and equals one-half the aiming deviation in range This is a somewhat greater ballistic error than occurs in practice, but it has been taken large to contrast with our earlier calculations, where we assumed zero ballistic deviation

Using Table III, we plot the mid-points of 25 salvos, using a range scale twice as large as the deflection scale Then, with further use of the table, we displace four points from each mid-point, thus arriving at a plot of 100 points, 25 salvos of 4 bombs each This is shown in Figure 15 The individual hits are represented by the numbered circles, the individual salvos have their 4 circles connected by straight lines and are labeled by letters a to y Here the ballistic error is large enough so that the patterns overlap.

To compute the probability of hitting a target of known size and shape, when bombed by four bombs in salvo, we superpose on this pattern a drawing of the target having a size corresponding to the ratio between the actual target size and the normal deviations, an orientation related to the direction of the plane's track over the target and having the point of aim at the center of the figure

A mere counting of the circles whose centers are inside the target gives the number of bombs hitting the target in 25 passes Dividing by 25 gives the chance of a bomb hitting in one pass.

Some of the hits may be two (or three or four) out

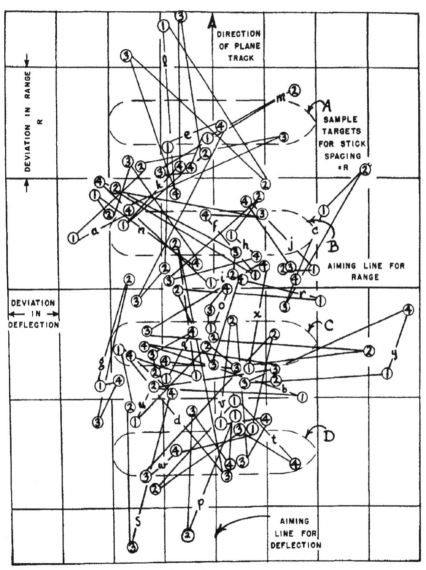

FIGURE 15. Random salvos a to y of 4 bombs each Ballistic dispersion equals deflection dispersion equals one-half range dispersion, R

TABLE 2 Bombing calculation by sampling method ($D = 0.5$)

Stick spacing	Zero	(R/2)	R
N_1, no sticks with only 1 hit in an area	Does not apply	17	21
N_{11}, no sticks with 1 hit in each of 2 areas	"	3	1
N_{111}, no. sticks with 1 in each of 3 areas	"	1	1
N_{21}, no sticks with 1 in one area, 2 in another	"	3	0
N_{31}, no sticks with 1 in one area, 3 in another	"	1	0
No salvos which result in 1 hit $n_1 = 6N_1 + 8N_{11} + 9N_{111} + 10N_{21} + 12N_{31}$	4	177	143
No salvos which result in 2 hits $n_2 = 2N_{11} + 3N_{111} + 4N_{21} + 6N_{31}$	6	27	5
No salvos which result in 3 hits $n_3 = N_{111}$	0	1	1
Total no sticks in sample $= N$	25	600	600
Expected total hits per salvo (or stick) $= (1/N)(n_1 + 2n_2 + 3n_3)$	0 640	0 390	0 260
Expected fraction salvos which resulted in at least 1 hit $= (1/N)(n_1 + n_2 + n_3)$	0 400	0 342	0 248
Probability of sinking ship $= (1/N)(0.5n_1 + 0.75n_2 + 0.875n_3)$	0 260	0 183	0 127

of one salvo Such pairs (or triplets or quadruplets) should only count as a single, if we wish to compute the chance that the target is hit at least once in a salvo On the other hand, if the target is a ship, with probability of sinking given by equation (2), the chance of sinking the ship with a single salvo is approximately

$$S \approx \frac{1}{25} \{ n_1 D + n_2[1 - (1 - D)^2] + n_3[1 - (1 - D^3)] + n_4[1 - (1 - D)^4] \},$$

where n_1 is the number of salvos having only one hit inside the target, n_2 the number having two hits inside, etc When a target of the shape and size shown in Figure 15 is placed over the point of aim, the count is that shown in the column marked *Zero* (stick spacing) in Table 2 The other two columns will be explained below

To use the same figure for a *stick* of four bombs, we can imagine displacing each circle marked 1 by 1 5 times the stick spacing downward, the circles marked 3 by 0 5 times the spacing upward and those marked 4 by 1 5 times the spacing upward Rather than redraw the figure, we can draw 4 *targets*, as shown by (A, B, C, D), displaced in the opposite direction by similar amounts, and count all the circles marked 1 which are in area A, all circles marked 2 in area B, and so on

Of course we could have considered the circles marked 2 as being the first bombs in the train, in which case we would have counted the number of circles marked 2 in area A, etc.

There are 24 different ways that $(1, 2, 3, 4)$ can fit into areas (A, B, C, D), so that we can consider the samples as representing $24 \times 25 = 600$ trials These trials are not all independent of each other, so that the result will not be as accurate (on the average) as if we had drawn 600 independent salvos, but the result will be less subject to fluctuations than if we had taken only the number of 1's in A, 2's in B, etc

The rules for computing the result are worked out by setting down all 24 permutations and counting which of the permutations corresponds to what result They are

1 We count the number of *circles* in each area which belong to sticks having hits *in only one area* (for instance stick e has $e4$ in area A and no other in another area, and stick u has $u2$ and $u4$ in area C but none in another area) Call this number N_1

2 We count the number of *pairs* of circles belonging to one stick, one of which is in one area and one in another (for instance stick w has $w2$ in area C and $w4$ in area D) Call this number N_{11}

3 Count the number of triplets belonging to one stick, two of which are in one area and one in another area (If $w3$ were displaced slightly upward, it also would be in area D, along with $w4$) Call this number N_{12}

4 Count the number of triplets belonging to one stick, each of which is in a different area ($d2$ is in area B, $d4$ in area C, and $d3$ in area D) Call this number N_{111}

5 The extension of these definitions to N_{21}, N_{111}, etc., should by now be obvious.

We then count over the various 24 permutations of

1, 2, 3, 4 which make the above combinations into single, double, etc , hits, and arrive at the following rules· Out of the 600 sample sticks·

The number of sticks resulting in a single hit is
$$n_1 = 6N_1 + 8N_{11} + 9N_{111} + 10N_{21}$$
$$+ 9N_{1111} + 10N_{211} + 12N_{31} + 8N_{22}$$
The number of sticks resulting in two hits is
$$n_2 = 2N_{11} + 3N_{111} + 4N_{21} + 6N_{1111}$$
$$+ 4N_{211} + 6N_{31} + 8N_{22} \qquad (39)$$
The number of sticks resulting in three hits is
$$n_3 = N_{111} + 2N_{211}$$
The number of sticks resulting in four hits is
$$n_4 = N_{1111}$$

In the case shown in Figure 15 the circles inside the target areas are

A; $a3, e4, m1$
B; $d2, f3, f4, h1, j3, k1$
C, $b4, d4, o1, o2, q3, q4, r3, s1, u2, u4, w2, x3$
D; $d3, p4, t4, v3, w4$

The numbers N are therefore

N_1 $= 21; A - a, e, m; B - f(2), h, i, k; C - b,$
$\qquad o(2), q(2), r, s, u(2), x; D - p, t, v$
N_{11} $= 1; C, D - w$
N_{111} $= 1, B, C, D - d$

These are entered in Table 2 in the third column and the resulting calculations are obvious Another count was made for a spacing of 0 5R, and the results shown It can be seen that, for such a large ballistic dispersion compared to the aiming dispersion, it is somewhat better to drop the bombs in salvo rather than with any appreciable stick spacing The ballistic dispersion does enough spreading without needing any additional amount

Similar calculations can be made for the target areas rotated about their centers, to determine the effect of approach bearing on the probabilities When the areas overlap, circles in the common area must be counted in both areas The same chart can be used for sticks of three or two, by revising equations (39)

Chapter 7

OPERATIONAL EXPERIMENTS WITH EQUIPMENT AND TACTICS

IN TIME OF WAR the measures of effectiveness of weapons used in various ways must ultimately be determined from experience on the field of battle, for only in this way can we be sure of their actual behavior in the face of the enemy, and only then can we devise tactics which we can be sure are effective in practice Constant scrutiny of operational data is necessary to see whether changes in training procedures make possible more effective utilization, and to see whether changes in enemy tactics require modifications of ours

However, operational data are *observational*, rather than *experimental* data Conditions cannot be changed at will, pertinent variables cannot be held constant, and the results give overall effectiveness with usually little chance to gain insight into the adequacy of various components of the tactic The check, by operational data alone, of an analytical theory of the effectiveness of a given tactic, is not often detailed enough to be able to determine the correctness of all the component parts of the analysis To obtain such a confirmation, an independent variation of each of the component variables is always desirable and usually necessary, a procedure which the enemy is seldom kind enough to allow us to carry out on the field of battle

To gain insight into the detailed workings of a given operation, therefore, so that one can redesign tactics *in advance* of changing conditions, it is necessary to supplement the operational data with data obtained from *operational experiments*, done under controlled conditions with a specially designated task force These additional data can never take the place of the figures obtained from battle, for one can never be sure what the enemy is likely to do, or how our own forces will react to battle conditions Nevertheless, suitable experimental data, obtained under controlled conditions approximating as closely as possible to actual warfare, can be of immense assistance in providing more detailed knowledge of the complex interrelations between men and equipment which make up even the simplest operation They are the only available data during peacetime, so it is important that they be gathered as carefully as possible

This idea of operational experiments, performed primarily not for training but for obtaining a quantitative insight into the operation itself, is a new one, and is capable of important results Properly implemented, it should make it possible for the military forces of a country to keep abreast of new technical developments during peace, rather than to have to waste lives and energy catching up after the next war has begun Such operational experiments are of no use whatever if they are dealt with as ordinary tactical exercises, however, and they must be planned and observed by trained scientists as valid *scientific experiments* Here, then, is an important and useful role for operations research for the armed forces in peacetime

7 1 PLANNING THE OPERATIONAL EXPERIMENTS

The carrying out of operational experiments is a difficult problem, because of the large number of variables involved, but the fundamental principles are the same as for any other scientific experiment The results to be aimed at are a series of *numerical* answers, representing the dependence of the measures of effectiveness on the pertinent variables The behavior of these variables should be known, and they should be varied independently, as far as possible, during the experiment Since operational behavior depends on the crew as well as the equipment, the state of training of this crew should be investigated In fact, the learning curves for the crews should be determined as fully as possible, so that as one changes from crew to crew the effect of training can be taken into account These measurements on training will also be valuable in indicating the amount of training which will be necessary when the equipment is put into actual operation. The maintenance problems of the equipment must also be investigated, and simple checks must be found to determine the state of maintenance of the gear during each portion of the test.

Since the tests are to determine the behavior of equipment and men, average crews must be used to handle *all gear* entering into the operation. The scientific observers must confine themselves to observing, and should not interfere in the operation itself. If, for instance, an antiaircraft fire director is being tested, the usual crew must be put in charge of the director and of the gun, and the usual orders given them This crew must not be allowed to know any more about the position of the incoming test plane than do usual crews in combat The observers should occupy themselves with photographing, or otherwise recording, the actions of the crew and the results of the firing There should be many observers specially trained for this task, but the observers must keep themselves outside the experiment itself

7 1.1   Preliminary Theory

Another important requirement is that one should have some general theory of the operation before the experiment is started This requirement is in common with other scientific experiments, one does not usually blindly measure anything and everything concerned with a test, one usually knows enough about the phenomena to be able to say that such and such variables are the crucial ones, and that the effect of others is less important One should know approximately where the errors are likely to be the largest, and should be able to get the range of the variables over which the greatest number of measurements must be made It is not necessary that the theory be completely correct, for the theory merely provides a framework for planning the experiments If the measurements turn out to disagree with the theory, this will be almost as helpful as if they agreed. In fact, an investigation of the disagreement between the measurements and the preliminary theory sometimes provides the most fruitful results of the whole experiment

Not only should there be many extraoperational observers to keep track of all of the variables involved, but there also should be enough computers available so that the data can be reduced as fast as the experiment goes ahead It is extremely dangerous to take all the data without reducing any of them and to allow the crews and equipment to disband before any results are obtained It is practically certain that the results will show that certain further measurements should have been made, measurements which could have easily been made while the equipment was assembled, but which are extremely difficult to obtain later A continuing, though preliminary, analysis of the results can tell when the measurements are inadequate, when a new crew has not been sufficiently

trained, etc , and can indicate deviations from the preliminary theory so that this can be analyzed in time

7.1 2   Preliminary Write-up

In drawing up a plan for an operational experiment it has been found by experience that the following five items should be written down in detail
1 Subject
2 Authorization
3. Purpose and Aims of Testing.
4 Present Status of Available Data
5 Plan of Procedure
Items 1, 2, and 3 are self-evident requirements Since the work concerns equipment already in existence there will be certain performance data already accumulated by the technical experts who were responsible for its development and production If the equipment is newly designed the chances are that the technical experts had been told some of the requirements and tactical uses Therefore, there exists some performance data from the development and acceptance stage If the equipment has already been in service, the evaluation called for would either be in connection with some new tactical use or due to unfavorable reports from the field Thus there exist known facts about its performance, and these should be assembled under item 4 of the above outline The Plan of Procedure called for in item 5 needs some explanation.

7 1 3   Plan of Procedure

This calls for an itemized account of how the needed data are to be obtained It is a detailing of the duties of various observers, of their training beforehand, etc It has been found expedient in this type of work to gather more data during the tests than might seem necessary The old adage of "penny wise and pound foolish" should be remembered and a really adequate program carried out It is a cardinal principle that *facts* are *recorded* and not impressions, so every possible use is to be made of stop watches, range finders, thermometers, etc The limitations of all equipment must be determined This is not in order to find a fault, but to govern tactics

A generous use of movie cameras and still cameras has been found extremely valuable when used properly, i e , camera focal length, frame frequency, and altitude, must be known and recorded if data are to be taken from camera evidence Thirty seconds of movies showing equipment performance is more convincing to fleet commanders than volumes of reports All these things and more must be thought through well in advance, so that the testing goes off smoothly

Experience has shown that the data must be gathered in such a way that they can be understood *during* the testing period, even if this requires a group of men doing nothing but recording, tabulating, computing, and constructing graphs In this way the technical director of the project knows whether his data are significant, and whether he has completed testing before the experimental facilities are diverted to other efforts One other reason for this should the data from a given set of conditions give an unexpected result, the experiment with these conditions can be repeated at once Finally, in the plan for procedure some consideration for the time of completion and urgency of the project should play a role Interim instructions or a report of first findings may expedite a fleet commander's decision

7 1 4 Significant Data

Keeping in mind the tactical use of the equipment should in itself insure that the data taken are significant At least one person with field experience should be assigned to the project for this reason A few examples will indicate how one must distinguish significant data from other kinds

In rocket firing from an aircraft with a newly developed sight a pilot is assigned a plane, and proceeds to fire several hundred rounds on a land range over a period of several weeks Do the data from this effort constitute a measure of equipment performance from an operational point of view? Obviously there are reasons to doubt that equipment performance would be the same as it would be under battle conditions Operational data on such a sight should come from several squadrons with respectively different types of aircraft The rockets should be fired on a towed target at sea to prevent range or azimuth correction made possible by fixed objects on a land range In addition, the pilots should fire at the target from several directions relative to the wind, and the firing should be spread over enough days to allow for reasonable variations in wind and sea conditions In other words, to evaluate the rocket-sight performance the project officer must keep in mind that the rocket sight will be used tactically in such a way that the

aircraft will make one or, at most, two passes at the target.

An evaluation of the experimental data should have some tactical conclusions The fighting forces and the planners will find conclusions on the performance of the sight useful in order to judge how many planes are required to knock out a given target It would also be the duty of the operations research worker to seek further confirmation of performance of the sight from combat information, if this is possible

Sometimes it is not necessary to get such a spread of data Let us consider the firing of torpedoes from a destroyer, and the evaluation of the performance of a new torpedo The data needed are the comparative performance with other torpedoes under various tactical conditions, and the data can be obtained by one or two destroyers Operational success can then be inferred, since data on the launching errors are already available A similar study might be adequate in the case of airborne torpedoes

Considerable care must be taken that the data from performance of sound or radar equipment are significant In the case of sound gear, the performance is influenced by temperature gradients, density layers, and depths of the water In the case of radar, the performance is altered by moisture, temperature gradients, etc Thus care must be taken that data reported on performance are properly qualified, so that tactics designed for their use will be properly varied to meet the conditions In addition to the tricks played by the elements on such gear, there is the large variable of equipment maintenance by fleet personnel Every effort should be made to allow the equipment to age or even disintegrate under the maintenance of those personnel whom the fleet expects to service it Having done this, the tests should then be conducted for performance In this way it will be possible to assess the maintenance effort required by the fighting forces to keep the equipment effective, and thus to estimate whether the advantages of the new gear are sufficient to warrant the maintenance and training effort

7 1 5 Conclusions

The data gathered in evaluating equipment for tactical use will be useless to the operational commands unless there is, in the report, an interpretation of the data and conclusions The theater commander, faced with peculiar conditions, may not agree with the conclusions in the report, but a summing up, along with the data, will help him reach the correct conclusions for his theater's requirements

7.2   ACCURACY MEASUREMENTS

One of the commonest types of test programs is that in which the accuracy of a weapon is to be measured Such programs may be test firings of rockets to determine the distribution of aiming and ballistic errors, practice firing of guns to determine gun and director errors, practice runs by destroyers on submarines to determine the errors in dropping depth charges when various approach tactics and attack directors are used, test firings of torpedoes from submarines, and so on In each case there is a target at which projectiles are fired, and in each case the measure of effectiveness desired is the distribution of the projectiles around the target In many cases it is also necessary to analyze the sources of error with the object of improving the accuracy

Whenever it can be arranged (it is not always possible), arrangements should be made to record the position of each projectile fired relative to the target This is not usually easy, and requires the closest cooperation with experimental laboratories and with operating personnel Sometimes when a land target is used, the positions of the hits can be measured directly by a surveying party after each salvo When the target is on the surface of water, photographic recording is usually used (When possible a Fleet Camera Party should be used) The bursts of AA shells around air targets have also been recorded photographically With underwater targets, underwater sound methods can sometimes be used. The interpretation of photographs and the calculation of underwater sound data both require careful study if accurate measurements are to be made Even when direct measurements are made on land, it is frequently necessary to introduce corrections for uneven terrain

In order to separate the effects of aiming errors and ballistic errors, the projectiles should be fired in salvos of at least two at a time Larger salvos would be better in some cases, but considerations of economy frequently keep the salvo down to two projectiles However, unless it is known that either the aiming error or the ballistic error can be neglected (very rarely the case), salvo firing is absolutely essential

In recording the data, the salvo to which each pro-

jectile belongs must be recorded This is most easily done by means of a salvo number It should go without saying that all other pertinent data should be recorded target, ship or plane firing, wind or weather conditions if relevant.

7.2.1   Calculation of Standard Deviations

The first step in working up the data is to calculate the mean point of impact [MPI] of each salvo, by averaging the positions of the projectiles in the salvo The distribution of the projectile positions about the MPI is obviously independent of the aiming error,

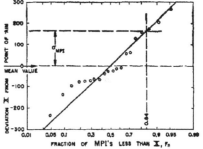

FIGURE 1   Use of probability paper Deviations from MPI, $\sigma = 18$, $\sigma_b = 18\sqrt{2} = 25$

and so may be used to determine the ballistic error. Ballistic errors are almost always normally distributed (but not necessarily circularly), and it is easily shown that if the errors are normally distributed about the point of aim, they are also normally distributed about the MPI, with a standard deviation which is less than that about the point of aim by a factor $\sqrt{(n-1)/n}$, where n is the number of projectiles in the salvo

The standard deviations of the ballistic errors in range and deflection are most easily found by the use of "probability paper" This paper is ruled with a linear scale along one axis, and graduated on the other axis according to the normal distribution function $F_n(x)$ (see Chapter 2) To use the paper, the fraction of a population of values of a stochastic variable ξ with values less than a given value x, is plotted against x, plotting the value of x on the linear scale and the fraction on the F_n scale. If the population has a normal distribution, the result will be a straight line The mean value is then found at the point $F_n = 0\,5000$, while the standard deviation is

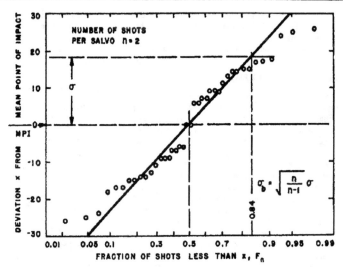

FIGURE 2   Use of probability paper   Distribution of MPI, $\sigma_{MPI} = 161$

the difference between this value and the value corresponding to $F_n = 0\ 8413$

A plot of this kind for the difference in range (or deflection) between each projectile and the MPI of its salvo, as shown in Figure 1, therefore gives an immediate test of whether the errors follow the normal distribution law, and, if the normal law is obeyed, gives the mean (which will, of course, be zero) and standard deviation The standard deviation σ_b of the ballistic errors about the point of aim instead of the MPI is found by multiplying the MPI by $\sqrt{n/(n-1)}$

If probability paper is not available, the standard deviation of the errors from the MPI may be found by the arithmetic method of finding the square root of the mean of the squares of the deviation This process, however, is laborious, and does not check the normality of the population

When the distribution of ballistic errors has been determined, the distribution of aiming errors can be found from the distribution of the MPI's as shown in Figure 2 If both the aiming and ballistic errors are normally distributed, the MPI's should be normally distributed, with a standard deviation given by

$$\sigma_{MPI}{}^2 = \sigma_a{}^2 + \frac{1}{n}\sigma_b{}^2, \qquad (1)$$

where σ_a is the standard deviation of the aiming error, σ_b is that of the ballistic error, and n is the number of projectiles per salvo The value of σ_{MPI} can be found by the use of probability paper, or arithmetically.

7.2 2   An Example

To show the details of calculation, the following table represents a series of 20 salvos of two bombs The value of x_1 and x_2 are the range errors of the bombs in feet The third column gives the MPI's found by averaging the first two columns The next two columns are the deviations of the individual bombs from the MPI The 40 values of Δx were arranged in ascending order of magnitude from -26 to $+26$, and plotted on probability paper as shown in Figure 1, the lowest being plotted at $F_n = \frac{1}{41}$, and the highest being plotted at $F_n = \frac{40}{41}$. The resulting curve is about as good an approximation to a straight line as we can expect from a sample this small, so it was assumed that the distribution was normal, and the best straight line drawn in by eye. From the points at $F_n = 0\ 5000$ and $F_n = 0\ 8413$, σ is found to be 18 feet Since $n = 2$, the standard ballistic dispersion σ_b is $18\sqrt{2} = 25$ feet The distribution of the

MPI's was then plotted as shown in Figure 2 This also seems to be normal, with $\sigma_{\text{MPI}} = 161$ feet. Hence

$$\sigma_a = \sqrt{\sigma_{\text{MPI}}^2 - \frac{1}{2}\sigma_b^2} = 160 \text{ feet.}$$

A similar calculation could have been made for the deflection errors

Record of deviations of hits from aiming point

Salvo	x_1	x_2	MPI	Δx_1	Δx_2
1	−124	−142	−133	9	−9
2	−68	−82	−75	7	−7
3	−52	−88	−70	18	−18
4	184	162	173	11	−11
5	−220	−254	−237	17	−17
6	−42	−14	−28	−14	14
7	218	200	209	9	−9
8	−6	−20	−13	7	−7
9	−52	−78	−65	13	−13
10	276	264	270	6	−6
11	−108	−78	−93	−15	15
12	48	82	65	−17	17
13	156	128	142	14	−14
14	−38	−8	−23	−15	15
15	−52	−102	−77	25	−25
16	−90	−42	−66	−24	24
17	−8	−60	−34	26	−26
18	−16	−4	−10	−6	6
19	66	48	57	9	−9
20	154	154	154	0	0

7 3   EVALUATION OF DETECTION EQUIPMENT

The field testing of detection equipment should be conducted to determine the numerical values of the measures of effectiveness of the equipment in the tactical situations in which the equipment is to be used For some equipment the only important measure to be determined is its sweep width against the most important target or targets it is designed to detect In other cases, however, the sweep width is not sufficient An early warning radar, for example, must not only detect aircraft, but do so at a long enough range to enable an interception to be made In such a case it is necessary to know the "survival curve," i e , the probability of a plane approaching to a given range without being detected In other cases the accuracy of range and bearing information is important and must be determined

7.3.1   Sweep Width

From a theoretical standpoint the most direct method of determining a sweep width is from direct trial For airborne radar such trials might be carried out by having the equipment flown a distance L in an area A containing n targets If the flying and the placing of the targets are done perfectly at random, and C contacts are made, the sweep width W is given by

$$W = \frac{CA}{nL}. \qquad (2)$$

In actual practice, however, randomness is very difficult to achieve, and to avoid difficulties with edge effects, the area A must be of dimensions large compared to W This requires a great amount of flying

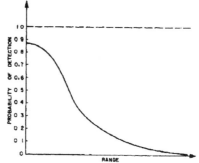

FIGURE 3   Range distribution curve

to be done to make C large enough to avoid trouble with statistical fluctuations Because of these difficulties the method of direct trial is very rarely used

The most common method of evaluating search equipment is what might be called the *range distribution* method In this method the equipment is carried toward a target (or the target made to approach the equipment) until the target is detected, and the range of first detection is recorded From a sufficiently large number of such runs, a distribution curve can be constructed showing the probability that the target has been detected as a function of range A typical form for such a curve is shown in Figure 3 In many cases the probability of detection approaches unity as the range approaches zero, but this is by no means always the case The only universal characteristic of such a curve is that the probability is a monotonic decreasing function of range

7.3.2 Detection Expectancy

As shown in Chapter 5, the probability of detection is related to the "detection expectancy," ϕ, by the relation

$$P = 1 - e^{-\phi} \tag{3}$$

By means of this equation, a plot of ϕ as a function of range can be constructed In Figure 4 the ϕ versus

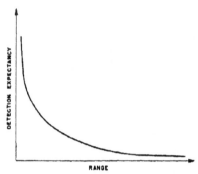

FIGURE 4 Variation of detection expectancy with range If f is the slope of the curve, then $-f dR$ is the probability of detecting a target between ranges R and $R + dR$

R plot corresponding to the P versus R plot of Figure 3 is shown If P approaches unity as R approaches zero, then ϕ approaches infinity

The negative slope, $f = -d\phi/dR$ of the ϕ versus R curve represents the probability of detecting a hitherto undetected target in an element of range dR, divided by dR It is therefore a direct measure of the detecting power of the equipment at a given range Examination of this quantity will frequently reveal "bad spots" in the performance of the equipment

In actual service the target motion is seldom straight toward the detection equipment The most common situation is that in which the target tracks are straight lines passing the target at random If the doubtful (but usually unavoidable) assumption is made that the detecting power ϕ is independent of the target aspect and bearing, then the curve of detection probability as a function of the lateral range of the target track can be found If the observed relationship between f and R can be approximated

analytically, then for a track whose lateral range is x, the detection expectancy is given by the integral

$$\bar{\phi}(x) = \int_{-\infty}^{\infty} f(\sqrt{x^2 + y^2})\,dy, \tag{4}$$

and the probability of detection is as usual given by

$$P(x) = 1 - e^{-\phi(x)} \tag{5}$$

If no analytical expression for f can be found, or if the integral (4) proves difficult, then $\phi(x)$ can be found graphically by plotting a series of curves for $f(\sqrt{x^2 + y^2})$ as functions of y, and measuring their areas with a planimeter The sweep width can then be found by

$$W = \int_{-\infty}^{\infty} P(x)\,dx \tag{6}$$

Examples of such calculations can be found in Division 6, Volume 2B If the target aspect produces an effect on sighting, this can be introduced as an additional factor in the integrations It is, of course, highly important to set up the experiments so any aspect effect will be apparent

7.4 SURVIVAL PROBLEMS IN GUNNERY

A type of analysis very similar to that above has been used in gunfire evaluation, particularly the evaluation of AA fire In the AA case the pertinent measure of effectiveness is the probability of shooting down a plane before it reaches a position to drop bombs or torpedoes. The situation is similar in other cases where the object of the gunfire is to prevent the approach of enemy forces

7.4.1 AA Gunnery

The evaluation is based on practice firings in which a target (e g , a drone) is made to approach the gun position, using evasive maneuvers similar to those which an actual enemy might be expected to employ Firing is continued at a known rate throughout the entire run The range of each hit (or burst of proximity-fuzed ammunition) is recorded. The target need not be of the same size as the enemy craft against which the effectiveness is to be measured, but, if it is not the same, the ratio of the effective target areas must be known Different types of run (varying altitude, speed, line of approach, etc) should be tried, and the results of each type analyzed separately

As the firing rate and quality of the ammunition may vary from run to run, these must be recorded during the firing practice. In analyzing the results, a standard firing rate and quality of ammunition are chosen If, in a given run, the firing rate was j times the standard, and the quality of the ammunition (fraction of shells not duds) was q times the standard, then the run is given a weight jq, that is, it is considered that jq standard runs were made during the actual run

The first step in the analysis is to find the average number of hits per standard run outside each range, as a function of the range This is conveniently done by arranging all the hits in order of decreasing range, and numbering them serially The quotient of the serial number of each hit by the total number of standard runs then gives the average number of hits outside the range of the hit The result is now plotted against range to give the *hit expectancy* curve for a standard run

7.4 2   Hit Expectancy

The hit expectancy curve is the analogue of the detection expectancy curve for the detection problem It should be proportional to the firing rate, so that the effect of a change in the number of guns or a change in the firing rate per gun is easily found It is also directly proportional to the quality of the ammunition Its negative slope is a measure of the effectiveness of the fire as a function of range, and can be used to find the weak spots of any given method of

firing Moreover the hit expectancy is directly proportional to the effective target area, so that the curve is easily translated from the practice target to the actual target being considered

If E is the hit expectancy at range R, the probability that the target will be hit before it reaches a given range is given by

$$P = 1 - e^{-E} \qquad (7)$$

In most cases, however, it is not this probability which is of interest, but the probability that the target will be destroyed To find this it is necessary to introduce the damage coefficients, D_n (Chapter 6) To a sufficient degree of approximation the probability of n hits, if E are expected, is given by the Poisson law

$$P_n = \frac{E^n e^{-E}}{n!}$$

The probability of destruction is therefore

$$P_D = \sum_n D_n \frac{E^n e^{-E}}{n!} \qquad (8)$$

Given the D_n, this may be evaluated as a function of E once and for all, and the resulting curve used to convert the hit expectancy curve into a probability of destruction curve When the "vital spot" hypothesis can be used

$$1 - D_n = (1 - D)^n,$$

and

$$P_D = 1 - e^{-DE}. \qquad (9)$$

In this equation DE is evidently the expected number of times the plane will be destroyed

Chapter 8

ORGANIZATIONAL AND PROCEDURAL PROBLEMS

REFERRING AGAIN to the first sentence of Chapter 1, we may emphasize at this point that operations research is not a pure research activity separated from all else, it is an integral part of an operating organization It is a part of the thinking process of the operating organization, so to speak, the summing up of the facts bearing on the problem before a decision is made Separate existence, by itself, would be as anomalous as the separate existence of the frontal lobe of a brain without the rest of the brain and body

It is thus obvious that problems concerning the organization of a group to carry out operations research and concerning its relationships with the executive branch of the operating organization are far from trivial They have been touched on in Chapter 1 and are discussed in more detail in this chapter It should also be obvious that the details of these organizational matters will depend considerably on the sort of organization involved, whether it be industrial, governmental, or military, for example Consequently only general comments on principles of organization, which seem to have general validity, can be given here, together with a few examples of the way these general principles have been applied in particular cases Most of the examples are in connection with military applications, because of the greater amount of experience amassed here and because of the continuing importance of these applications

As a matter of fact, in World War II, a great deal of time and energy was spent, by scientists and officers, in finding workable solutions to the organizational problems involved in setting up operations research It took careful organizational planning and detailed indoctrination of workers to insure that technical information could be sent freely across command boundaries without short-circuiting the usual chain of command in regard to orders It took a great deal of missionary work to persuade security officers that it was important to release highly secret information to the operations research worker, even though he did nothing more than *think* about the information for the time being

By the end of the war, most of these organizational problems had been worked out, in one way or another Several possible types of organization had been evolved, and the possible procedural methods for some of the specialized operations research work (such as the working up of operational statistics, or research in the field) had been determined The first section of this chapter discusses some of the solutions and indicates some of the problems requiring special consideration The applicability of the discussion with respect to industrial or other governmental applications is then taken up, the differences and similarities between the organizational solutions being indicated

An important requirement for an operations research worker in starting a new study is that he become familiar at first hand with the operations involved To do this he must go into the field he must fly in the bomber plane, travel in the bus, operate the early-warning radar, and make purchases in the store, as the case may be Sometimes this field work involves extensive travel, sometimes it involves living away from the central operations research group for some time In these instances the organization of field work involves special problems This is particularly true with respect to military applications, but it is also true in some nonmilitary examples These special problems are discussed in section 8 2

8 1 ORGANIZATION OF AN OPERATIONS RESEARCH GROUP FOR MILITARY SERVICE

Many of the necessary procedures of an operations research group run directly contrary to long-established precedents of line of command, as usually encountered in military or industrial organizations Ordinarily, breadth of knowledge of a military situation, command responsibility, and power go hand in hand in the military organization The soldier in the lower echelon is supposed to know just enough to get his own job done, and his power and responsibility are commensurate with his knowledge The high command, on the other hand, has access to all of the information concerning the military situation and concurrently has broad command powers and responsibilities It is a fundamental property of operations research that operations research groups *must* have broad knowledge but should have *very little* power and responsibility Operations research workers must be able to think about the military situation impersonally and impartially, and this can be done best if they are relieved of the responsibility of issuing orders Their conclusions must take the form of advice to some high-ranking officer, *for him to make the orders* (if he sees fit)

Because of the close interconnection between breadth of knowledge and breadth of responsibility and power in military organizations, the principle of "normal channels" is particularly strong in such organizations In order that the system work effectively in times of great stress, the system of hierarchy of power and responsibility must be clear-cut Each officer must be answerable to only one superior, and the men under him must be answerable only to him, otherwise conflicting orders arise, and the system falls to pieces Since breadth of knowledge usually coincides with breadth of power and responsibility, it has been taken for granted that the channel for the transmission of intelligence must be identical with the channel for transmission of orders and requests This communalization of the intelligence channels with the command channels is satisfactory as long as the intelligence is not overly technical or is not urgent If the information is to be transmitted from headquarters to the field or from the field to headquarters is both technical *and* urgent, however, experience in the last war indicates that the normal command channels are quite inadequate They are too long, and the links in the chain usually consist of officers with little technical knowledge, and technical knowledge *cannot be transmitted* via nontechnical intermediaries

8 1 1   Importance of Contacts with Several Echelons

Let us now see what implications these general comments have on the problem of organizing an operations research group Ideally, such a group should have available all possible information concerning a given type of operation, the results of its work could be findings and recommendations on the conduct of all aspects of this type of operation, from minor details of maintenance and training to overall strategical questions Owing to the usual hierarchy of responsibility, power, and knowledge, this output must be fed into the military organiza-

tion at several different levels, depending on the level of the corresponding findings The group, therefore, should have access to several different levels in the command hierarchy

An operations research group, moreover, cannot work insulated from direct experience It probably is impossible, and it certainly would be inefficient, to have the group segregated in a single room or building, with all its data and all requests for studies pushed through a slot from the outside An extremely important part of the functions of an operations research group is to determine what are the important problems to be solved as well as to solve them It is true in operations research, as it is in other parts of science, that the proper enunciation of the problem to be solved often requires a higher order of scientific ability than does the solving of the problem, once it has been formulated It is not to be expected that nontechnical officers, immersed in the pressures of command responsibilities, should be able to formulate the problems for the operations research group to work on effectively, such a division of labor would drastically reduce the group's usefulness The operations research worker himself must get close enough to the action to be able to help formulate the problem as well as to work on its solution

Both in the interests of rapid formulation of the problems and rapid dissemination of the solutions, therefore, it is important that the operations research group have contact with a number of different echelons in the military hierarchy This inevitably means the cutting across of command boundaries The experience of World War II has shown that operations research can only function effectively and adequately by and through such cross connections The problem of the supplementing of "normal channels" is therefore a fundamental one in the organization of an operations research group either for military or for other problems In fact, one can say that it is a waste of valuable technical talent to form an operations research group without having worked out a solution of this problem that is satisfactory both to the scientists and to the executive officers involved

8 1 2   Assignment of Group

It must also be apparent that an operations research group must be attached to the *operational* commands in a military organization The logistic and technical commands of the organization also have their problems requiring scientific personnel for their solution, but this sort of work is not what is meant by operations research The operations research worker must be the scientific adviser of the fighting force itself and must never degenerate into a salesman for a laboratory or a service branch He must be able to render impartial judgments on various equipment, so as to pick the one most effective for the operation at hand, not the one that happens to be urged by a bureau It is important, not only that the operations research worker feel that he is part of the fighting team (even to the extent of being somewhat suspicious of bureaus and laboratories) but also that the operational command be thoroughly persuaded that the worker is really a member of the fighting team The operations research group should therefore be assigned directly to the operating command and should make its reports and recommendations directly to the various echelons in this command

8.1.3   Sub-Groups in the Field

It should be clear from the foregoing that an operations research group should be attached to a high echelon in the headquarters staff but should also have points of contact with lower echelons in the field With the U S Navy this was achieved by assigning the group as a whole to the Readiness Division of the Headquarters of the Commander-in-Chief, U S Fleet, and by reassigning parts of the group to the strategic planning officer, or the operations officer, of subordinate commands in the field The central group at headquarters was answerable only to headquarters and distributed its reports only on headquarters authorization The sub-groups, however, were assigned to their respective theater commands, and distributed their reports only with the authorization of these commands Thus contact was made with several different echelons in the military hierarchy

Intercommunication between the sub-group and the headquarters group was carried on directly and frequently, with the approval of headquarters and of the theater commands Toward the end of the war, biweekly teletype conferences were held between the central group and the sub-groups at Pearl Harbor, with a resulting improvement in this important intercommunication Formal reports sent from the central group to the sub-group were subject to the approval of headquarters, similarly, reports

sent from the sub-group back to headquarters were subject to the approval of the local theater commander Informal communication also went on, giving *facts*, not gossip or personal opinions Information gained by such intercommunication was not disseminated outside the group until permission had been obtained from the source Thus, with a well-indoctrinated group, technical data could be obtained rapidly without disturbing the normal channels for command

It was also found important to circulate the personnel between field assignment and headquarters group Much information can only be "soaked up" in person in the field, but such information can often be most useful back in headquarters Conversely, the headquarters worker is likely to lose touch with reality unless he is "sent to the front," once in a while A period of rotation of about six months seems to be healthy Such rotation often is opposed by the field commands, particularly when they have a good man assigned them, but the rotation is important enough for the homogeneity of the group and for the alertness of its individuals to risk local displeasure by maintaining the rotation

8.1 4   Reports and Memoranda

The output of an operations research group consists of reports and memoranda, the reports embodying the results of major studies, and the memoranda consisting of comments on various aspects of the changing military situations and of suggestions for action The reports generally come from the central or headquarters group, where the members have the leisure and facilities to carry out long-term studies The sub-groups at the outlying bases usually apply the results of these basic studies, and their output is more likely to consist of shorter notes and memoranda All this output must be scrutinized carefully to see that the material is consistent with other previous reports and with latest group opinion, as well as to see that the material does not conflict with current military doctrines or criticize unduly certain military actions

Allegorically, the group might be considered to be separated from the rest of the military organization by a semipermeable membrane From each one of its contacts with the military organization, at headquarters and at the theater commands, data concerning military operations are absorbed through the membrane into the group Inside the group these data should promote a rapid flow of ideas and suggestions, and these related ideas, suggestions, criticisms, and theories should circulate outside the group Only in this way can the proper atmosphere of freedom of thought be built up, without which no scientific advance can be made

Because of the great difference between military procedure and scientific procedure, however, this interplay of suggestions, criticism, and theory should be kept *within* the group until the new ideas and concepts have crystallized A military organization, by nature, finds it difficult to understand such an interplay, and a broadcast of the procedure to the service at large only produces misunderstanding and suspicion Therefore, the semipermeable membrane must be so designed that it will allow material to go from the group out to the service at large *only* if this material has come to represent the considered opinion of the group as a whole, on the basis of all available data at that time

Consequently, the written material of the group must be of two sorts internal studies and notes, representing preliminary theories and suggestions, which circulate freely within the group and to the sub-groups, but which are not distributed to the rest of the service except under very special circumstances, and the reports and memoranda mentioned previously, which are written primarily for circulation to the rest of the service These reports and memoranda must be carefully edited and refereed They must embody the considered opinion of the group as a whole and should not contradict previous reports (or, if they do so contradict, an explanation should be included as to why the group has changed its mind) *They must be brief* They should be written so as to be understandable and easy to read for the operational officer These officers are usually overworked and should not be expected to take the time to absorb complicated arguments or unclear writing Great effort must be made by the group to make the major points easy to understand and the reasons simple to grasp in all reports and memoranda written for distribution outside the group Oral briefing, by the group, of the operational staff on the major points of a report is often a useful means of insuring detailed understanding of its conclusions

8 1.5   Status of Group Members

In order to emphasize the difference in function between the operations research worker and the

staff officer, in military applications, it has usually been found best to leave the operations research worker in a civilian status, at least within the continental United States In an outlying theater of operations, however, it is usually necessary for the worker to be in uniform Sometimes the worker has been given a temporary rank, sufficient for him to perform his functions without undue embarrassment This temprary rank has some disadvantages, however, for it immobilizes him in the military hierarchy and makes it more difficult for him to approach lower echelons on terms of equality Sometimes it has been possible to avoid the question of temporary rank and give the worker some special insignia This also has difficulties, for proper accommodations and entrance into necessary headquarters are often only available to officers, and the special insignia may not be recognized as being the equivalent of an officer

Most of these problems are individual ones, and no general solution can be offered More comments on the status of the worker in the field are given in the next section

8 1 6   Implications for Nonmilitary Application

Many of the statements made here and in Chapter 1 concerning organizational problems and solutions for military application can be translated immediately to groups working on nonmilitary problems For example, the problem of by-passing the command channels is often present in any large organization whether it is military or not In nearly every operations research problem (except the most trivial) contacts must be made with several echelons in the operational hierarchy The group must have contact with the actual workers, carrying on parts of the operation, in order to see what the real problems are, at the same time it must have contact with the higher echelons in order to see the problem as a whole and in order to be conversant with the decisions that need to be made It is important in all cases that the group be attached directly to the operating executive in charge and not to a subsidiary or parallel research branch The reasons for this, given in section 8 1 2, are just as valid and as important in nonmilitary operations research as they are in the military instances

Few nonmilitary operations research groups will need as complex a field organization as is needed for military application in time of war In some problems, however, it will be useful and important to assign a part of the group temporarily to some outlying plant or part of the organization under study. In such a case the principles enunciated in section 8.1.3 will apply The comments concerning formal reports and internal memoranda also apply to great extent, though they need not be so fully formalized for a small group.

8 1.7 Recruiting and Training the Operations Research Worker

No particular correlation has been found between the particular scientific specialty in which the operations research worker was trained and his subsequent excellence in the field of operations research No university has at present a unified course of training in this field, so that workers in operations research must be recruited from men trained in other branches of science It is obvious that their previous training should be in science, and experience shows that graduate training, including training in scientific research, is quite important It is not certain which branch of science provides the best training for such workers; in fact it appears that each science has its own usefulness.

Men with training in physics are particularly valuable since most operations, both military and non-military, involve equipment operating on physical principles A great number of these evaluations of equipment performance must be made by men with training in physics or electrical engineering, and physicists seem to be useful in helping to design operational experiments Training in chemistry, particularly in physical chemistry, also has proved to be a good background Mathematicians are particularly useful, especially if they have training in the field of probability (which does *not* mean the usual course in statistics). Their capacity for abstract thought makes them valuable in analytic studies, though an interest in practical application seems to be more useful than a bent toward complete abstraction. Training in biology also seems to be useful in certain cases, since the data of operations research often have the same refractory quality as the data of biology Psychologists and economists have their special spheres of usefulness

A few universities are now instituting courses in operations research It should be obvious, however, that only the bare fundamentals of the subject can be learned from a formal course After having been trained in scientific research in the university, the worker must learn operations research by doing operations research Consequently, even though an introductory formal course will be of use, the important background will be one in science in general and, in particular, in scientific research The apprentice method will be the most important means of giving the final training Most operations research groups of any size have a regular training program, involving reading of reports and performing of specific jobs, which they give to all new recruits It is important that such an introductory training program be planned early in the existence of any operations research group

8 2 OPERATIONS RESEARCH IN THE FIELD

As has been mentioned in the previous section, activities in the field form an important part of operations research This section attempts to formulate and illustrate some of the aspects of field work. As before, examples are drawn chiefly from military applications, since experience has been greatest in this line In particular, the examples are drawn from the experience of the Operations Research Group (ORG) assigned to and functioning with the headquarters of the Commander-in-Chief, U S Fleet It is believed, however, that the lessons to be drawn are probably general in nature and, with appropriate modifications for particular situations, will be typical of many other types of work

Work of the field representatives serves several purposes (1) to provide help directly to the service units to which they may be temporarily attached, (2) to secure information that might otherwise be difficult to obtain and transmit it to the parent operations research body, (3) to give the individual members of the operations research group a practical background which is indispensable in avoiding the pitfalls to which the pure theorist may be subject

The value of maintaining representatives with operating military units throughout the course of an operations research group's activities is thus made apparent

8 2.1   Assignments

The principal types of field assignment include

1 Liaison
2 Staff
3 Operations
4 Training.
5 Experimental (operational)
6 Experimental (equipment)

Representatives of all types are desirable in the field In actual practice, it is seldom that a field man is restricted to work in any one of these types, indeed, his assignment is likely to represent a mixture

The *liaison type* is best illustrated by the representatives of ORG in London, where their primary mission was to secure information for the parent body and indirectly for the Navy This information was obtained from British operations research groups and from the British military services The ORG representatives also kept the British units posted on the work of the ORG home office (to the extent permitted by the naval staff) and thus helped to minimize a duplication of research

In the *staff type*, the representative is assigned directly to the staff of a commander of some operations unit, such as a sea frontier, a fleet, or an area. This representative acts as a small operations research group in his own right, seeking solutions to problems appropriate to his duties that are proposed to him by the staff commander In addition, his location at headquarters proves extremely useful in the collection and systematization of operations statistics and in forwarding them to the central ORG This type of assignment has been found very fruitful and has been used often both in Atlantic antisubmarine work and in the Pacific

Perhaps the best example of the staff type of work is found in a Pearl Harbor sub-group, consisting of several men assigned to Commander Submarines, Pacific This sub-group conducted the bulk of its work at the command headquarters, getting into the "field" and participating in operations in connection with such projects as required such activity

In most staff-type assignments, such as to sea frontiers, the men have also engaged in operations-type activities, going on operational missions to observe the techniques involved. This contact with lower-echelon operating personnel was used to disseminate directly such technical information as seemed desirable. Thus, a representative at a sea frontier could spend a considerable portion of his time visiting various bases where he studied the local records, lectured and talked informally with the personnel, and gained personal knowledge of the technicalities of the operations Purely operations-type assignments have been infrequent, perhaps the closest approximation to these were assignments to an aircraft carrier escort (CVE), during an antisubmarine cruise, to a submarine on war patrol and to a task force during a landing operation

The *training-type* assignment has also been infrequent, but some excellent work has been done by men assigned to such training bases as at Langley Field, Va , in connection with Army ASW work, and at Kaneohe, with Fleet Air Wing 2 On such assignments studies were made of improving operators' techniques through training, with an eye to the best methods At such locations it was also frequently possible to find approximations to operational data by studying the results of training for the operation under study, which were quite useful when it happened to be difficult to obtain operational results For example, a study of ASW bombing errors from operational data was difficult because of the scarcity of well-recorded data, whereas data on training-bombing errors were available in statistically significant quantity.

An example of the *experimental-(operational-) type* of work was to be found in the assignment of members to the Antisubmarine Development Detachment, Atlantic Fleet (ASDevLant), the official unit that made experimental studies of proposed operational techniques in the field of antisubmarine warfare Here the operations research representatives contributed importantly, through their study of the results of operational tests A somewhat similar assignment was at Langley Field, to the Army Air Forces development unit for antisubmarine work In general, it is regarded as desirable to maintain one or more operations research representatives at stations devoting their efforts to experimental operational study This sort of activity has expanded considerably in importance and scope since the war

The sixth type, *experimental (equipment)*, is not properly part of an operations research group's work Of necessity, however, it has been found frequently that this type of work can be done expediently by the group's men, because of location or other reasons Such work has been carried on at ASDevLant, at Langley Field, and, toward the end of the war, at the naval ordnance test station (NOTS) at Inyokern

All six types of work might typically be included at a single base. A man assigned to a sea frontier, in addition to staff duties, would observe operational work in the field and function as liaison between his station and the headquarters group, might make some studies of training results, and might occasionally carry out experimentation on a minor scale at the request of the commanding officer

Of the six types, a combination of the staff and operations types has been found most fruitful in providing assistance to the commands and information to the central group Although each type has obvious merit within its defined scope, the assignment to the staff of the commander of a fairly large operating unit has proved of greatest value and should probably constitute the bulk of the field work in a future war

Assignment of field men to the Trinidad Sector of the Caribbean Sea Frontier, in the early stages of the antisubmarine effort, is cited as an excellent example They reported directly to the commander of the sector and thus may be regarded as having a staff assignment There they were available for consultation on planning and the results of operations As in most broadly organized bases, there was ample variety of operations to require of the men a certain amount of the five other types of work Proximity to operating squadrons enabled the men to keep in close contact with the field Studies were made of the training results in these same squadrons Liaison was carried on, both in forwarding operational needs to Washington and in explaining doctrine developed in Washington to the operating forces At various times, experimental work was done for instance, on the study of the effects of German search receivers and of the use of American search receivers in searching for German radar

The types of field assignments possible and feasible for nonmilitary application will depend considerably on the operation under study A study of railroad operations, for example, might profitably involve assignment of several operations research workers to various shipping centers on a staff or liaison-type assignment to a subordinate office of the organization to which the worker is attached Operations research for a large merchandising concern, on the other hand, may only have the opportunity to carry on field work of the training type mentioned previously, studying the elements of the operation in connection with the training courses for operational personnel

8.2.2 **Types of Field Work**

An operations research man on field assignment encounters various types of work, which fall into these primary divisions·

1. Analytical
2 Statistical
3 Liaison
4 Experimental
5 Educational
6 Publication

The *analytical* type of problem consists of the study of an operation, major or minor, before its execution, or at least before data on the results of the operation are available for examination Examples of this are numerous the design of aircraft barrier patrols in the Fourth Fleet Area to intercept submarines, or the study of antitorpedo-evasive maneuvers by the Submarine Operations Research Group, SubPac

An operation can also be studied by a *statistical* examination of the operational results As typical examples of the numerous studies of this sort carried on during the war may be mentioned the examination of contacts to determine the probable use of search receivers against radar, or studies of the relative hazards to convoy and independent merchant vessels. A more complete discussion of specialized statistical techniques is given in the next section

Liaison work has been discussed to some extent previously and hardly needs amplifying here This work is a natural necessity, and a certain amount of it must be done at each base

A certain amount of *experimental* work is a necessary and proper function of an operations research field man This does not mean that it is his proper duty to indulge in the design or development of new equipment, but he can play an important role in studying the use of new equipment or new operations. When a new piece of equipment, such as a radar set or a bombsight, is first available for field use, it is desirable to assign, if possible, the first output to units operating in an area serviced by an operations research man Then the initial use of the equipment can be scientifically observed and suggestions formulated to aid in introducing the innovation elsewhere in the field Similarly, when a new operational technique is provided, such as the use of flares in a night aircraft attack on a submarine or surface vessel, it is again desirable to try it out under careful observation and to make suggestions for the elimination of imperfections that may appear.

The *educational* aspect of field work is twofold: education of the operations research man in the methods of the field, and such instruction work in the field as he is able to provide The first, self-educational, aspect is of extreme importance to the success of an operations research group and should be encouraged at every opportunity It is only by gaining intimate practical acquaintance with operations problems that successful operations research can be done

The educational contributions to the service personnel which are within the sphere of activity of the field representative include both formal and informal instruction It is not unusual for him to be called upon to deliver a lecture or series of lectures to operational squadron personnel either at a school or at their own base Informally, he has frequent contacts with operational personnel, both professionally and socially, which present opportunities for fruitful discussions

The field man is occasionally called upon to aid in the *publication* of professional periodicals issued by the command to which he is attached. Examples of this are the *Statistical Summary* published monthly by the Trinidad Sector of the Caribbean Sea Frontier, the *Submarine Bulletin* published by the Commander Submarines, Pacific Fleet, and the monthly *Antisubmarine Bulletin of the Seventh Fleet*. Representatives of the Antisubmarine Warfare Operations Research Group have had important roles in the formation and continued publication of these bulletins This type of work is regarded as most valuable, inasmuch as it acquaints a wide circle of readers with statistical and analytical studies

A different method of subdividing operations research work would be into strategic and tactical work. A great deal of the operations research in the recent war, but by no means all, has been in the tactical field, and this has been even more true of field men If a field man, however, is attached to a sufficiently high-echelon command, he may be called upon to study strategic problems For example, an ORG man at Argentia worked on the question of routing convoys, and ORG men at London worked on the problems of optimum size of convoys and the Bay of Biscay antisubmarine offensive.

The following general comments concerning field assignments are made on the basis of the experience of the ORG during the past war It is to be remembered that, although these suggestions probably would apply to other cases, situations might well develop that would demand entirely different treatment

Selection of the location for a new field assignment and the initial installation of a man depend on several factors Considerations apart from operations research determine the location of some types, such as liaison, training, or research, and such assignments are almost automatic On the other hand, the location of a combined staff-operations-type assignment requires careful consideration Selection of regions of extensive activity in the operations under study should be made with considerable care

It must be understood that assignment is made only upon direct invitation of the officer to whom the man will be ordered This requires formal or informal machinery to inform the proper officials of the existence and availability of operations research men and of the type of service they can perform

Assignment to as high a command as possible, compatible with the area and type of problem under study, is generally desirable This permits the widest distribution of the field man's work.

In reporting to a new assignment, the field man should try to take with him a carefully chosen library of material bearing on his proposed work Usually the parent body can supply a wider variety of literature than is available in the local command This library should be kept up to date during the assignment

After being assigned, a field man works on problems presented to him by the commanding officer of the staff as well as on problems originating with himself The ultimate decision as to the work to be done remains with the commanding officer The field man should reach an agreement with this officer that, as a scientist, he should have complete access to the data pertaining to an assigned problem. He is to make all official reports to the same officer, with such distribution as the latter approves. However, informal communication with ORG headquarters should be arranged for, as this is highly desirable for the interchange of ideas These informal communications are generally shown to the officer in charge, for his information rather than for censorship.

Provision for opportunities for frequent trips about the operational area and to the operations research central headquarters at least every six months should be arranged, to stimulate further the exchange of ideas

The field man is enjoined to remember that these assignments should be terminated as well as started. Once he is well established in a given location, natural inertia may be counted upon to slow the process of terminating the assignment and completing the work in that field. It should be understood that operations are continually changing, and assignments must be shifted to keep field men in appropriately active regions The supply of such men is limited and should not be wasted in dead-end streets.

In the last analysis, the success or failure of a field assignment is fundamentally determined by the personality of the man involved His background should include a certain amount of physics, engineering, and mathematics, including statistical theory He should, moreover, be well trained in most phases of the operation under study And, above all, he should have a personality that will permit him to talk successfully to all ranks, from the bottom to the top, as the measure of his achievement may depend on this basic ability to adapt himself to all grades of personnel.

TABLE I   Random sequence of digits

Derived from Tippett, *Random Sampling Numbers*, Cambridge University Press, 1927 (See Section 2 1, Table 1 of Chapter 2, and Section 6 4)

					34829	12006	51850	01054	55930
					09655	44407	72675	10410	22229
					29974	68015	40277	55815	90984
					52490	09053	35850	32398	53650
					06538	69698	49007	23532	38896
57705	13094	60835	36014	35950					
71618	35193	42323	38612	03235	33690	45040	45744	98683	27307
73710	64580	25732	93857	73606	61708	87590	96911	60166	15298
70131	64559	93364	33749	66090	36074	10144	60456	97834	33252
16961	68008	63407	08921	31842	56365	78064	61446	05141	83928
					88288	18915	01484	42971	23435
53324	39848	72028	07721	22807	65421	84885	58127	84117	12627
43166	33851	25496	58577	41476	67798	74145	14569	48861	30367
26275	80586	83761	39303	74473	69184	26754	16211	09156	23333
05926	69939	58568	19302	78489	59886	21304	99988	01241	60360
66289	98351	27409	17068	14142	90654	37385	53211	34771	69359
35483	32673	64789	59201	75975	69921	03959	66049	65690	45320
09393	12949	78992	18688	55604	57959	76536	71359	53990	73195
30304	14644	67388	73449	80702	63609	58656	02834	56855	50876
55186	66887	75316	41734	11027	98462	84131	30962	16608	32627
64003	43042	73673	17033	34559	63578	50128	71712	70101	70556
20514	49110	21681	18664	73345	92500	97454	32388	46167	93500
00188	18170	32763	94722	02783	03289	01648	69834	55659	16023
55709	19187	50983	55024	54095	95414	93649	22686	26319	20078
86977	02464	98359	85143	29373	30781	56663	67117	05596	92740
31303	55739	38440	28594	96006	28838	07809	64571	68116	43583
11578	52992	78142	76086	69351	31502	60309	74417	30379	76145
93045	86513	25730	97570	07995	93655	23699	59729	24354	69477
93011	10480	30454	26292	00900	91757	82052	60805	51929	34027
42844	56437	19106	07120	29396	17901	85317	91288	13396	23426
52906	13647	58222	11851	17727	05558	09792	41101	50527	70231
09461	57910	45818	24806	25424	31648	65813	70855	25154	61461
99602	54062	96748	90506	38695	08183	90183	34523	06277	72870
69962	23767	45732	39116	02624	04408	57276	35855	08366	85109
31311	43191	91542	35745	36522	97706	72549	42280	46410	32961
27004	03283	78115	82713	56461	14925	83202	50674	19199	75530
65339	46250	18186	07938	62250	00994	07555	82548	10664	91269
93382	28366	61450	51275	73071	43496	32443	70353	89865	63191
05758	16074	74582	32203	59362	03051	66017	06433	65211	52786
00336	98951	80004	51925	98178	11444	47321	05789	61382	06016
88222	54686	49538	24693	40526	06864	35326	82795	41116	95670
98585	87615	22917	16837	74412	85993	08367	49336	45915	25019
52103	44968	99135	78155	79033	92473	64742	94781	65421	65952
91827	27709	58274	97412	62192	75906	66400	01912	77234	77311
07069	59560	01940	00892	90942	98187	66808	01330	23430	93999
13928	00799	87397	84299	34623	13830	49703	12138	11171	14363
66674	76151	84445	96036	48259	50518	48680	87881	78118	88178
99279	61716	86012	48472	12634	85445	08606	40057	26616	26825
24202	59298	51625	42687	93997	19323	18011	62325	48154	15821
94010	89923	71881	89434	32799	10514	36580	21041	33802	53561
60981	20327	64466	67912	04011	55961	12790	66413	32462	27047
75626	90180	89489	50359	98156	29560	95580	08834	43767	15735
77367	28023	62721	97152	23640	37295	07771	01100	23449	30044
62046	54017	91319	03727	45005	20270	11113	74904	89595	22767
69759	22721	36524	16443	76193	03878	27161	62190	00088	79130
70600	23292	90567	86755	54159	73133	90578	05308	70756	90830

	TABLE I—(Continued)			
56656	74058	79714	33580	49320
28995	31970	39110	71164	74969
83635	48160	46799	71120	63317
91719	58831	70122	47229	59911
60112	45549	23508	47961	96059
90722	25293	85013	45087	20376
17557	37568	04058	01851	88070
30266	86373	19069	22246	62328
78543	37058	89772	27159	46158
20980	41329	04998	88478	94797
76762	95282	46440	01328	66375
23542	80262	02462	71287	29772
99512	12069	49701	18345	72659
67839	06330	28240	69027	11868
64594	96862	16958	50558	89049
59559	89230	39081	56032	50874
42957	47491	28028	39521	07309
69161	27766	43883	40266	38074
19660	24412	57042	34137	91103
17323	47446	61047	81370	31174
85144	01109	14180	06475	51450
14284	40876	42047	09332	02897
99106	17378	20375	13116	01359
48956	51457	41422	81782	98690
02438	23725	58885	29126	88618
10712	00829	08793	77802	39699
94918	07866	19220	09379	71119
37052	31862	96291	28953	97538
99343	78243	72801	24279	41276
76178	37668	53493	62114	34825
19748	59795	38219	49232	10148
36708	24299	45132	92481	44499
96428	85178	70368	91546	29881
42829	18331	96411	21303	36397
78388	21440	53420	31554	83349

19268	73248	81305	07701	19415
14078	90001	88821	56944	92014
75825	16401	20301	70654	46231
42705	14426	12088	90910	86701
45709	49315	63916	59272	37804
62509	19795	24528	56275	09077
35964	55927	28935	99538	20821
98225	46074	42975	90799	44421
89995	16835	68290	92188	25552
47202	25233	21637	51827	14084
66414	93439	00550	65926	85223
27671	90798	56370	22726	83527
67780	99540	27914	23458	97548
58418	91310	94209	07136	84089
71261	27258	35317	04121	53460
56061	65853	87865	01757	99359
46275	81178	58592	93289	05065
37907	60879	78292	48656	17171
28329	81037	10070	56832	50895
82877	17434	77931	56768	38316
54306	49594	30046	56677	09312
12803	54403	13160	62353	82501
74173	40297	52041	19082	15843
39539	89717	45036	60698	46286
70937	18423	20323	97672	82885
06256	41832	39121	94175	09627
61618	92582	04569	28897	51244
83223	23505	22187	44185	64919
34877	69215	51377	86341	55073
27107	96364	25416	66339	40116
09312	15960	06929	96272	41919
82501	62062	72868	49368	77275
15843	33995	51332	53150	59071
46286	11459	43599	73166	00626
82885	43910	37202	21139	10557

TABLE II   Random sequence of angles, from 000 to 359
Derived from Table I (See Sections 2 1 and 6 4)

143	243	012	184	359	243	015	343	094	312	319	031	059	178	232	221	262	031	280	345
307	034	083	125	211	051	160	036	115	106	008	000	142	165	120	302	174	290	350	332
001	218	004	325	211	168	164	307	346	144	144	317	104	022	246	115	197	155	151	292
070	002	130	191	106	322	043	087	317	268	086	103	036	248	339	339	324	018	204	009
044	095	032	335	319	089	245	350	246	078	199	156	055	227	275	149	242	170	204	118
158	025	246	018	316	104	343	070	342	051	063	272	246	001	272	144	083	080	297	128
348	061	276	130	309	251	017	147	066	178	258	174	286	293	121	041	078	020	104	033
258	316	037	127	174	337	192	319	303	073	252	109	130	071	272	010	339	323	007	340
205	183	171	032	117	246	120	352	156	223	127	303	349	069	136	262	271	290	342	221
057	225	014	001	277	263	343	346	259	133	214	210	094	343	211	122	183	261	035	156
250	088	205	045	007	083	037	263	011	306	126	204	244	064	133	156	154	226	299	040
313	091	272	180	028	193	017	146	019	343	338	007	273	347	219	147	118	008	060	266
270	272	058	045	127	285	143	052	042	202	114	002	237	319	254	194	159	088	288	018
262	034	299	241	222	012	220	036	213	112	332	092	075	125	037	156	328	010	065	026
059	108	018	296	274	194	259	334	219	270	116	045	120	269	359	121	289	106	055	258
115	009	267	342	135	186	036	287	309	275	166	112	168	255	110	234	164	090	316	041
336	067	294	096	049	010	140	090	278	173	171	110	164	356	316	092	027	231	270	025
179	111	164	025	288	303	293	333	027	187	341	117	184	012	191	006	288	278	032	280
081	269	304	002	359	323	341	274	102	052	116	069	353	232	012	053	087	159	313	167
169	149	329	021	012	166	159	342	000	244	185	159	159	268	213	163	345	292	114	035
315	116	254	050	280	170	171	225	159	284	320	055	159	262	083	323	252	137	026	023
354	051	048	011	074	098	126	089	120	225	079	235	083	219	028	116	111	116	119	170
149	106	018	089	359	248	103	262	299	266	089	077	062	296	076	256	318	134	056	175
003	210	331	260	115	186	311	358	123	261	191	118	333	023	182	329	177	030	031	303
303	085	309	136	103	101	135	279	056	275	250	133	202	323	275	295	272	032	253	137
242	216	232	278	186	164	277	055	219	323	191	298	274	184	337	161	114	279	000	188
094	291	200	334	101	062	120	082	040	286	347	079	323	222	269	173	180	218	023	287
139	258	319	273	323	170	035	325	106	107	091	348	212	007	134	011	253	163	062	279
093	144	328	290	049	262	213	278	089	071	071	192	251	262	170	164	077	232	277	082
096	194	030	030	142	357	102	102	061	061	037	027	098	280	206	235	277	124	247	150

TABLE III   Random normal deviates in units of standard errors.

Based upon tables of E L Dodd, *Bollettino di Matematica*, 1942, pages 76–77 (See equation (26) of Chapter 2 and Section 6 4)

z	z²	z	z²	z	z²	z	z²	z	z²	(z²)
0 80	0 640	−0 69	0 476	0 38	0 144	0 13	0 017	1 73	2 993	
−0 54	0 292	−0 21	0 044	−0 60	0 360	−1 59	2 528	−0 60	0 360	
0 42	0 176	1 67	2 789	0 67	0 449	0 06	0 004	1 37	1 877	0 75
−0 48	0 230	−1 13	1 277	0 50	0 250	−0 19	0 036	1 18	1 392	
0 16	0 026	−0 61	0 372	0 74	0 548	1 16	1 346	0 37	0 137	
1 95	3 803	1 57	2 465	−1 19	1 416	−1 47	2 161	0 35	0 122	
1 87	3 497	1 41	1 988	−0 37	0 137	−0 25	0 062	−0 25	0 063	
0 63	0 397	1 17	1 369	0 25	0 062	−0 24	0 058	−0 31	0 096	1 11
−1 48	2 190	0 46	0 212	−1 28	1 638	−1 36	1 850	−0 83	0 689	
−0 49	0 240	−0 27	0 073	1 04	1 082	−1 41	1 988	0 38	0 144	
−2 92	8 526	1 53	2 341	−0 51	0 260	−1 02	1 040	−0 78	0 608	
1 72	2 958	−0 08	0 006	1 29	1 664	−0 96	0 922	0 91	0 828	
−0 90	0 810	−1 75	3 063	0 15	0 023	−1 09	1 188	−0 12	0 014	1 06
−0 24	0 058	1 16	1 346	0 21	0 044	−0 22	0 048	1 23	1 513	
0 24	0 058	0 16	0 026	0 28	0 078	0 75	0 563	0 96	0 922	
0 34	0 116	0 06	0 004	−0 72	0 518	0 44	0 194	−2 27	5 153	
−0 88	0 774	0 14	0 020	0 89	0 792	−0 14	0 020	−0 39	0 152	
−1 07	1 145	0 54	0 292	−0 46	0 212	0 81	0 656	1 16	1 346	0 80
0 47	0 221	−0 25	0 063	−0 01	0 000	0 59	0 348	0 56	0 314	
1 46	2 132	−1 53	2 341	1 51	2 280	0 54	0 292	0 71	0 504	
−0 67	0 449	−2 01	4 040	−0 52	0 270	0 67	0 449	0 05	0 003	
0 61	0 372	−0 70	0 490	1 04	1 082	−2 01	4 040	−0 91	0 828	
1 15	1 322	2 08	4 326	0 60	0 360	0 81	0 656	−0 77	0 593	
−0 19	0 036	−0 95	0 903	0 56	0 314	−0 29	0 084	−0 22	0 048	
−0 90	0 810	1 93	3 725	−0 57	0 325	−0 61	0 372	−1 61	2 592	1 07
−0 70	0 490	−0 97	0 941	1 36	1 850	−0 02	0 000	0 87	0 757	
−0 36	0 130	1 38	1 904	−1 24	1 538	−0 68	0 462	−0 92	0 846	
0 05	0 003	−1 08	1 166	−0 49	0 240	−0 29	0 084	0 81	0 656	
0 56	0 314	0 45	0 202	−0 37	0 137	0 26	0 068	2 37	5 617	
1 28	1 638	1 25	1 563	1 34	1 796	0 83	0 689	−0 52	0 270	
−1 18	1 392	−0 28	0 078	−1 23	1 513	−0 91	0 828	0 31	0 096	
−0 66	0 436	−0 08	0 006	−0 76	0 578	0 75	0 563	1 75	3 062	
−0 68	0 462	0 78	0 608	−0 96	0 922	0 15	0 023	1 78	3 168	
1 76	3 098	0 39	0 152	−0 74	0 548	0 57	0 325	−0 80	0 640	
−2 47	6 101	1 35	1 823	−0 33	0 109	1 66	2 756	0 75	0 562	1 13
−0 32	0 102	−0 48	0 230	0 91	0 828	−1 99	3 960	−0 81	0 656	
2 22	4 928	−0 22	0 048	−1 11	1 232	0 77	0 593	0 01	0 000	
0 02	0 000	−0 35	0 123	−1 06	1 124	0 19	0 036	−1 59	2 528	
−0 55	0 303	0 14	0 020	−1 12	1 254	0 28	0 078	0 00	0 000	
2 62	6 864	0 73	0 533	0 06	0 004	−0 40	0 160	1 13	1 277	

Each group of 25 or 50 deviates has been adjusted by a small amount so that the mean value of z for the group is exactly zero The mean square deviate for each group is given at the extreme right For a large enough group this average should approach unity

TABLE IV Binomial distribution function $F_b(s, n) = 1 - I_p(s + 1, n - s)$ Probability of s or fewer successes in n trials, and the probability that it will take more than n trials to achieve $s + 1$ successes Probability of success per trial is p (See equation (21) of Chapter 2)

	$p=0.1$	$p=0.2$	$p=0.3$	$p=0.4$	$p=0.5$	$p=0.6$	$p=0.7$	$p=0.8$	$p=0.9$
$n = 2$, $s = 0$	0 8100	0 6400	0 4900	0 3600	0 2500	0 1600	0 0900	0 0400	0 0100
$s = 1$	9900	9600	9100	8400	7500	6400	5100	3600	1900
$s = 2$	1 0000	1 0000	1 0000	1 0000	1 0000	1 0000	1 0000	1 0000	1 0000
$n = 5$, $s = 0$	0 5905	0 3277	0 1681	0 0778	0 0512	0 0102	0 0024	0 0003	0 0000
$s = 1$	9185	7373	5282	3370	.1875	0949	0347	0067	0005
$s = 2$	9914	9421	8369	6826	5000	3174	1631	0579	0086
$s = 3$	9995	9933	9692	9130	8125	6630	4718	2627	0815
$s = 4$	1 0000	9997	9976	9898	9088	9222	8319	6723	4095
$s = 5$	1 0000	1 0000	1 0000	1 0000	1 0000	1 0000	1 0000	1 0000	1 0000
$n = 10$, $s = 0$	0 3487	0 1074	0 0282	0 0060	0 0010	0 0001	0 0000	0 0000	0 0000
$s = 1$	7361	4068	1493	0464	0107	0017	0001	0000	0000
$s = 2$	9298	6778	3828	1673	0547	0123	0016	0001	0000
$s = 3$	9872	8791	6496	3823	1719	0548	0129	0012	0000
$s = 4$	9990	9672	8497	6331	3770	1662	0463	0064	0001
$s = 5$	9999	9936	9527	8338	6230	3669	1503	0328	0016
$s = 6$	1 0000	9992	9894	9452	8281	6177	3504	1209	0128
$s = 7$	1 0000	9999	9984	9877	9453	8327	6172	3222	0702
$s = 8$	1 0000	1 0000	9999	9983	9893	9536	8507	6242	2639
$s = 9$	1 0000	1 0000	1.0000	9999	9990	9940	9718	8926	6513
$s = 10$	1 0000	1 0000	1 0000	1 0000	1 0000	1 0000	1 0000	1 0000	1 0000
$n = 20$, $s = 0$	0 1216	0 0115	0 0008	0 0000	0 0000	0 0000	0 0000	0 0000	0 0000
$s = 2$	6769	2161	0355	0036	0002	0000	0000	0000	0000
$s = 4$	9568	6296	2375	0510	0059	0003	0000	0000	0000
$s = 6$	9976	9133	6080	2500	0577	0064	0003	0000	0000
$s = 8$	9999	9900	8867	5956	2517	0565	0051	0001	0000
$s = 10$	1 0000	9994	9829	8725	5881	2447	0480	0026	0000
$s = 12$	1 0000	1 0000	9987	9790	8684	5841	2277	0321	0004
$s = 14$	1 0000	1 0000	1 0000	9984	9793	8744	5836	1958	0113
$s = 16$	1 0000	1 0000	1 0000	1 0000	9987	9840	8929	5886	1330
$s = 18$	1 0000	1 0000	1 0000	1 0000	1 0000	9995	9924	9308	6083
$s = 20$	1 0000	1 0000	1 0000	1 0000	1 0000	1 0000	1 0000	1 0000	1 0000
$n = 50$, $s = 0$	0 0052	0 0000	0 0000	0 0000	0 0000	0 0000	0 0000	0 0000	0 0000
$s = 5$	6161	0480	0007	0000	0000	0000	0000	0000	0000
$s = 10$	9906	5836	0789	0021	0000	0000	0000	0000	0000
$s = 15$	1 0000	9692	5692	0955	0033	0000	0000	0000	0000
$s = 20$	1 0000	9997	9522	5610	1013	0034	0000	0000	0000
$s = 25$	1 0000	1 0000	9991	9427	5561	.0978	0024	0000	0000
$s = 30$	1 0000	1 0000	1 0000	9986	9405	5535	0848	0009	0000
$s = 35$	1 0000	1 0000	1 0000	1 0000	9987	9460	5532	0607	0001
$s = 40$	1 0000	1 0000	1 0000	1 0000	1 0000	9992	9598	5563	0245
$s = 45$	1 0000	1 0000	1 0000	1 0000	1 0000	1 0000	9998	9815	5688
$s = 50$	1 0000	1 0000	1 0000	1 0000	1 0000	1 0000	1 0000	1 0000	1 0000

TABLE V   Normal distribution functions

$$f_n(x) = \frac{1}{\sqrt{2\pi}} e^{-(x^2/2)}, \; F_n(x) = \frac{1}{\sqrt{2\pi}} \int_{-\infty}^{x} e^{-(u^2/2)} du$$

(See equation (24) of Chapter 2.)

x	$f_n(x)$	$F_n(x)$	x	$f_n(x)$	$F_n(x)$
−4 0	0 0001	0 0000	0 0	0 3989	0 5000
−3 8	0003	0001	0 2	3910	5793
−3 6	.0006	.0002	0 4	3683	6554
−3 4	0012	0004	0 6	3332	7257
−3 2	0024	0007	0 8	2897	7881
−3 0	0044	0014	1 0	2420	8413
−2 8	0079	0026	1 2	1942	8847
−2 6	0136	0047	1 4	1497	9193
−2 4	0224	0082	1 6	1109	9452
−2 2	0355	0139	1 8	0790	9641
−2 0	0 0540	0 0228	2 0	0 0540	0 9772
−1 8	0790	0359	2 2	0355	9861
−1 6	1109	0548	2 4	0224	9918
−1 4	1497	0807	2 6	0136	9953
−1 2	1942	.1151	2 8	0079	9974
−1 0	2420	1587	3 0	0044	9986
−0 8	2897	2119	3 2	0024	9993
−0 6	3332	2743	3 4	0012	9996
−0 4	3683	3446	3 6	0006	9998
−0 2	3910	4207	3 8	0003	9999
0 0	0 3989	0 5000	4 0	0 0001	1 0000

$F_n(x)$	x	$f_n(x)$	$F_n(x)$	x	$f_n(x)$	$F_n(x)$	x	$f_n(x)$
0 00	− ∞	0 0000	0 30	−0 525	0 3477	0 70	0 525	0 3477
02	−2 053	0486	32	− 468	3576	72	583	3363
04	−1 742	0874	34	− 412	3665	74	644	3242
06	−1 554	1193	36	− 359	3741	76	707	3109
08	−1 405	.1489	38	− 306	3807	78	773	2900
10	−1 281	1754	40	− 253	3862	80	842	2799
12	−1 175	0 1998	42	−0 202	0 3906	82	0 916	0 2620
14	−1 080	2227	44	− 151	3943	84	0 995	2430
16	−0 995	2430	46	− 101	3969	86	1 080	2227
18	− 916	2620	48	− 050	3983	88	1 175	1998
20	− 842	2799	50	0 000	3989	90	1 281	1754
22	−0 773	0 2900	52	+0 050	0 3983	92	1 405	0 1489
24	− 707	3109	54	101	3969	94	1 554	1193
.26	− 644	3242	56	151	3943	96	1 742	0874
28	− 583	3363	58	202	3906	98	2 053	0486
30	− 525	3477	60	253	3862	1 00	∞	0000
			62	0 306	0 3807			
			64	359	3741			
			66	412	3665			
			68	468	3576			
			70	525	3477			

TABLE VI   Poisson distribution function $F_p(m, E) = \sum_{n=0}^{m} \frac{E^n}{n!} e^{-E} = \int_E^\infty \frac{x^m}{m!} e^{-x} dx$ Probability that m points or fewer are in an interval when the expected number is E (See equation (30) of Chapter 2)

	E=0.1	E=0.2	E=0.3	E=0.4	E=0.5	E=0.6	E=0.7	E=0.8	E=0.9
m = 0	0 9048	0 8187	0 7408	0 6703	0 6065	0 5488	0 4966	0 4493	0 4066
1	9953	9825	9631	9385	9098	8781	8442	8088	7725
2	9998	9989	9964	9921	9856	9769	9659	9526	9371
3	1 0000	9999	9997	9992	9982	.9966	9942	9909	9865
4	1 0000	1 0000	1 0000	9999	9998	9996	9992	9986	9977
5			1 0000	1 0000	1 0000	1 0000	9999	9998	9997
6	.			1 0000	1 0000	1 0000	1 0000	1 0000	1 0000
7							1 0000	1 0000	1 0000

	E=1.0	E=1.1	E=1.2	E=1.3	E=1.4	E=1.5	E=1.6	E=1.7	E=1.8	E=1.9
n = 0	0 3679	0 3329	0 3012	0 2725	0 2466	0 2231	0 2019	0 1827	0 1653	0 1496
1	7358	6990	6626	6268	5918	5578	5249	4932	4628	4337
2	9197	9004	8795	8571	8335	8088	7834	7572	7306	7037
3	9810	9743	9662	9569	9463	9344	9212	9068	8913	8747
4	9963	9946	9923	9893	9857	9814	9763	9704	9636	9559
5	9994	9990	9985	9178	9968	9955	9940	9920	9896	9868
6	9999	9999	9997	9996	9994	9991	9987	9981	9974	9966
7	1 0000	1 0000	1 0000	9999	9999	9998	9997	9996	9994	9992
8	1 0000	1 0000	1 0000	1 0000	1 0000	1 0000	1 0000	9999	9999	9998
9				1 0000	1 0000	1 0000	1 0000	1 0000	1 0000	1 0000

	E=2.0	E=2.1	E=2.2	E=2.3	E=2.4	E=2.5	E=2.6	E=2.7	E=2.8	E=2.9
m = 0	0 1353	0 1225	0 1108	0 1003	0 0907	0 0821	0 0743	0 0672	0 0608	0 0550
1	4060	3796	3546	3309	3084	2873	2674	2487	2311	2146
2	6767	6496	6227	5960	5697	5438	5184	4936	4695	4460
3	8571	8386	8194	7993	7787	7576	7360	7141	6919	6696
4	9473	9379	9275	9102	9041	8912	8774	8629	8477	8318
5	9834	9796	9751	9700	9643	9580	9510	9433	9349	9258
6	9955	9941	9925	9906	9884	9858	9828	9794	9756	9713
7	9989	9985	9980	9974	9967	9958	9947	9934	9919	9912
8	9998	9997	9995	9994	9991	9989	9985	9981	9976	9969
9	1 0000	9999	9999	9999	9998	9997	9996	9995	9993	9991
10	1 0000	1 0000	1 0000	1 0000	1 0000	9999	9999	9999	9998	9998
12		1 0000	1 0000	1 0000	1 0000	1 0000	1 0000	1 0000	1 0000	1 0000
14						1 0000	1 0000	1 0000	1 0000	1 0000

	E=3.0	E=3.2	E=3.4	E=3.6	E=3.8	E=4.0	E=4.2	E=4.4	E=4.6	E=4.8
m = 0	0 0498	0 0408	0 0334	0 0273	0 0224	0 0183	0 0150	0 0123	0 0101	0 0082
1	1991	1712	1468	1257	1074	0916	0780	0663	0563	0477
2	4232	3799	3397	3027	2689	2381	2102	1851	1626	1425
3	6472	6025	5584	5152	4735	4335	3954	3594	3257	2942
4	8153	7806	7442	7064	6678	6288	5898	5512	5132	4763
5	9161	8946	8705	8441	8156	7851	7531	7199	6858	6510
6	9665	9554	9421	9267	9091	8893	8675	8436	8180	7908
7	9881	9832	9769	9692	9599	9489	9361	9214	9050	8867
8	9962	9943	9917	9883	9840	9786	9721	9642	9549	9442
9	9989	9982	9973	9960	9942	9919	9889	9851	9805	9749
10	9997	9995	9992	9987	9981	9972	.9959	.9943	9922	9896
12	1 0000	1 0000	9999	9999	9998	9997	9996	9993	9990	9986
14	1 0000	1 0000	1 0000	1 0000	1 0000	1 0000	1 0000	9999	9999	9999
16								1 0000	1 0000	1 0000
18						.			1 0000	1 0000

TABLE VI—(Continued)

	E=50	E=52	E=54	E=56	E=58	E=60	E=65	E=70	E=75	E=80
n = 0	0 0067	0 0055	0 0045	0 0037	0 0030	0 0025	0 0015	0 0009	0 0006	0 0003
1	0404	0342	0289	0244	0206	0174	0113	0073	0047	0030
2	1247	1088	0948	0824	0715	0620	0430	0296	0203	0137
3	2650	2381	2133	1906	1700	1512	1118	0818	0591	0424
4	4405	4061	3733	3422	3127	2851	2237	1730	1321	0996
5	6160	5809	5461	5119	4783	4457	3690	3007	2414	1912
6	7622	7324	7017	6703	6384	6063	5265	4497	3782	3134
7	8666	8449	8217	7970	7710	7440	6728	5987	5246	4529
8	9319	9181	9027	8857	.8672	.8472	7916	7291	6620	5925
9	9682	9603	9512	9409	9292	9161	8774	8305	7764	7166
10	9863	9823	9775	9718	9651	9574	9332	9015	8622	8159
12	9980	9972	9962	9949	9932	9912	9840	9730	9573	9362
14	9998	9997	9995	9993	9990	9986	9970	9943	9897	9827
16	1 0000	1 0000	9999	9999	9999	9998	9996	9990	9980	9963
18	1 0000	1 0000	1 0000	1 0000	1 0000	1 0000	9999	9999	9997	9993
20		1 0000	1 0000	1 0000	1 0000	1 0000	1 0000	1 0000	1 0000	9999
22							1 0000	1 0000	1 0000	1 0000
24										1 0000

	E=85	E=90	E=95	E=10		E=85	E=90	E=95	E=10
m = 0	0 0002	0 0001	0 0001	0 0000	m = 10	7634	7060	6453	5830
1	0019	0012	0008	0005	12	9091	8758	8364	7916
2	0093	0062	0042	0028	14	9726	9585	9400	9165
3	0301	0212	.0149	0103	16	9934	9889	.9823	9730
4	0744	0550	0403	0293	18	9987	9976	9957	9928
5	1496	1157	0885	0671	20	9998	9996	9991	9984
6	2562	2068	1650	1301	22	1 0000	9999	9999	9997
7	3856	3239	2687	2202	24	1 0000	1 0000	1 0000	1 0000
8	5231	4557	3918	3328	26		1 0000	1 0000	1 0000
9	6530	5874	5218	4579					

BIBLIOGRAPHY

1 *Operational Research*, P M S Blackett, Advance of Science, April 1948

The Nature and Development of Operations Research, Charles Kittel, *Science*, **105**, 150 (1947)

Operational Research, Sir Charles Goodeve, *Nature*, **161**, 377 (1948)

Operations Research—A Scientific Basis for Executive Decisions, W Horvath, *The American Statistician*, **2**, No 5, 6 (1948)

2 *The Causes of Evolution*, J B S Haldane, Harper and Brothers, London, 1934

3 *The Genetical Theory of Natural Selection*, R A Fisher, Clarendon Press, Oxford, 1930

4 *Theory of Games and Economic Behavior*, John Von Neumann and Oskar Morgenstern, Princeton University Press, Princeton, 1944

5 *Probability and Its Engineering Uses*, Thornton C Fry, D Van Nostrand and Co , New York, 1928

6 *Tables of the Incomplete Beta-Function*, Karl Pearson, editor, University College, London, 1934

7 *Handbook of Chemistry and Physics*, Charles D Hodgman, editor, Chemical Rubber Publishing Co , Cleveland, 29th edition, 1945

8 *Handbook of Mathematical Tables and Formulas*, compiled by Richard Stevens Burington, Handbook Publishers, Sandusky, Ohio, 2d edition, 1940

9 *Aircraft in Warfare, the Dawn of the Fourth Arm*, F W Lanchester, Constable and Co , London, 1916

10 *A Quantitative Aspect of Combat*, B O Koopman, OEMsr-1007, Applied Mathematics Panel, Note 6, AMG-Columbia, August 1943, AMP-900-M2 *

11 *Leçons sur la théorie mathematique de la lutte pour la vie*, Vita Volterra, Gauthier-Villars et cie , Paris, 1931

12 *Elements of Physical Biology*, Alfred J Lotka, Williams and Wilkins Co , Baltimore, 1925

13 *A Treatise on the Theory of Bessel Functions*, G N Watson, University Press, Cambridge, 2d edition, 1944

14 *Random Sampling Numbers*, arranged by L H C Tippett, Cambridge University Press, London, 1927

15 E L Dodd, *Bollettino di Matematica*, 1942, pp 76–77

16 *Analysis of Air Traffic at Kingsford-Smith Airport, Mascot, Sydney*

17 Delays in the Flow of Air Traffic, *Journal of the Royal Aeronautical Society*, 1943, p. 51

18 Operational Research into the Air Traffic Problem, *Journal of the Institute of Navigation*, 1, No 4, 338–341

19 *Statistical Methods in Research and Production*, O L Davies, Oliver & Boyd, London, 1947

20 *Science at War*, J G Crowther, and R Whiddington, H M Stationery Office, London, 1948

21 Operational Analysis in Relation to Administration of Government-Sponsored Research, J R Loofbourow, *Science*, **106**, No 2745, 113–117

22 Science and Statecraft, Marshall H Stone, *Science*, **105**, No 2733, May 16, 1947

23 The Role of Operations Research in the Navy, Jacinto Steinhardt, Jr , *United States Naval Institute Proceedings*, **72**, 649 (1946)

24 Of Men and Machines, P M Morse, *The Technology Review*, **49**, November 1946

25 *Operational Research*, Robert Watson-Watt

Operational Research in Peace, J D Bernal

Operational Research in Social Medicine and Biology, F A E Crew

Operational Research and Strategic Planning, S Zuckerman

The Work of a Medical Research Section in the Field, W C Wilson

The Contribution of Operational Research to the Army in War and Peace, O H Wansborough-Jones

Talks delivered before the British Association for the Advancement of Science, 1948

* This number indicates that this document has been microfilmed and that its title appears in the microfilm index printed in a separate volume For access to the index volume and to the microfilm, consult the Office of the Chief of Naval Operations, Navy Department, Washington 25, D C

INDEX